W9-CLL-332

grzimek's
Student Animal Life Resource

• • • •

grzimek's
Student Animal Life Resource

• • • •

Mammals
volume 3

Primates to True Seals

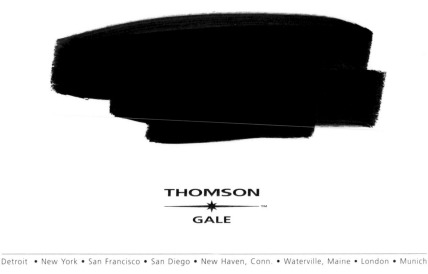

THOMSON

GALE

Detroit • New York • San Francisco • San Diego • New Haven, Conn. • Waterville, Maine • London • Munich

THOMSON

GALE

Grzimek's Student Animal Life Resource
Mammals

Project Editor
Melissa C. McDade

Editorial
Julie L. Carnagie, Madeline Harris, Elizabeth Manar, Heather Price

Indexing Services
Synapse, the Knowledge Link Corporation

Rights and Acquisitions
Sheila Spencer, Mari Masalin-Cooper

Imaging and Multimedia
Randy Bassett, Michael Logusz, Dan Newell, Chris O'Bryan, Robyn Young

Product Design
Tracey Rowens, Jennifer Wahi

Composition
Evi Seoud, Mary Beth Trimper

Manufacturing
Wendy Blurton, Dorothy Maki

© 2005 Thomson Gale, a part of The Thomson Corporation.

Thomson and Star Logo are trademarks and Gale and UXL are registered trademarks used herein under license.

For more information, contact
Thomson Gale
27500 Drake Rd.
Farmington Hills, MI 48331-3535
Or you can visit our Internet site at http://www.gale.com

ALL RIGHTS RESERVED
No part of this work covered by the copyright hereon may be reproduced or used in any form or by any means—graphic, electronic, or mechanical, including photocopying, recording, taping, Web distribution, or information storage retrieval systems—without the written permission of the publisher.

For permission to use material from this product, submit your request via Web at http://www.gale-edit.com/ permissions, or you may download our Permissions Request form and submit your request by fax or mail to:

Permissions
Thomson Gale
27500 Drake Rd.
Farmington Hills, MI 48331-3535
Permissions Hotline:
248-699-8006 or 800-877-4253, ext. 8006
Fax: 248-699-8074 or 800-762-4058

While every effort has been made to ensure the reliability of the information presented in this publication, Thomson Gale does not guarantee the accuracy of the data contained herein. Thomson Gale accepts no payment for listing; and inclusion in the publication of any organization, agency, institution, publication, service, or individual does not imply endorsement of the editors or publisher. Errors brought to the attention of the publisher and verified to the satisfaction of the publisher will be corrected in future editions.

LIBRARY OF CONGRESS CATALOGING-IN-PUBLICATION DATA

Grzimek's student animal life resource. Mammals / Melissa C. McDade, project editor.
    p. cm.
  Includes bibliographical references and index.
  ISBN 0-7876-9183-6 (set hardcover : alk. paper) — ISBN 0-7876-9184-4 (volume 1) — ISBN 0-7876-9185-2 (volume 2) — ISBN 0-7876-9187-9 (volume 3) — ISBN 0-7876-9188-7 (volume 4) — ISBN 0-7876-9234-4 (volume 5)
  1. Mammals—Juvenile literature. I. Grzimek, Bernhard. II. McDade, Melissa C.
  QL703.G79 2005
  599—dc22
                          2004015604

ISBN 0-7876-9402-9 (21-vol set), ISBN 0-7876-9183-6 (Mammals set),
ISBN 0-7876-9184-4 (v.1), ISBN 0-7876-9185-2 (v.2), ISBN 0-7876-9187-9 (v.3),
ISBN 0-7876-9188-7 (v.4), ISBN 0-7876-9234-4 (v.5)

This title is also available as an e-book
Contact your Thomson Gale sales representative for ordering information.

Printed in Canada
10 9 8 7 6 5 4 3 2 1

Contents

MAMMALS: VOLUME 5

Reader's Guide

Grzimek's Student Animal Life Resource: Mammals offers readers comprehensive and easy-to-use information on Earth's mammals. Entries are arranged by taxonomy, the science through which living things are classified into related groups. Order entries provide an overview of a group of families, and family entries provide an overview of a particular family. Each entry includes sections on physical characteristics; geographic range; habitat; diet; behavior and reproduction; animals and people; and conservation status. Family entries are followed by one or more species accounts with the same information as well as a range map and photo or illustration for each species. Entries conclude with a list of books, periodicals, and Web sites that may be used for further research.

ADDITIONAL FEATURES

Each volume of *Grzimek's Student Animal Life Resource: Mammals* includes a pronunciation guide for scientific names, a glossary, an overview of Mammals, a list of species in the set by biome, a list of species by geographic location, and an index. The set has 540 full-color maps, photos, and illustrations to enliven the text, and sidebars provide additional facts and related information.

NOTES

The classification of animals into orders, families, and even species is not a completed exercise. As researchers learn more about animals and their relationships, classifications may change. In some cases, researchers do not agree on how or whether to make a change. For this reason, the heading "Number of species" in the introduction of an entry may read "About 36 species" or "34 to 37 species." It is not a question of whether some animals exist or not, but a question of how they are classified. Some researchers are more likely to "lump" animals into the same species classification, while others may "split" animals into separate species.

Grzimek's Student Animal Life Resource: Mammals has standardized information in the Conservation Status section. The IUCN Red List provides the world's most comprehensive inventory of the global conservation status of plants and animals. Using a set of criteria to evaluate extinction risk, the IUCN recognizes the following categories: Extinct, Extinct in the Wild, Critically Endangered, Endangered, Vulnerable, Conservation Dependent, Near Threatened, Least Concern, and Data Deficient. These terms are defined where they are used in the text, but for a complete explanation of each category, visit the IUCN web page at http://www.iucn.org/themes/ssc/redlists/RLcats2001booklet.html.

ACKNOWLEDGEMENTS

Special thanks are due for the invaluable comments and suggestions provided by the *Grzimek's Student Animal Life Resource: Mammals* advisors:

- Mary Alice Anderson, Media Specialist, Winona Middle School, Winona, Minnesota
- Thane Johnson, Librarian, Oklahoma City Zoo, Oklahoma City, Oklahoma
- Debra Kachel, Media Specialist, Ephrata Senior High School, Ephrata, Pennsylvania
- Nina Levine, Media Specialist, Blue Mountain Middle School, Courtlandt Manor, New York
- Ruth Mormon, Media Specialist, The Meadows School, Las Vegas, Nevada

COMMENTS AND SUGGESTIONS

We welcome your comments on *Grzimek's Student Animal Life Resource: Mammals* and suggestions for future editions of this work. Please write: Editors, *Grzimek's Student Animal Life Resource: Mammals*, U•X•L, 27500 Drake Rd., Farmington Hills, Michigan 48331-3535; call toll free: 1-800-877-4253; fax: 248-699-8097; or send e-mail via www.gale.com.

Pronunciation Guide for Scientific Names

Abrocoma cinerea AB-ruh-KOH-muh sin-EAR-ee-uh

Abrocomidae ab-ruh-KOH-muh-dee

Acomys cahirinus ak-OH-meez kay-hih-RYE-nuhs

Acrobates pygmaeus ak-CROW-bah-teez pig-MEE-uhs

Acrobatidae ak-crow-BAH-tuh-dee

Agouti paca ah-GOO-tee PAY-cuh

Agoutidae ah-GOO-tuh-dee

Ailuropoda melanoleuca AYE-lur-uh-POD-uh MEL-uh-noh-LYOO-kuh

Ailurus fulgens AYE-lur-uhs FULL-jens

Alces alces AL-ceez AL-ceez

Alouatta seniculus ah-loo-AH-tuh se-NIH-kul-uhs

Anomaluridae ah-nuh-mah-LOOR-uh-dee

Anomalurus derbianus ah-nuh-MAH-loor-uhs der-BEE-an-uhs

Antilocapra americana AN-til-uh-KAP-ruh uh-mer-uh-KAN-uh

Antilocapridae an-til-uh-KAP-ruh-dee

Antrozous pallidus an-tro-ZOH-uhs PAL-uh-duhs

Aotidae ay-OH-tuh-dee

Aotus trivirgatus ay-OH-tuhs try-VER-gah-tuhs

Aplodontia rufa ap-loh-DON-shuh ROO-fah

Aplodontidae ap-loh-DON-tuh-dee

Arctocephalus gazella ARK-tuh-SEFF-uh-luhs guh-ZELL-uh

Artiodactyla AR-tee-uh-DAK-til-uh

Asellia tridens ah-SELL-ee-uh TRY-denz

Ateles geoffroyi ah-TELL-eez JEFF-roy-eye

Atelidae ah-TELL-uh-dee

Babyrousa babyrussa bah-bee-ROO-suh bah-bee-ROO-suh

Balaena mysticetus bah-LEE-nuh mis-tuh-SEE-tuhs

Balaenidae bah-LEE-nuh-dee

Balaenoptera acutorostrata bah-lee-NOP-teh-ruh uh-KYOOT-uh-ROS-trah-tuh

Balaenoptera musculus bah-lee-NOP-teh-ruh muhs-KU-luhs

Balaenopteridae bah-lee-nop-TEH-ruh-dee

Barbastella barbastellus bar-buh-STELL-uh bar-buh-STELL-uhs

Bathyergidae bath-ih-ER-juh-dee

Bettongia tropica bee-ton-JEE-uh TROP-ik-uh

Bison bison BI-sun BI-sun

Bovidae BOH-vuh-dee

Bradypodidae brad-ih-POD-uh-dee

Bradypus variegatus BRAD-ih-puhs vair-ee-uh-GAH-tuhs

Bubalus bubalis BYOO-bal-uhs BYOO-bal-is

Burramyidae bur-ruh-MY-uh-dee

Cacajao calvus KA-ka-jah-oh KAL-vuhs

Caenolestes fuliginosus kee-NOH-less-teez fyoo-li-JEH-noh-suhs

Caenolestidae kee-noh-LESS-tuh-dee

Callicebus personatus kal-luh-SEE-buhs per-SON-ah-tuhs

Callimico goeldii kal-luh-MEE-koh geel-DEE-eye

Callitrichidae kal-luh-TRIK-uh-dee

Camelidae kam-EL-uh-dee

Camelus dromedarius KAM-el-uhs drom-uh-DARE-ee-uhs

Canidae KAN-uh-dee

Canis lupus KAN-is LYOO-puhs

Caperea marginata kay-per-EE-uh mar-JIN-ah-tuh

Capricornis sumatraensis kap-rih-KOR-nis soo-mah-TREN-sis

Capromyidae kap-roh-MY-uh-dee

Capromys pilorides KAP-roh-meez pi-LOH-ruh-deez

Carnivora kar-NIH-voh-ruh

Castor canadensis KAS-tor kan-uh-DEN-sis

Castoridae kas-TOR-uh-dee

Caviidae kave-EYE-uh-dee

Cebidae SEE-buh-dee

Cebuella pygmaea see-boo-ELL-uh pig-MEE-uh

Cebus capucinus SEE-buhs kap-oo-CHIN-uhs

Cebus olivaceus SEE-buhs ah-luh-VAY-see-uhs

Ceratotherium simum suh-rah-tuh-THER-ee-um SIM-um

Cercartetus nanus ser-kar-TEE-tuhs NAN-uhs

Cercopithecidae ser-koh-pith-EEK-uh-dee

Cervidae SER-vuh-dee

Cervus elaphus SER-vuhs EL-laff-uhs

Cetacea sih-TAY-she-uh

Cheirogaleidae KY-roh-GAL-uh-dee

Cheiromeles torquatus ky-ROH-mel-eez TOR-kwah-tuhs

Chinchilla lanigera chin-CHILL-uh la-NIJ-er-uh

Chinchillidae chin-CHILL-uh-dee

Chironectes minimus ky-roh-NECK-teez MIN-ih-muhs

Chiroptera ky-ROP-ter-uh

Chlamyphorus truncatus klam-EE-for-uhs TRUN-kah-tuhs

Choloepus hoffmanni koh-LEE-puhs HOFF-man-eye

Chrysochloridae krih-soh-KLOR-uh-dee

Chrysocyon brachyurus krih-SOH-sigh-on bra-kee-YOOR-uhs

Civettictis civetta sih-VET-tick-tis SIH-vet-uh

Coendou prehensilis SEEN-doo prih-HEN-sil-is

Condylura cristata KON-dih-LUR-uh KRIS-tah-tuh

Connochaetes gnou koh-nuh-KEE-teez NEW

Craseonycteridae kras-ee-oh-nick-TER-uh-dee

Craseonycteris thonglongyai kras-ee-oh-NICK-ter-is thong-
  LONG-ee-aye

Cricetomys gambianus kry-see-TOH-meez GAM-bee-an-uhs

Cricetus cricetus kry-SEE-tuhs kry-SEE-tuhs

Crocuta crocuta kroh-CUE-tuh kroh-CUE-tuh

Cryptomys damarensis krip-TOH-meez DAM-are-en-sis

Cryptoprocta ferox krip-TOH-prok-tuh FAIR-oks

Cryptotis parva krip-TOH-tis PAR-vuh

Ctenodactylidae ten-oh-dak-TIL-uh-dee

Ctenomyidae ten-oh-MY-uh-dee

Ctenomys pearsoni TEN-oh-meez PEAR-son-eye

Cyclopes didactylus SIGH-kluh-peez die-DAK-til-uhs

Cynocephalidae sigh-nuh-seff-UH-luh-dee

Cynocephalus variegatus sigh-nuh-SEFF-uh-luhs VAIR-ee-
  uh-GAH-tus

Cynomys ludovicianus SIGH-no-mees LOO-doh-vih-SHE-an-
  uhs

Dasypodidae das-ih-POD-uh-dee

Dasyprocta punctata das-IH-prok-tuh PUNK-tah-tuh

Dasyproctidae das-ih-PROK-tuh-dee

Dasypus novemcinctus DAS-ih-puhs noh-VEM-sink-tuhs

Dasyuridae das-ih-YOOR-uh-dee

Dasyuromorphia das-ih-yoor-oh-MOR-fee-uh

Daubentoniidae daw-ben-tone-EYE-uh-dee

Daubentonia madagascariensis daw-ben-TONE-ee-uh mad-uh-GAS-kar-EE-en-sis

Delphinapterus leucas del-fin-AP-ter-uhs LYOO-kuhs

Delphinidae del-FIN-uh-dee

Dendrohyrax arboreus den-droh-HI-raks are-BOHR-ee-uhs

Dendrolagus bennettianus den-droh-LAG-uhs BEN-net-EE-an-uhs

Dermoptera der-MOP-ter-uh

Desmodus rotundus dez-MOH-duhs ROH-tun-duhs

Dicerorhinus sumatrensis die-ser-uh-RHY-nuhs soo-mah-TREN-sis

Didelphidae die-DELF-uh-dee

Didelphimorphia die-delf-uh-MOR-fee-uh

Didelphis virginiana DIE-delf-is ver-JIN-ee-an-uh

Dinomyidae die-noh-MY-uh-dee

Dinomys branickii DIE-noh-meez BRAN-ick-ee-eye

Dipodidae dih-POD-uh-dee

Dipodomys ingens dih-puh-DOH-meez IN-jenz

Diprotodontia dih-pro-toh-DON-she-uh

Dipus sagitta DIH-puhs SAJ-it-tuh

Dolichotis patagonum doll-ih-KOH-tis pat-uh-GOH-num

Dromiciops gliroides droh-MISS-ee-ops gli-ROY-deez

Dugong dugon DOO-gong DOO-gon

Dugongidae doo-GONG-uh-dee

Echimyidae ek-ih-MY-uh-dee

Echinosorex gymnura EH-ky-noh-SORE-eks JIM-nyoor-uh

Echymipera rufescens ek-ee-MIH-per-uh ROO-fehs-sens

Ectophylla alba ek-toh-FILE-luh AHL-buh

Elephantidae el-uh-FAN-tuh-dee

Elephas maximus EL-uh-fuhs MAX-im-uhs

Emballonuridae em-bal-lun-YOOR-uh-dee

Equidae EK-wuh-dee

Equus caballus przewalskii EK-wuhs CAB-uh-luhs prez-VAL-skee-eye

Equus grevyi EK-wuhs GREH-vee-eye

Equus kiang EK-wuhs KY-an

Eremitalpa granti er-uh-MIT-ahl-puh GRAN-tie

Erethizon dorsatum   er-uh-THY-zun DOR-sah-tum

Erethizontidae er-uh-thy-ZUN-tuh-dee

Erinaceidae er-ih-nay-SIGH-dee

Erinaceus europaeus   er-ih-NAY-shuhs yoor-uh-PEE-uhs

Eschrichtiidae ess-rick-TIE-uh-dee

Eschrichtius robustus ess-RICK-shuhs roh-BUHS-tuhs

Eubalaena glacialis yoo-bah-LEE-nuh glay-SHE-al-is

Felidae FEE-luh-dee

Furipteridae fur-ip-TER-uh-dee

Galagidae gal-AG-uh-dee

Galago senegalensis   GAL-ag-oh sen-ih-GAHL-en-sis

Galidia elegans   ga-LID-ee-uh EL-uh-ganz

Gazella thomsonii   guh-ZELL-uh TOM-son-ee-eye

Genetta genetta   JIN-eh-tuh JIN-eh-tuh

Geomyidae gee-oh-MY-uh-dee

Giraffa camelopardalis   JIH-raf-uh KAM-el-uh-PAR-dal-is

Giraffidae jih-RAF-uh-dee

Glaucomys volans   glo-KOH-meez VOH-lans

Glossophaga soricina   glos-SUH-fag-uh sore-ih-SEE-nuh

Gorilla gorilla guh-RILL-uh guh-RILL-uh

Hemicentetes semispinosus   hemi-sen-TEE-teez semi-PINE-oh-
   suhs

Herpestidae her-PES-tuh-dee

Heterocephalus glaber   HEH-tuh-roh-SEFF-uh-luhs GLAH-ber

Heteromyidae HEH-tuh-roh-MY-uh-dee

Hexaprotodon liberiensis   hek-suh-PRO-tuh-don lye-BEER-ee-
   en-sis

Hippopotamidae HIP-poh-pot-UH-muh-dee

Hippopotamus amphibius   HIP-poh-POT-uh-muhs am-FIB-ee-
   uhs

Hipposideridae HIP-poh-si-DER-uh-dee

Hominidae hom-IN-uh-dee

Homo sapiens HOH-moh SAY-pee-enz

Hyaenidae hi-EE-nuh-dee

Hydrochaeridae hi-droh-KEE-ruh-dee

Hydrochaeris hydrochaeris hi-droh-KEE-ris hi-droh-KEE-ris

Hydrodamalis gigas   hi-droh-DAM-uhl-is JEE-guhs

Hylobates lar hi-loh-BAY-teez lahr

Hylobates pileatus   hi-loh-BAY-teez pie-LEE-ah-tuhs

Hylobatidae hi-loh-BAY-tuh-dee

Hylochoerus meinertzhageni hi-loh-KEE-ruhs MINE-ertz-hah-gen-eye

Hyperoodon ampullatus hi-per-OH-uh-don am-PUH-lah-tuhs

Hypsiprymnodontidae HIP-see-PRIM-nuh-DON-shuh-dee

Hypsiprymnodon moschatus hip-see-PRIM-nuh-don MOS-kah-tuhs

Hyracoidea HI-rah-koy-DEE-uh

Hystricidae hiss-TRIK-uh-dee

Hystrix africaeaustralis HISS-triks AF-rik-ee-au-STRA-lis

Hystrix indica HISS-triks IN-dik-uh

Indri indri IN-dri IN-dri

Indriidae in-DRY-uh-dee

Inia geoffrensis in-EE-uh JEFF-ren-sis

Iniidae in-EYE-uh-dee

Insectivora IN-sek-TIV-uh-ruh

Kerodon rupestris KER-uh-don ROO-pes-tris

Kogia breviceps koh-JEE-uh BREV-ih-seps

Lagomorpha LAG-uh-MOR-fuh

Lagothrix lugens LAG-uh-thriks LU-jens

Lama glama LAH-muh GLAH-muh

Lama pacos LAH-muh PAY-kuhs

Lemmus lemmus LEM-muhs LEM-muhs

Lemur catta LEE-mer KAT-tuh

Lemur coronatus LEE-mer KOR-roh-nah-tuhs

Lemuridae lee-MYOOR-uh-dee

Lepilemur leucopus lep-uh-LEE-mer LYOO-koh-puhs

Lepilemur ruficaudatus lep-uh-LEE-mer ROO-fee-KAW-dah-tuhs

Lepilemuridae LEP-uh-lee-MOOR-uh-dee

Leporidae lep-OR-uh-dee

Lepus americanus LEP-uhs uh-mer-uh-KAN-uhs

Lepus timidus LEP-uhs TIM-id-uhs

Lipotes vexillifer lip-OH-teez veks-ILL-uh-fer

Lipotidae lip-OH-tuh-dee

Lorisidae lor-IS-uh-dee

Loxodonta africana LOK-suh-DON-tuh AF-rih-kan-uh

Loxodonta cyclotis LOK-suh-DON-tuh SIGH-klo-tis

Lutra lutra LOO-truh LOO-truh

Lynx rufus LINKS ROO-fuhs

Macaca mulatta muh-KAY-kuh MYOO-lah-tuh

Macroderma gigas ma-CROW-der-muh JEE-guhs

Macropodidae ma-crow-POD-uh-dee

Macropus giganteus ma-CROW-puhs jy-GAN-tee-uhs

Macropus rufus ma-CROW-puhs ROO-fuhs

Macroscelidea MA-crow-sel-uh-DEE-uh

Macroscelididae MA-crow-sel-UH-duh-dee

Macrotis lagotis ma-CROW-tis la-GO-tis

Macrotus californicus ma-CROW-tuhs kal-uh-FORN-uh-kuhs

Madoqua kirkii ma-DOH-kwah KIRK-ee-eye

Mandrillus sphinx man-DRILL-uhs SFINKS

Manidae MAN-uh-dee

Manis temminckii MAN-is TEM-ink-ee-eye

Marmota marmota MAR-mah-tuh MAR-mah-tuh

Massoutiera mzabi mas-soo-TEE-er-uh ZA-bye

Megadermatidae meg-uh-der-MUH-tuh-dee

Megalonychidae meg-uh-loh-NICK-uh-dee

Megaptera novaeangliae meg-uh-TER-uh NOH-vee-ANG-lee-dee

Meles meles MEL-eez MEL-eez

Mephitis mephitis MEF-it-is MEF-it-is

Microbiotheria my-crow-bio-THER-ee-uh

Microbiotheriidae my-crow-bio-ther-EYE-uh-dee

Microcebus rufus my-crow-SEE-buhs ROO-fuhs

Micropteropus pusillus my-crop-TER-oh-puhs pyoo-SILL-uhs

Miniopterus schreibersi min-ee-OP-ter-uhs shry-BER-seye

Mirounga angustirostris MIR-oon-guh an-GUHS-tih-ROS-tris

Molossidae mol-OS-suh-dee

Monachus schauinslandi MON-ak-uhs SHOU-inz-land-eye

Monodon monoceros MON-uh-don mon-UH-ser-uhs

Monodontidae mon-uh-DON-shuh-dee

Monotremata mon-uh-TREEM-ah-tuh

Mormoopidae mor-moh-UP-uh-dee

Moschus moschiferus MOS-kuhs mos-KIF-er-uhs

Muntiacus muntjak mun-SHE-uh-kuhs MUNT-jak

Muridae MUR-uh-dee

Mustela erminea MUS-tuh-luh er-MIN-ee-uh

Mustelidae mus-TUH-luh-dee

Myocastor coypus MY-oh-KAS-tor COI-puhs

Myocastoridae MY-oh-kas-TOR-uh-dee

Myotis lucifugus my-OH-tis loo-SIFF-ah-guhs

Myoxidae my-OKS-uh-dee

Myoxus glis MY-oks-uhs GLIS

Myrmecobiidae mur-mih-koh-BYE-uh-dee

Myrmecobius fasciatus mur-mih-KOH-bee-uhs fah-SHE-ah-tuhs

Myrmecophaga tridactyla mur-mih-KOH-fag-uh try-DAK-til-uh

Myrmecophagidae mur-mih-koh-FAJ-uh-dee

Mystacina tuberculata miss-tih-SEE-nuh too-ber-KYOO-lah-tuh

Mystacinidae miss-tih-SEE-nuh-dee

Myzopoda aurita my-zoh-POD-uh OR-it-uh

Myzopodidae my-zoh-POD-uh-dee

Nasalis larvatus NAY-zal-is LAR-vah-tuhs

Natalidae nay-TAL-uh-dee

Natalus stramineus NAY-tal-uhs struh-MIN-ee-uhs

Neobalaenidae nee-oh-bah-LEE-nuh-dee

Noctilio leporinus nok-TIHL-ee-oh leh-por-RYE-nuhs

Noctilionidae nok-tihl-ee-ON-uh-dee

Notomys alexis noh-TOH-meez ah-LEK-sis

Notoryctemorphia noh-toh-rik-teh-MOR-fee-uh

Notoryctes typhlops noh-TOH-rik-teez TIE-flopz

Notoryctidae noh-toh-RIK-tuh-dee

Nycteridae nik-TER-uh-dee

Nycteris thebaica NIK-ter-is the-BAH-ik-uh

Nycticebus pygmaeus nik-tih-SEE-buhs pig-MEE-uhs

Nyctimene robinsoni nik-TIM-en-ee ROB-in-son-eye

Ochotona hyperborea oh-koh-TOH-nuh hi-per-BOHR-ee-uh

Ochotona princeps oh-koh-TOH-nuh PRIN-seps

Ochotonidae oh-koh-TOH-nuh-dee

Octodon degus OK-tuh-don DAY-gooz

Octodontidae ok-tuh-DON-tuh-dee

Odobenidae oh-duh-BEN-uh-dee

Odobenus rosmarus oh-DUH-ben-uhs ROS-mahr-uhs

Odocoileus virginianus oh-duh-KOI-lee-uhs ver-JIN-ee-an-nuhs

Okapia johnstoni oh-KAH-pee-uh JOHNS-ton-eye

Ondatra zibethicus ON-dat-ruh ZIB-eth-ih-kuhs

Onychogalea fraenata oh-nik-uh-GAL-ee-uh FREE-nah-tuh

Orcinus orca OR-sigh-nuhs OR-kuh

Ornithorhynchidae OR-nith-oh-RIN-kuh-dee

Ornithorynchus anatinus OR-nith-oh-RIN-kuhs an-AH-tin-uhs

Orycteropodidae or-ik-ter-uh-POD-uh-dee

Orycteropus afer or-ik-TER-uh-puhs AF-er

Otariidae oh-tar-EYE-uh-dee

Otolemur garnettii oh-tuh-LEE-mer GAR-net-ee-eye

Ovis canadensis OH-vis kan-uh-DEN-sis

Pagophilus groenlandicus pa-GO-fil-luhs GREEN-land-ih-cuhs

Pan troglodytes PAN trog-luh-DIE-teez

Panthera leo PAN-ther-uh LEE-oh

Panthera tigris PAN-ther-uh TIE-gris

Paucituberculata paw-see-too-ber-KYOO-lah-tuh

Pedetidae ped-ET-uh-dee

Peramelemorphia per-uh-mel-eh-MOR-fee-uh

Peramelidae per-uh-MEL-uh-dee

Perameles gunnii PER-uh-MEL-eez GUN-ee-eye

Perissodactyla peh-RISS-uh-DAK-til-uh

Perodicticus potto per-uh-DIK-tuh-kuhs POT-toh

Perognathus inornatus PER-ug-NAH-thuhs in-AWR-nah-tuhs

Peropteryx kappleri per-OP-ter-iks KAP-ler-eye

Peroryctidae per-uh-RIK-tuh-dee

Petauridae pet-OR-uh-dee

Petauroides volans pet-or-OY-deez VOH-lanz

Petaurus breviceps PET-or-uhs BREV-ih-seps

Petrogale penicillata pet-ROH-gah-lee pen-ih-SIL-lah-tuh

Petromuridae pet-roh-MUR-uh-dee

Petromus typicus PET-roh-muhs TIP-ih-kuhs

Phalanger gymnotis FAH-lan-jer jim-NOH-tis

Phalangeridae fah-lan-JER-uh-dee

Phascogale tapoatafa fas-KOH-gah-lee TAP-oh-uh-TAH-fuh

Phascolarctidae fas-koh-LARK-tuh-dee

Phascolarctos cinereus fas-KOH-lark-tuhs sin-EAR-ee-uhs

Phocidae FOE-suh-dee

Phocoena phocoena FOE-see-nuh FOE-see-nuh

Phocoena spinipinnis FOE-see-nuh SPY-nih-PIN-is

Phocoenidae foe-SEE-nuh-dee

Pholidota foe-lih-DOH-tuh

Phyllostomidae fill-uh-STOH-muh-dee

Physeter macrocephalus FY-se-ter ma-crow-SEFF-uh-luhs

Physeteridae fy-se-TER-uh-dee

Piliocolobus badius fill-ee-oh-KOH-loh-buhs BAD-ee-uhs

Pithecia pithecia pith-EEK-ee-uh pith-EEK-ee-uh

Pitheciidae pith-eek-EYE-uh-dee

Plantanista gangetica plan-TAN-is-tuh gan-JET-ik-uh

Platanistidae plan-tan-IS-tuh-dee

Pongo pygmaeus PON-goh pig-MEE-uhs

Pontoporia blainvillei pon-toh-POR-ee-uh BLAIN-vill-ee-eye

Pontoporiidae PON-toh-por-EYE-uh-dee

Potoroidae pot-uh-ROY-dee

Primates PRY-maytes

Proboscidea proh-BOS-see-uh

Procavia capensis proh-CAVE-ee-uh KAP-en-sis

Procaviidae proh-kave-EYE-uh-dee

Procyon lotor proh-SIGH-on LOH-tor

Procyonidae proh-sigh-ON-uh-dee

Proechimys semispinosus proh-EK-ih-meez sem-ih-SPY-noh-suhs

Propithecus edwardsi proh-PITH-eek-uhs ED-werds-eye

Proteles cristatus PROH-tell-eez KRIS-tah-tuhs

Pseudocheiridae soo-doh-KY-ruh-dee

Pseudocheirus peregrinus soo-doh-KY-ruhs PEHR-eh-GRIN-uhs

Pteronotus parnellii ter-uh-NOH-tuhs PAR-nell-ee-eye

Pteropodidae ter-uh-POD-uh-dee

Pteropus giganteus ter-OH-puhs jy-GAN-tee-uhs

Pteropus mariannus ter-OH-puhs MARE-ih-an-uhs

Pudu pudu POO-doo POO-doo

Puma concolor PYOO-muh CON-kuh-luhr

Puripterus horrens PYOOR-ip-TER-uhs HOR-renz

Pygathrix nemaeus PIG-uh-thriks neh-MEE-uhs

Rangifer tarandus RAN-jih-fer TAR-an-duhs

Rhinoceros unicornis rye-NOS-er-uhs YOO-nih-KORN-is

Rhinocerotidae rye-NOS-er-UH-tuh-dee

Rhinolophidae rye-noh-LOH-fuh-dee

Rhinolophus capensis rye-noh-LOH-fuhs KAP-en-sis

Rhinolophus ferrumequinum rye-noh-LOH-fuhs FEHR-rum-EK-wy-num

Rhinopoma hardwickei rye-noh-POH-muh HARD-wik-eye

Rhinopomatidae rye-noh-poh-MAT-uh-dee

Rhynchocyon cirnei rin-koh-SIGH-on SIR-neye

Rodentia roh-DEN-she-uh

Rousettus aegyptiacus ROO-set-tuhs ee-JIP-tih-kuhs

Saccopteryx bilineata sak-OP -ter-iks BY-lin-EE-ah-tuh

Saguinus oedipus SAG-win-uhs ED-uh-puhs

Saimiri sciureus SAY-meer-eye sigh-OOR-ee-uhs

Sarcophilus laniarius SAR-kuh-FIL-uhs lan-ee-AIR-ee-uhs

Scalopus aquaticus SKA-loh-puhs uh-KWAT-ik-uhs

Scandentia skan-DEN-she-uh

Sciuridae sigh-OOR-uh-dee

Sciurus carolinensis SIGH-oor-uhs kar-uh-LINE-en-sis

Sigmodon hispidus SIG-muh-don HISS-pid-uhs

Sirenia sy-REEN-ee-uh

Solenodon paradoxus so-LEN-uh-don PAR-uh-DOCKS-uhs

Solenodontidae so-len-uh-DON-shuh-dee

Sorex palustris SOR-eks PAL-us-tris

Soricidae sor-IS-uh-dee

Stenella longirostris steh-NELL-uh LAWN-juh-ROS-tris

Suidae SOO-uh-dee

Sus scrofa SOOS SKRO-fuh

Sylvilagus audubonii SILL-vih-LAG-uhs AW-duh-BON-ee-eye

Symphalangus syndactylus SIM-fuh-LAN-guhs sin-DAK-til-uhs

Tachyglossidae TAK-ih-GLOS-suh-dee

Tachyglossus aculeatus TAK-ih-GLOS-suhs ak-YOOL-ee-ah-tuhs

Tadarida brasiliensis ta-DARE-ih-dah bra-ZILL-ee-en-sis

Talpidae TAL-puh-dee

Tamias striatus TAM-ee-uhs stry-AH-tuhs

Tapiridae tay-PUR-uh-dee

Tapirus indicus TAY-pur-uhs IN-dih-kuhs

Tapirus terrestris TAY-pur-uhs TER-rehs-tris

Tarsiidae tar-SIGH-uh-dee

Tarsipedidae tar-sih-PED-uh-dee

Tarsipes rostratus TAR-si-peez ROS-trah-tuhs

Tarsius bancanus TAR-see-uhs BAN-kan-uhs

Tarsius syrichta TAR-see-uhs STRIK-tuh

Tasmacetus shepherdi taz-muh-SEE-tuhs SHEP-erd-eye

Tayassu tajacu TAY-yuh-soo TAY-jah-soo

Tayassuidae tay-yuh-SOO-uh-dee

Tenrec ecaudatus TEN-rek ee-KAW-dah-tuhs

Tenrecidae ten-REK-uh-dee

Thomomys bottae TOM-oh-meez BOTT-ee

Thryonomyidae thry-oh-noh-MY-uh-dee

Thryonomys swinderianus THRY-oh-NOH-meez SWIN-der-EE-an-uhs

Thylacinidae thy-luh-SEEN-uh-dee

Thylacinus cynocephalus THY-luh-SEEN-uhs sigh-nuh-SEFF-uh-luhs

Thyroptera tricolor thy-ROP-ter-uh TRY-kuh-luhr
Thyropteridae thy-rop-TER-uh-dee
Tragulidae tray-GOO-luh-dee
Tragulus javanicus TRAY-goo-luhs jah-VAHN-ih-kuhs
Trichechidae trik-EK-uh-dee
Trichechus manatus TRIK-ek-uhs MAN-uh-tuhs
Trichosurus vulpecula TRIK-uh-SOOR-uhs vul-PEK-yoo-luh
Tubulidentata toob-yool-ih-DEN-tah-tuh
Tupaia glis too-PUH-ee-uh GLIS
Tupaiidae too-puh-EYE-uh-dee
Tursiops truncatus tur-SEE-ops TRUN-kah-tuhs
Uncia uncia UN-see-uh UN-see-uh
Ursidae UR-suh-dee
Ursus americanus UR-suhs uh-mer-uh-KAN-uhs
Ursus maritimus UR-suhs mar-ih-TIME-uhs
Vespertilionidae ves-puhr-TEEL-ee-UHN-uh-dee
Viverridae vy-VER-ruh-dee
Vombatidae vom-BAT-uh-dee
Vombatus ursinus VOM-bat-uhs ur-SIGH-nuhs
Vulpes vulpes VUHL-peez VUHL-peez
Xenarthra ZEN-areth-ruh
Yerbua capensis YER-byoo-uh KAP-en-sis
Zalophus californianus ZA-loh-fuhs kal-uh-FORN-uh-kuhs
Zalophus wollebaeki ZA-loh-fuhs VOLL-back-eye
Ziphiidae ziff-EYE-uh-dee

Words to Know

A

Aborigine: Earliest-known inhabitant of an area; often referring to a native person of Australia.

Adaptation: Any structural, physiological, or behavioral trait that aids an organism's survival and ability to reproduce in its existing environment.

Algae: Tiny plants or plantlike organisms that grow in water and in damp places.

Anaconda: A large snake of South America; one of the largest snakes in the world.

Aphrodisiac: Anything that intensifies or arouses sexual desires.

Aquatic: Living in the water.

Arboreal: Living primarily or entirely in trees and bushes.

Arid: Extremely dry climate, with less than 10 inches (25 centimeters) of rain each year.

Arthropod: A member of the largest single animal phylum, consisting of organisms with segmented bodies, jointed legs or wings, and exoskeletons.

B

Baleen: A flexible, horny substance making up two rows of plates that hang from the upper jaws of baleen whales.

Biogeography: The study of the distribution and dispersal of plants and animals throughout the world.

Bipedal: Walking on two feet.

Blowhole: The nostril on a whale, dolphin, or porpoise.

Blubber: A layer of fat under the skin of sea mammals that protects them from heat loss and stores energy.

Brachiation: A type of locomotion in which an animal travels through the forest by swinging below branches using its arms.

Brackish water: Water that is a mix of freshwater and saltwater.

Burrow: Tunnel or hole that an animal digs in the ground to use as a home.

C

Cache: A hidden supply area.

Camouflage: Device used by an animal, such as coloration, allowing it to blend in with the surroundings to avoid being seen by prey and predators.

Canine teeth: The four pointed teeth (two in each jaw) between the incisors and bicuspids in mammals; designed for stabbing and holding prey.

Canopy: The uppermost layer of a forest formed naturally by the leaves and branches of trees and plants.

Carnivore: Meat-eating organism.

Carrion: Dead and decaying animal flesh.

Cecum: A specialized part of the large intestine that acts as a fermentation chamber to aid in digestion of grasses.

Cervical vertebrae: The seven neck bones that make up the top of the spinal column.

Clan: A group of animals of the same species that live together, such as badgers or hyenas.

Cloud forest: A tropical forest where clouds are overhead most of the year.

Colony: A group of animals of the same type living together.

Coniferous: Refers to evergreen trees, such as pines and firs, that bear cones and have needle-like leaves that are not shed all at once.

Coniferous forest: An evergreen forest where plants stay green all year.

Continental shelf: A gently sloping ledge of a continent that is submerged in the ocean.

Convergence: In adaptive evolution, a process by which unrelated or only distantly related living things come to resemble one another in adapting to similar environments.

Coprophagous: Eating dung. Some animals do this to extract nutrients that have passed through their system.

Crepuscular: Most active at dawn and dusk.

Critically Endangered: A term used by the IUCN in reference to a species that is at an extremely high risk of extinction in the wild.

D

Data Deficient: An IUCN category referring to a species that is not assigned another category because there is not enough information about the species' population.

Deciduous: Shedding leaves at the end of the growing season.

Deciduous forest: A forest with four seasons in which trees drop their leaves in the fall.

Deforestation: Those practices or processes that result in the change of forested lands to non-forest uses, such as human settlement or farming. This is often cited as one of the major causes of the enhanced greenhouse effect.

Delayed implantation: A process by which the fertilized egg formed after mating develops for a short time, then remains inactive until later when it attaches to the uterus for further development, so that birth coincides with a better food supply or environmental conditions.

Den: The shelter of an animal, such as an underground hole or a hollow log.

Dentin: A calcareous material harder than bone found in teeth.

Desert: A land area so dry that little or no plant or animal life can survive.

Digit: Division where limbs terminate; in humans this refers to a finger or toe.

Digitigrade: A manner of walking on the toes, as cats and dogs do, as opposed to walking on the ball of the feet, as humans do.

Dingo: A wild Australian dog.

Diurnal: Refers to animals that are active during the day.

Domesticated: Tamed.

Dominant: The top male or female of a social group, sometimes called the alpha male or alpha female.

Dorsal: Located in the back.

Dung: Feces, or solid waste from an animal.

E

Echolocation: A method of detecting objects by using sound waves.

Ecotourist: A person who visits a place in order to observe the plants and animals in the area while making minimal human impact on the natural environment.

Electroreception: The sensory detection of small amounts of natural electricity by an animal (usually underwater), by means of specialized nerve endings.

Elevation: The height of land when measured from sea level.

Endangered: A term used by the U. S. Endangered Species Act of 1973 and by the IUCN in reference to a species that is facing a very high risk of extinction from all or a significant portion of its natural home.

Endangered Species Act: A U. S. law that grants legal protection to listed endangered and threatened species.

Endemic: Native to or occurring only in a particular place.

Erupt: In teeth, to break through the skin and become visible.

Estivation: State of inactivity during the hot, dry months of summer.

Estuary: Lower end of a river where ocean tides meet the river's current.

Eutherian mammal: Mammals that have a well-developed placenta and give birth to fully formed live young.

Evergreen: In botany, bearing green leaves through the winter and/or a plant having foliage that persists throughout the year.

Evolve: To change slowly over time.

Extinct: A species without living members.

Extinction: The total disappearance of a species or the disappearance of a species from a given area.

F

Family: A grouping of genera that share certain characteristics and appear to have evolved from the same ancestors.

Feces: Solid body waste.

Fermentation: Chemical reaction in which enzymes break down complex organic compounds into simpler ones. This can make digestion easier.

Forage: To search for food.

Forb: Any broad-leaved herbaceous plant that is not a grass; one that grows in a prairie or meadow, such as sunflower, goldenrod, or clover.

Fragment: To divide or separate individuals of the same species into small groups that are unable to mingle with each other.

Frugivore: Animal that primarily eats fruit. Many bats and birds are frugivores.

Fuse: To become joined together as one unit.

G

Genera: Plural of genus.

Genus (pl. genera): A category of classification made up of species sharing similar characteristics.

Gestation: The period of carrying young in the uterus before birth.

Gland: A specialized body part that produces, holds, and releases one or more substances (such as scent or sweat) for use by the body.

Gleaning: Gathering food from surfaces.

Grassland: Region in which the climate is dry for long periods of the summer, and freezes in the winter. Grasslands are characterized by grasses and other erect herbs, usually without trees or shrubs, and occur in the dry temperate interiors of continents.

Grooming: An activity during which primates look through each other's fur to remove parasites and dirt.

Guano: The droppings of birds or bats, sometimes used as fertilizer.

Guard hairs: Long, stiff, waterproof hairs that form the outer fur and protect the underfur of certain mammals.

Gum: A substance found in some plants that oozes out in response to a puncture, as plant sap, and generally hardens after exposure to air.

H

Habitat: The area or region where a particular type of plant or animal lives and grows.

Habitat degradation: The diminishment of the quality of a habitat and its ability to support animal and plant communities.

Hallux: The big toe, or first digit, on the part of the foot facing inwards.

Harem: A group of two or more adult females, plus their young, with only one adult male present.

Haul out: To pull one's body out of the water onto land, as when seals come out of the water to go ashore.

Herbivore: Plant-eating organism.

Hibernation: State of rest or inactivity during the cold winter months.

Hierarchy: A structured order of rank or social superiority.

Home range: A specific area that an animal roams while performing its activities.

I

Ice floe: A large sheet of floating ice.

Incisor: One of the chisel-shaped teeth at the front of the mouth (between the canines), used for cutting and tearing food.

Indigenous: Originating in a region or country.

Insectivore: An animal that eats primarily insects.

Insulate: To prevent the escape of heat by surrounding with something; in an animal, a substance such as fur or body fat serves to retain heat in its body.

Invertebrate: Animal lacking a spinal column (backbone).

IUCN: Abbreviation for the International Union for Conservation of Nature and Natural Resources, now the World Conservation Union. A conservation organization of government agencies and nongovernmental organizations best known for its Red Lists of threatened and endangered species.

K

Keratin: Protein found in hair, nails, and skin.

Krill: Tiny shrimp-like animals that are the main food of baleen whales and are also eaten by seals and other marine mammals.

L

Lactate: To produce milk in the female body, an activity associated with mammals.

Larva (pl. larvae): Immature form (wormlike in insects; fishlike in amphibians) of an organism capable of surviving on its own. A larva does not resemble the parent and must go through metamorphosis, or change, to reach its adult stage.

Leprosy: A disease of the skin and flesh characterized by scaly scabs and open sores.

Lichen: A complex of algae and fungi found growing on trees, rocks, or other solid surfaces.

Litter: A group of young animals, such as pigs or kittens, born at the same time from the same mother. Or, a layer of dead vegetation and other material covering the ground.

M

Malaria: A serious disease common in tropical countries, spread by the bites of female mosquitoes, that causes complications affecting the brain, blood, liver, and kidneys and can cause death.

Mammae: Milk-secreting organs of female mammals used to nurse young.

Mammals: Animals that feed their young on breast milk, are warm-blooded, and breathe air through their lungs.

Mangrove: Tropical coastal trees or shrubs that produce many supporting roots and that provide dense vegetation.

Marsupial: A type of mammal that does not have a well-developed placenta and gives birth to immature and under-developed young after a short gestation period. It continues to nurture the young, often in a pouch, until they are able to fend for themselves.

Matriarchal: Headed by a dominant female or females; said of animal societies.

Mechanoreceptor: Sensory nerve receptor modified to detect physical changes in the immediate environment, often having to do with touch and change of pressure or turbulence in water or air. In the platypus, mechanoreceptors in its bill may detect prey and obstacles.

Megachiroptera: One of the two groups of bats; these bats are usually larger than the microchiroptera.

Melon: The fatty forehead of a whale or dolphin.

Membrane: A thin, flexible layer of plant or animal tissue that covers, lines, separates or holds together, or connects parts of an organism.

Microchiroptera: One of two categories of bats; these make up most of the bats in the world and are generally smaller than the megachiroptera.

Migrate: To move from one area or climate to another as the seasons change, usually to find food or to mate.

Migratory pattern: The direction or path taken while moving seasonally from one region to another.

Molar: A broad tooth located near the back of the jaw with a flat, rough surface for grinding.

Mollusk: A group of animals without backbones that includes snails, clams, oysters, and similar hard-shelled animals.

Molt: The process by which an organism sheds its outermost layer of feathers, fur, skin, or exoskeleton.

Monogamous: Refers to a breeding system in which a male and a female mate only with each other during a breeding season or lifetime.

Muzzle: The projecting part of the head that includes jaws, chin, mouth, and nose.

Myxomatosis: A highly infectious disease of rabbits caused by a pox virus.

N

Near Threatened: A category defined by the IUCN suggesting that a species could become threatened with extinction in the future.

Nectar: Sweet liquid secreted by the flowers of various plants to attract pollinators (animals that pollinate, or fertilize, the flowers).

Neotropical: Relating to a geographic area of plant and animal life east, south, and west of Mexico's central plateau that includes Central and South America and the West Indies.

New World: Made up of North America, Central America, and South America; the western half of the world.

Nocturnal: Occurring or active at night.

Non-prehensile: Incapable of grasping; used to describe an animal's tail that cannot wrap around tree branches.

Noseleaf: Horseshoe-shaped flap of skin around the nose.

Nurse: To feed on mother's milk.

O

Old World: Australia, Africa, Asia, and Europe; in the eastern half of the world.

Omnivore: Plant- and meat-eating animal.

Opportunistic feeder: An animal that eats whatever food is available, either prey they have killed, other animals' kills, plants, or human food and garbage.

P

Pack ice: Large pieces of ice frozen together.

Patagium: The flap of skin that extends between the front and hind limbs. In bats, it stretches between the hind legs and helps the animal in flight; in colugos this stretches from the side of the neck to the tips of its fingers, toes, and tail.

Phylogenetics: Field of biology that deals with the relationships between organisms. It includes the discovery of these relationships, and the study of the causes behind this pattern.

Pinnipeds: Marine mammals, including three families of the order Carnivora, namely Otariidae (sea lions and fur seals), Phocidae (true seals), and Odobenidae (walrus).

Placenta: An organ that grows in the mother's uterus and lets the mother and developing offspring share food and oxygen through the blood.

Placental mammal: Any species of mammal that carries embryonic and fetal young in the womb through a long gestation period, made possible via the placenta, a filtering organ passing nutrients, wastes, and gases between mother and young.

Plantigrade: Walking on the heel and sole of the foot, instead of on the toes. Plantigrade species include bears and humans.

Plate tectonics: Geological theory holding that Earth's surface is composed of rigid plates or sections that move about the surface in response to internal pressure, creating the major geographical features such as mountains.

Poach: To hunt animals illegally.

Pod: In animal behavioral science (and in some zoology uses) the term pod is used to represent a group of whales, seals, or dolphins.

Pollen: Dust-like grains or particles produced by a plant that contain male sex cells.

Pollination: Transfer of pollen from the male reproductive organs to the female reproductive organs of plants.

Pollinator: Animal which carries pollen from one seed plant to another, unwittingly aiding the plant in its reproduction. Common pollinators include insects, especially bees, butterflies, and moths; birds; and bats.

Polyandry: A mating system in which a single female mates with multiple males.

Polyestrous: A female animal having more than one estrous cycle (mating period) within a year.

Polygamy: A mating system in which males and females mate with multiple partners.

Polygyny: A mating system in which a single male mates with multiple females.

Predator: An animal that eats other animals.

Prehensile: Able to control and use to grasp objects, characteristically associated with tails. Prehensile tails have evolved independently many times, for instance, in marsupials, rodents, primates, porcupines, and chameleons.

Prey: Organism hunted and eaten by a predator.

Primary forest: A forest characterized by a full-ceiling canopy formed by the branches of tall trees and several layers of smaller trees. This type of forest lacks ground vegetation because sunlight cannot penetrate through the canopy.

Promiscuity: Mating in which individuals mate with as many other individuals as they can or want to.

Puberty: The age of sexual maturity.

Q

Quadruped: Walking or running on four limbs.

R

Rabies: A viral infection spread through the bite of certain warm-blooded animals; it attacks the nervous system and can be fatal if untreated.

Rainforest: An evergreen woodland of the tropics distinguished by a continuous leaf canopy and an average rainfall of about 100 inches (250 centimeters) per year.

Regurgitate: Eject the contents of the stomach through the mouth; to vomit.

Rookery: A site on land where seals congregate to mate and raise the young.

Roost: A place where animals, such as bats, sit or rest on a perch, branch, etc.

S

Savanna: A biome characterized by an extensive cover of grasses with scattered trees, usually transitioning between areas dominated by forests and those dominated by grasses and having alternating seasonal climates of precipitation and drought.

Scavenger: An animal that eats carrion, dead animals.

Scent gland: Formed from modified, or changed, sweat glands, these glands produce and/or give off strong-smelling chemicals that give information, such as marking territory, to other animals.

Scent mark: To leave an odor, such as of urine or scent gland secretions, to mark a territory or as a means of communication.

Scrotum: The external pouch containing the testicles.

Scrub forest: A forest with short trees and shrubs.

Scrubland: An area similar to grassland but which includes scrub (low-growing plants and trees) vegetation.

Seamount: An underwater mountain that does not rise above the surface of the ocean.

Seashore: When referring to a biome, formed where the land meets the ocean.

Secondary forest: A forest characterized by a less-developed canopy, smaller trees, and a dense ground vegetation found on the edges of forests and along rivers and streams. The immature vegetation may also result from the removal of trees by logging and/or fires.

Semiaquatic: Partially aquatic; living or growing partly on land and partly in water.

Semiarid: Very little rainfall each year, between 10 and 20 inches (25 to 51 centimeters).

Sexually mature: Capable of reproducing.

Solitary: Living alone or avoiding the company of others.

Species: A group of living things that share certain distinctive characteristics and can breed together in the wild.

Spermaceti: A waxy substance found in the head cavity of some whales.

Steppe: Wide expanse of semiarid relatively level plains, found in cool climates and characterized by shrubs, grasses, and few trees.

Streamline: To smooth out.

Succulent: A plant that has fleshy leaves to conserve moisture.

Suckle: To nurse or suck on a mother's nipple to get milk.

Syndactyly: A condition in which two bones (or digits) fuse together to become a single bone.

T

Tactile: Having to do with the sense of touch.

Talon: A sharp hooked claw.

Taxonomy: The science dealing with the identification, naming, and classification of plants and animals.

Teat: A projection through which milk passes from the mother to the nursing young; a nipple.

Temperate: Areas with moderate temperatures in which the climate undergoes seasonal change in temperature and moisture. Temperate regions of the earth lie primarily between 30 and 60° latitude in both hemispheres.

Terrestrial: Relating to the land or living primarily on land.

Territorial: A pattern of behavior that causes an animal to stay in a limited area and/or to keep certain other animals of the same species (other than its mate, herd, or family group) out of the area.

Thicket: An area represented by a thick, or dense, growth of shrubs, underbrush, or small trees.

Threatened: Describes a species that is threatened with extinction.

Torpor: A short period of inactivity characterized by an energy-saving, deep sleep-like state in which heart rate, respiratory rate and body temperature drop.

Traction: Resistance to a surface to keep from slipping.

Tragus: A flap of skin near the base of the external ear.

Tributary: A small stream that feeds into a larger one.

Tropical: The area between 23.5° north and south of the equator. This region has small daily and seasonal changes in temperature, but great seasonal changes in precipitation. Generally, a hot and humid climate that is completely or almost free of frost.

Tundra: A type of ecosystem dominated by lichens, mosses, grasses, and woody plants. It is found at high latitudes (arctic tundra) and high altitudes (alpine tundra). Arctic tundra is underlain by permafrost and usually very wet.

Turbulent: An irregular, disorderly mode of flow.

U

Underfur: Thick soft fur lying beneath the longer and coarser guard hair.

Understory: The trees and shrubs between the forest canopy and the ground cover.

Ungulates: Hoofed animals, such as deer and elk.

Urine washing: A monkey behavior in which it soaks its hands with urine, then rubs the liquid on its fur and feet so as to leave the scent throughout its forest routes.

Uterus: A pear-shaped, hollow muscular organ in which a fetus develops during pregnancy.

V

Vertebra (pl. vertebrae): A component of the vertebral column, or backbone, found in vertebrates.

Vertebrate: An animal having a spinal column (backbone).

Vertical: Being at a right angle to the horizon. Up and down movements or supports.

Vestigial: A degenerate or imperfectly developed biological structure that once performed a useful function at an earlier stage of the evolution of the species.

Vibrissae: Stiff sensory hairs that can be found near the nostrils or other parts of the face in many mammals and the snouts, tails, ears, and sometimes feet of many insectivores.

Vocalization: Sound made by vibration of the vocal tract.

Vulnerable: An IUCN category referring to a species that faces a high risk of extinction.

W

Wallaby: An Australian marsupial similar to a kangaroo but smaller.

Wean: When a young animal no longer feeds on its mother's milk and instead begins to eat adult food.

Wetlands: Areas that are wet or covered with water for at least part of the year and support aquatic plants, such as marshes, swamps, and bogs.

Woodlands: An area with a lot of trees and shrubs.

Y

Yolk-sac placenta: A thin membrane that develops in the uterus of marsupials that does not fuse with the mother's uterus and results in short pregnancies with the young being born with poorly developed organs.

Getting to Know Mammals

MAMMALS

Mammals are found on all continents and in all seas. It isn't easy to tell that an animal is a mammal. A combination of special features separates mammals from other animals.

Mammal milk

Only mammals can feed their young with milk produced by their body. This milk comes from special glands called mammae. A female may have two mammary glands or as many as a dozen or more. Mammal milk is very healthy for infants and immediately available.

Body temperature

Mammals are warm-blooded, meaning they keep a constant body temperature. To keep their temperature fairly constant, a mammal needs some protective covering. Hair, made of a protein called keratin, serves several functions. One function is insulation, controlling the amount of body heat that escapes into the mammal's environment through the skin.

Mammal hair

All mammals have hair at some time of their life. Some have a lot, such as gorillas, and some have very little, such as the naked mole rats. There are three types of hair: a coarse long topcoat, a fine undercoat, and special sensory hairs, or whiskers.

In some mammals, hair has unusual forms. Porcupines have stiff, sharp, and thickened hairs called quills. Anteaters have

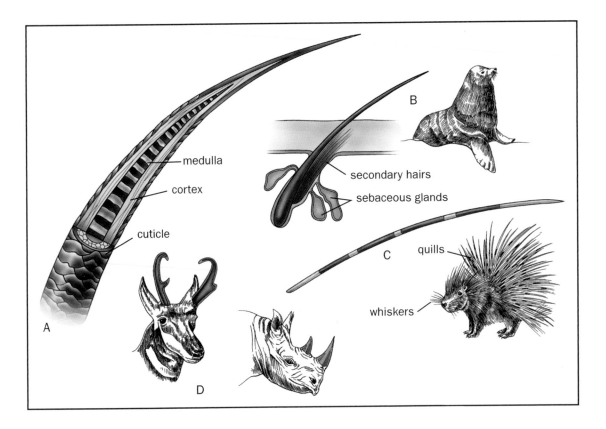

medulla

cortex

cuticle

A

B

secondary hairs

sebaceous glands

C

quills

whiskers

D

A. Cross section of a hair. B. Hairs may provide insulation and waterproofing. Specialized hair includes quills, whiskers (C), and horns (D). (Illustration by Patricia Ferrer. Reproduced by permission.)

sharp-edged scales made of modified hairs. These modified, or changed, hairs are protective against predators.

Mammals that live all or most of their lives in water, such as sea otters, may have a lot of dense, long hair, or fur. Others have much less hair, but a very thick hide, or skin, plus a thick layer of fat or blubber underneath the hide.

Hair color and pattern may vary. Males and females may have different fur colors. Special color patterns, such as a skunk's black and white fur, act as warnings. Hair color can also serve as camouflage, enabling the mammal to blend into its background.

Some mammals have fur color changes in summer and winter. Colors can be entirely different. Snowshoe rabbits and weasels can be brownish in summer, and almost pure white in winter. But this only happens if there is snow where they live. If it seldom snows, weasels and snowshoe rabbits stay brown.

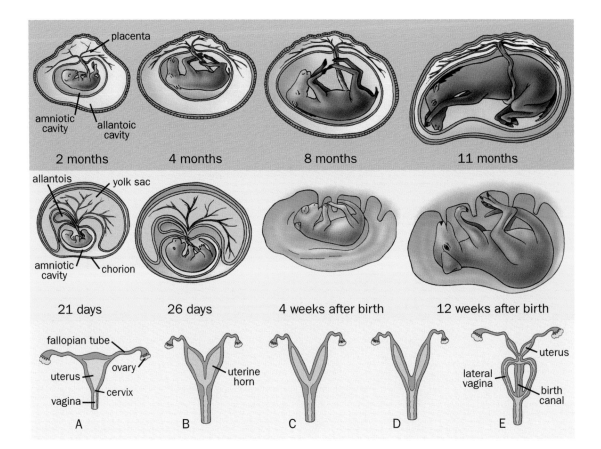

Reproduction

Mammals have two genetic sexes, male and female. Ninety percent of mammals are placental (pluh-SENT-ul). In placental mammals, the baby develops, or grows, within the mother's body before it enters the world. What about the other 10 percent? These mammals lay eggs. There are only three egg-laying mammals alive today.:

Other mammal features

Other bodily mammal features include their ability to breathe air through their lungs. Water-dwelling mammals, such as the whale and porpoise, do this too. Mammals have jaws, usually with teeth. Mammals usually have four limbs. Mammals have a four-chambered heart. Mammals have vertebrae, or back bones, unlike invertebrates such as insects, in which there is an outside shell or structure called an exoskeleton.

Top: Placental mammal development. Middle row: Marsupial mammal development. Types of uterus: A. Simplex; B. Bipartite; C. Bicornuate; D. Duplex; E. Marsupial. (Illustration by Patricia Ferrer. Reproduced by permission.)

This life-sized woolly mammoth model is kept in the Royal British Columbia Museum. Woolly mammoths were as tall as 10 feet (3 meters). (© Jonathan Blair/Corbis. Reproduced by permission.)

FOSSIL MAMMALS

Fossils are body parts of animals that lived very long ago. Not many long-ago mammals are preserved as fossils. But some entire mammal fossils have been discovered, such as a 10-foot (3-meter) woolly mammoth preserved in Siberian frozen ground, and an Ice Age woolly rhinoceros discovered in Poland, preserved in asphalt.

Many long-ago mammals lived in a warm, wet world. They ate soft, leafy plants. The earliest known mammals were possibly shrew-like creatures living about 190 million years ago. Later larger mammals occurred, then disappeared, or became extinct. These include the mesohippus, a three-toed horse only 24 inches (60 centimeters) high; a giant pig with a head that was 4 feet (1.22 meters) in length; and the smilodon, a huge saber-toothed cat with canine teeth that were 8 inches (20.3

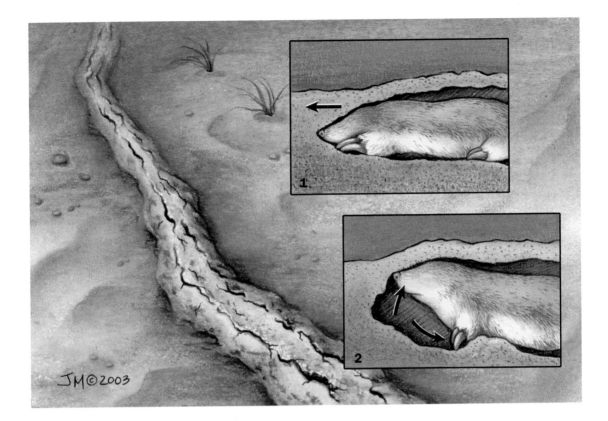

The Grant's desert mole uses its powerful forelimbs to burrow through the sands of the Namib Desert in southern Africa. The golden mole moves forward (1), and enlarges the tunnel by pushing dirt up with its head and back with its claws (2). (Illustration by Jacqueline Mahannah. Reproduced by permission.)

centimeters) in length. By about 15,000 years ago, long-ago people were hunting mammals with stone-pointed spears. Most of the animals they hunted are extinct for various reasons, some known, and some unknown.

WHERE MAMMALS LIVE

Underground mammals

Some small mammals spend all or most of their lives living underground. These include many species of prairie dogs, chipmunks, moles, groundhogs, Greenland collared lemmings, and Peruvian tuco-tucos. Each of these mammals has a special body design enabling it to survive underground.

Moles have large, powerful shoulders and short, very powerful forelimbs. Spade-like feet have claws, enabling quick digging. Hind feet have webbed toes, enabling the mole to kick soil backwards effectively. Velvety-type fur enables a mole to slip easily through its tunnels. And, although moles

A RECENT DISCOVERY

A bright orange, mouse-like mammal, weighing 0.5 ounces (15 grams) and measuring 3.12 inches (8 centimeters) plus a long tail, has recently been discovered in the Philippines. It has whiskers five times longer than its head. It can open and eat very hard tree nuts that no other mammal in the area can eat.

have almost no eyes, they can rely on touch, smell, and sensitivity to vibration to find underground insects and earthworms.

Sea mammals

Some mammals live in the sea, including manatees, whales, seals, and dolphins. While some need air every few minutes, a sperm whale can remain underwater for an hour and a half. How is this possible? Some sea mammals have a very low metabolism. They don't use up the their oxygen quickly and can store large amounts of oxygen in their bodies.

Tree mammals

Some mammals spend all or most of their lives in trees. Tree-dwelling mammals are often hidden from sight by leaves, vines, and branches. Tree-dwelling mammals include the Eastern pygmy possum, which nests in small tree hollows; the koala; Lumholtz's tree kangaroo, which leaps from branch to branch; the three-toed sloth; and the clouded leopard.

Flying mammals

The only truly flying mammals are bats. The sound of bat wings was first heard about 50 million years ago. Some bats are large, with a wingspan almost 7 feet (21.3 meters) wide. Some are small, as the Philippine bamboo bat, whose body is just 2 inches (5.08 centimeters) long.

Other mammals only appear to fly, such as the southern flying squirrel and the colugo, or Malayan flying lemur. These mammals have gliding membranes, skin folds from body front to legs, that, when spread out, act almost like a parachute. For example, the feathertail glider, a tiny possum, crawls along narrow branches. At branch end, it leaps out and slightly downward. Spreading its gliding membranes, it speeds through the air, landing on a nearby tree.

Mountain mammals

Some mammals spend most of their lives on mountain peaks. These include Asian corkscrew-horned markhor goats, North

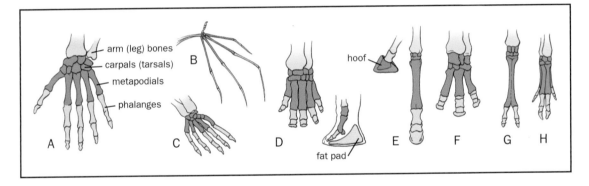

American Rocky Mountain bighorn sheep, and Siberian ibex. Siberian ibex can stand anyplace on any pinnacle with just enough room for its four feet. North American mountain goats can climb up a mountain peak, almost going straight up. Specially shaped hooves help.

Other high mountain dwelling mammals include snow leopards and Asian pikas that can survive at 19,685 feet (6,000 meters). Gunnison's prairie dogs do well up to 11,500 feet (3,505 meters).

Desert mammals

Some mammals spend most of their lives in arid, or very dry areas. Not all deserts are sandy like Death Valley or the Sahara. Some are rocky. Other arid areas are mountainous. Desert dwelling mammals include the North African elephant shrew, white-tailed antelope squirrel, and the desert kangaroo rat. No mammal can live without water. Desert rodents have a way to extract, or get, water from their own body functions. Rodents may also get water by eating plants, seeds, roots, and insects that contain water.

Larger mammals live in arid regions too. The striped hyena can survive in stony desert as long as it is within 6 miles (9.7 kilometers) of water. Fennecs, a very small fox living near sand dunes, can go a long time without drinking. Camels can use body fluids when no water is available.

WHAT DO MAMMALS EAT?

Insect-eaters

Some mammals have mostly insect meals. Insect-eating mammals include the moles, aye-ayes and aardvarks. The aardvark

Mammals' hands and feet differ depending on where the animal lives and how it gets around. A. A hominid hand is used for grasping objects; B. A bat's wing is used for flight; C. A pinniped's flipper helps move it through the water. Hoofed animals move around on all fours: D. Elephant foot; E. Equid (horse family) foot; F. Odd-toed hoofed foot; G. Two-toed hoofed foot; H. Four-toed hoofed foot. (Illustration by Patricia Ferrer. Reproduced by permission.)

has a sticky tongue that can reach out as long as 1 foot (0.3 meters) to capture its ant and termite meals.

Plant eaters

Some mammals eat nothing but plants. Plant eaters include pandas, the West Indian manatee, and the red-bellied wallaby. Some mammals have a single stomach that breaks the plant food down into small pieces. Other mammals, such as cows and camels, have a large stomach made of several parts. Each part does a separate job of breaking down difficult-to-digest plants.

Some mammals eat both plants and fruit. These include the 14-ounce (400-gram) Eurasian harvest mouse, the 100-pound (45-kilogram) South American capybara, and the African elephant. An elephant can eat up to 500 pounds (227 kilograms) of grass, plants, and fruit per day.

Meat eaters

Mammals eating mostly meat or fish are carnivorous. Carnivorous mammals have long, pointed, and very strong incisor teeth. Carnivores include polar bears, hyenas, walruses, and Eu-

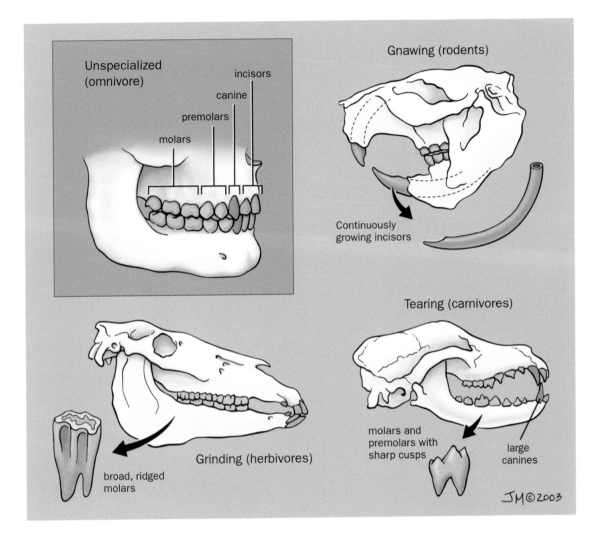

Mammals have different tooth shapes for different functions. Herbivores typically have large, flattened teeth for chewing plants. Rodents' ever-growing incisors are used for gnawing. Carnivores have teeth for holding and efficiently dismembering their prey. (Illustration by Jacqueline Mahannah. Reproduced by permission.)

ropean wild cats. The European wild cat may be an ancestor of our house cats.

Omnivores

Some mammals eat just about anything. They are omnivorous. Omnivorous mammals include wolverines, raccoons, and wild pigs. Wild pigs are the ancestors of our domestic pigs.

MAMMAL SLEEPING HABITS

Day or night

Some mammals sleep during the night, others sleep during the day. The night sleepers are diurnal, active during the day.

THE BIGGEST, THE TALLEST, AND THE SMALLEST

The largest and heaviest mammal alive today is the blue whale. One adult female measured 110.2 feet (33.6 meters). Blue whale weight can reach 268,400 pounds (121,853 kilograms).

The largest living land animal is the African bush elephant. From trunk tip to tail tip, a male has measured 33 feet (10 meters). Body weight was 24,000 pounds (10,886 kilograms).

The smallest non-flying mammal is the Savi's white-toothed pygmy shrew. An adult's head and body together measure only 2 inches (5.1 centimeters) long. Maximum weight is 0.09 ounces (2.5 grams).

How small is this? This pygmy shrew can travel through tunnels left by large earthworms!

The smallest flying mammal is the rare Kitti's hog-nosed bat, or "bumblebee bat," from Thailand. Head and body length is just 1.14 to 1.29 inches (29 to 33 millimeters). Weight is just 0.06 to 0.07 ounces (1.75 to 2 grams). This tiny bat was only discovered in 1973.

The tallest living animal is the giraffe. The average adult male, or bull, is 16 feet (4.9 meters) high, from front hoof to head horn tip. This size male weighs 2,376 to 2,800 pounds (1,078 to 1,270 kilograms).

The day sleepers are nocturnal, active at night. They may have special night vision. Many desert animals are nocturnal, moving about when it is cooler.

Hibernation

Some bat species hibernate through an entire winter. Hibernation is like a very long deep sleep. When a mammal hibernates, it uses up body fat that has accumulated from food eaten in good weather. Hibernators include the North African jird, groundhogs or woodchucks, and several dormice species. Dormice enter a tree hollow or ground burrow in autumn, and don't come out until springtime.

Bears don't truly hibernate. Their sleep isn't deep. They slow down quite a bit, and nap a lot, but do not sleep through an entire winter.

A new hibernating pattern has just been discovered. Madagascar fat-tailed lemurs hibernate in tree holes when winter daytime temperatures rise above 86° Fahrenheit (30° Celsius). They sleep for seven months. Scientists belief these dwarf lemurs find less food in what is the dry season in Madagascar, so they go to into deep sleep to preserve energy until a better food supply appears.

REPRODUCTION

Mating

Some mammals mate for life, such as wolves and sometimes coyotes. More commonly, a male may mate with several females each breeding period. Or a female may mate with several males.

Some mammals have one litter each year. Others have a litter only every two or three years. But the North American meadow mouse can have seventeen litters per year. That's a group of babies about every three weeks!

There may be one or more infants in a litter. Bats, giraffes, and two-toed sloths have just one baby per year. However, the Madagascar tenrec can produce thirty-two babies in just one litter.

Opossums are marsupial animals. The mother has a pouch in which the young continue to develop after they're born. (© Mary Ann McDonald/Corbis. Reproduced by permission.)

Child care

All mammal infants need protection. They are very small compared to their parents. They may be blind and hairless. Usually females provide care. However, in a few mammal species, such as the golden lion marmoset, the male does most of the care.

Female marsupial mammals, such as opossums, koalas, and kangaroos, have a pouch, like a pocket, on the front or under the body. Their tiny babies are incompletely developed when they are born. At birth, an opossum baby is about the size of a dime. It crawls immediately into its mother's pouch and stays there until ready to survive outside. The pouch contains mammary glands so babies can feed.

SOCIAL LIFE

Solitary mammals

Some mammals are solitary. They keep company with another of the same kind only when mating or when raising young. Solitary mammals include the giant anteaters, European bison, and right whales.

Japanese macaques are social animals, and groom each other regularly. (© Herbert Kehrer/OKAPIA/Photo Researchers, Inc. Reproduced by permission.)

Group living

Many mammals live in groups. In large groups, some eat, some rest, and some keep guard. Baboons, for example, may have from twenty to 300 animals in a group. One or more adult males lead each group. If a predator, such as a leopard, approaches, the males take action against it, while the females and young escape.

Some mammals travel in herds. Musk oxen travel in closely packed herds of fifteen to 100 individuals. These herds include males and females. Bighorn sheep females travel in herds of five to fifteen, with a dominant ewe, or female, as the leader.

Pack mammals get their food by cooperation. They work together to bring down much larger prey. Dingoes, killer whales, and lions hunt in packs.

MAMMALS AND PEOPLE

Domesticated mammals

About 14,000 years ago, humans began controlling, or domesticating, certain animals. This made humans' lives easier.

Horses have been domesticated for practical uses, such as transportation, and for entertainment, such as horse riding and racing. (© Kevin R. Morris/Corbis. Reproduced by permission.)

The earliest domesticated mammal was probably the dog. Some scientists think hunters adopted wolf cubs and trained them to smell out game, animals they hunted for food.

People use mammals for many purposes. Cows provide meat, milk, cheese, butter, and hide. Camels, yaks, and Indian elephants carry or pull heavy items. Water buffaloes do hauling and can provide milk. Horses provide transportation and racing activities. Other domesticated animals include rabbits, pigs, goats, sheep, cavies, and capybaras.

People keep animals as pets. Common mammal pets are dogs, cats, guinea pigs, and hamsters.

Pest mammals

Some mammals are considered pests. These include rats, mice, and, depending where they live, gophers, rabbits, and ground squirrels. Rats can transmit disease-carrying fleas. Rabbits and gophers eat garden and food plants.

ENDANGERED MAMMALS

Mammals in danger

Of about 5,000 mammal species currently existing, over 1,000 are seriously endangered. Few wild mammals can live outside their natural habitat. When land is cleared for farming or housing, animals making homes there must leave, if there is any place for them to go. If not, they die from starvation or (because they are easily seen) from predators. Slowly, or quickly, the mammal species disappears.

Many human habits lead to endangerment. Hunting for amusement, killing for fur or body parts, native and commercial killing for food, fishing gear entrapment, land-destructive wars, and the illegal pet trade all take their toll. So do chemicals.

Some mammals are probably on the way to extinction, or total elimination. There are only about sixty Java rhinoceros left in the world. The Seychelles sheath-tailed bat has only about fifty individuals remaining. Yellow-tailed woolly monkeys number no more than 250 individuals. Mediterranean monk seals may be killed by scuba divers, and number only 600 individuals.

Saving endangered animals

Today many people are trying to save endangered animals. Methods include zoo breeding, establishing forest reserves, and training native populations that animals can be an economic benefit. Ecotourism, people visiting a country to see its animals in their natural habitat, is increasing. There are laws against importing and exporting endangered species. And, in some parts of the world, there are laws against land destruction.

Some mammals have possibly been rescued from immediate extinction. The American bison once roamed the North American prairies, numbering about 50 million. After slaughter by soldiers and settlers for food and sport, by 1889 only 541 remained alive. Now, in the United States, there are about 35,000 in protected areas. California northern elephant seals were once reduced to fewer than 100 members due to hunting. Today, protected, there are about 50,000. The ibex was once hunted for supposedly curative body parts and few were left. But in 1922, a National Park was established in the Italian Alps, where several thousand now live. The Mongolian wild horse, once thought to be extinct, now has a special reserve in Mongolia.

Too late to save

Some mammals became extinct only recently. Recently extinct animals include Steller's sea cows, which became extinct in about 1768. The Tasmanian wolf was last seen in 1933, eliminated by bounty hunters. The African bluebuck disappeared from Earth in 1880. The quagga, from southern Asia, was hunted for hides and meat. The last known quagga, a relative of the zebra, died in a Dutch zoo in 1883.

FOR MORE INFORMATION

Books

Boitani, Luigi, and Stefania Bartoli. *Guide to Mammals.* New York: Simon and Schuster, 1982.

Booth, Ernest S. *How to Know the Mammals.* Dubuque, IA: Wm. C. Brown Company Publishers, 1982.

Embery, Joan, and Edward Lucaire. *Joan Embery's Collection of Amazing Animal Facts.* New York: Dell Publishing, 1983.

Jones, J. Knox Jr., and David M. Armstrong. *Guide to Mammals of the Plains States.* Lincoln, NE: University of Nebraska Press, 1985.

Kite, L. Patricia. *Raccoons.* Minneapolis: Lerner Publications Company, 2004.

Kite, L. Patricia. *Blood-Feeding Bugs and Beasts.* Brookfield, CT: Millbrook Press, 1996.

Line, Les, and Edward Ricciuti. *National Audubon Society Book of Wild Animals.* New York: H. L. Abrams, 1996.

Nowak, Ronald M., and John L. Paradiso. *Walker's Mammals of the World.* Baltimore and London: The Johns Hopkins University Press, 1983.

Vogel, Julia, and John F. McGee. *Dolphins (Our Wild World.* Minnetonka, MN: Northword Press, 2001.

Walters, Martin. *Young Readers Book of Animals.* New York, London, Toronto, Sydney, and Tokyo: Simon & Schuster Books for Young Readers, 1990.

Whitaker, John O. Jr. *National Audubon Society Field Guide to North American Mammals.* New York: Alfred A. Knopf, 2000.

Wilson, D. E., and D. M. Reeder. *Mammal Species of the World.* Washington, DC: Smithsonian Institution Press, 1993.

Wood, Gerald L. *Animal Facts and Feats.* New York: Sterling Publishing, 1977.

Woods, Samuel G., and Jeff Cline. *Amazing Book of Mammal Records: The Largest, the Smallest, the Fastest, and Many More!* Woodbridge, CT: Blackbirch Press, 2000.

Periodicals

Allen, Leslie. "Return of the Pandas." *Smithsonian Magazine* (April 2001): 44–55.

Chadwick, Douglas H. "A Mine of Its Own." *Smithsonian Magazine* (May 2004): 26–27.

Cheater, Mark. "Three Decades of the Endangered Species Act." *Defenders* (Fall 2003): 8–13.

Conover, Adele. "The Object at Hand." *Smithsonian Magazine* (October 1996).

Gore, Rick. "The Rise of Mammals." *National Geographic* (April 2003): 2–37.

Mitchell, Meghan. "Securing Madagascar's Rare Wildlife." *Science News* (November 1, 1997): 287.

Pittman, Craig. "Fury Over a Gentle Giant." *Smithsonian Magazine* (February 2004): 54–59.

"Prehistoric Mammals." *Ranger Rick* (October 2000): 16.

Sherwonit, Bill. "Protecting the Wolves of Denali." *National Parks Magazine* (September/October 2003): 21–25.

Sunquist, Fiona. "Discover Rare Mystery Mammals." *National Geographic* (January 1999): 22–29.

Weidensaul, Scott. "The Rarest of the Rare." *Smithsonian Magazine* (November 2000): 118–128.

"Wildlife of Tropical Rain Forests." *National Geographic World* (January 2000): 22–25.

Web sites

Animal Info. http://www.animalinfo.org/ (accessed on June 6, 2004).

"Class Mammalia." Animal Diversity Web. http://animaldiversity.ummz.umich.edu/site/accounts/information/Mammalia004 (accessed on June 5, 2004).

"Hibernating Primate Found in Tropics." CNN Science & Space. http://www.cnn.com/2004/TECH/science/06/24/science.hibernation.reuit/inex.html (accessed on June 24, 2004).

"Ice Age Mammals." National Museum of Natural History. http://www.mnh.si.edu/museum/VirtualTour/Tour/First/IceAge/index.html (accessed on June 6, 2004).

"Mammary Glands." Animal Diversity Web. http://animaldiversity.ummz.umich.edu/site/topics/mammal_anatomy/mammary_glands.html (accessed on June 6, 2004).

order

CHAPTER

PHYSICAL CHARACTERISTICS

There are many different types of primates. Some are very small—the smallest primate is the pygmy mouse lemur, which weighs only one ounce (30 grams). Others are very large—the largest primate is an adult male gorilla. A full-grown male gorilla can weigh 375 pounds (170 kilograms) or more, and be as tall as 6 feet (1.8 meters). Primates include the lemurs, lorises and bushbabies, tarsiers, New World monkeys, Old World monkeys, apes, and humans.

Because there are so many different types of primates, appearance varies quite a bit. Body hair may be long, as in the orangutan or the golden lion tamarin. Other primates have short fur all over the body, such as the chimpanzee or pygmy marmoset. There are many quite colorful primates. The male mandrill of Central Africa has bright red and blue on his face and red, blue, and violet coloration on his rump. The Japanese macaque is medium brown with a red face. The golden langur of China has flame orange fur with a bright blue face.

But even though primates may be quite different in size and color, they do have many things in common. Primates tend to have longer arms and legs in relation to body size than other mammals. Their hands and feet are shaped so that they can hold on to objects very well. On a primate's foot, the big toe is set far apart from the other four digits, or toes. This allows an especially strong wraparound grasp on branches. Every primate has this special grasping action of its feet except humans. The ventral or bottom surface of both hands and feet have special pads that help

phylum

class

subclass

● **order**

monotypic order

suborder

family

primates grip. This is another way that enables primates to achieve a better hold on tree limbs. Also, primates usually have rounded skulls with a large brain for their body size. Their eyes are set forward in the face for stereoscopic vision, which allows them to see things around them in three-dimensions (or "3-D"), rather than two-dimensions, like a page in a book.

GEOGRAPHIC RANGE

Primates are found in Africa, Asia, and South and Central America. The largest number of primates live in Africa, including the pottos, bushbabies, guenons, mangabeys, colobus monkeys, chimpanzees, gorillas, and baboons. Tarsiers, macaques, lorises, and most of the leaf monkeys live in Asia. Lemurs and aye-ayes are found only on the island of Madagascar. The New World monkeys, such as the marmosets, tamarins, and squirrel monkeys, live in South and Central America.

HABITAT

Primates live in a variety of habitats, including evergreen tropical rainforests with rain throughout the year, dry scrub forests, dry areas that have forests along river banks, coastal scrublands, bamboo stands, and dry deciduous forests where trees lose their leaves each year. For example, the mandrills and chimpanzees can be found in rainforests, and the ring-tailed lemurs live in dry woodlands. Rainforests are evergreen forests with a short dry season and high rainfall. Woodlands are areas with a lot of trees and shrubs.

DIET

Primates eat a wide variety of foods. All primates may eat insects, leaves, nuts, seeds, plant gums or fluids, and fruits. But each primate may have a food preference. The indri prefers young plants and leaves, fruit, and seeds. The aye-aye eats fruit and insect larvae (LAR-vee), or young. The blue monkey eats fruits, leaves, and slow-moving insects, as well as occasional birds and small animals.

BEHAVIOR AND REPRODUCTION

Most primates are arboreal, living in trees. Some are active during the day, such as the black lemurs and chimpanzees. Others are active only at night, such as the owl monkeys and lesser bushbabies. A few primates live primarily on the ground, such as mandrill baboons and gorillas, even though they may sleep in trees for protection.

A few primates live alone most of the time, such as the orangutan and the potto. However, most primates are quite social, living together in small or large groups. Verreaux's sifaka lives in groups of about six animals. The moustached monkey lives in groups of up to thirty-five animals. The savanna baboon may have 200 animals in its group. Depending on species, the groups have different numbers of males and females. The indri has equal numbers of males and females. The guenons, or forest monkeys, have one male to each group of adult females. This is sometimes called a harem (HARE-um) group. The gray-cheeked mangabey groups have two adult females to one adult male.

Primate females give birth to live young. Compared to other animal species of the same size, they have long pregnancies. Bushbabies are pregnant four to five months, and may have one to three babies each time. Baboons are pregnant for six months, and usually have one baby each time. Gorillas are pregnant for eight and a half months and have one baby each time. Babies are usually born covered with fur, and with their eyes and ears open.

Dedicated care by one or both parents is usual for primates. Babies nurse for a long time. There is a lot of physical contact between the infant and the mother—this is often because the infants travel with the mother, clinging to her fur. In some primate species, such as the cotton-top tamarin and Goeldi's monkey, they travel with the father too. They may ride clinging to a parent's front, belly, or back.

Primates often interact with each other in social ways. Grooming, or cleaning, each other is one example. Depending on species, grooming may be done with the teeth, with hands, or with a finger, or grooming claw, which has a long nail specialized for grooming. Primates also interact with sound communication. Each sound is a form of communication.

SOUNDING OFF

Primates make a wide variety of vocalizations, or sounds. The dourocouli (or night monkeys) of South America grunt. Howler monkeys sound their loud howl from the trees at dawn, during territorial arguments, and when they hear loud noises. Long-haired spider monkeys squeak, grunt, hoot, wail, moan, and scream. The sifakas get their name from the clear "si-fak!" call that they make. Male mandrills both grunt and make high-pitched crowing sounds. The Bornean orangutan male makes a booming sound that can be heard a half mile away. Tamarin monkeys and marmosets make a bird-like twittering sound. Marmosets can make ultrasonic sounds that humans can't hear.

THE ORGAN GRINDER'S MONKEY

In the early 1900s, the 6-pound (2.7-kilogram), brown, pale-fronted capuchin monkey would hold out its hand for money when its organ grinder owner played music in the streets of New York and Boston. The capuchin is a very intelligent primate. It has a large brain relative to its small size, and excellent eye-to-hand coordination, enabling it to accurately pick up the tiniest items. It would grab fruit and coins from passers-by on the street.

PRIMATES AND PEOPLE

People hunt some non-human primate species for meat, unproven medicinal uses of their body parts, or capture them for pets. Zoos collect primates as exhibit animals. Some primates, such as the baboon, rhesus monkey, and the common marmoset, are used in laboratory biomedical research. Current breeding programs have slowed the practice of taking these animals from the wild. A few primates, in close contact with human living areas, have become crop pests, such as the macaques who raid fruit trees that humans grow.

If not threatened, primates seldom bother human beings. However, some may harbor viruses that can be transmitted to human beings, such as Ebola, a usually fatal disease.

CONSERVATION STATUS

About one-third of all primate species are threatened. Of these, 120 species are Critically Endangered, facing an extremely high risk of extinction in the wild; Endangered, facing a very high risk of extinction; or Vulnerable, facing a high risk of extinction. Critically Endangered species include the Sumatran orangutan, one species of snub-nosed monkey, three lion tamarin species, and two gentle lemur species. Most of the problems for these tree-dwelling animals come from deforestation, or tree destruction and removal. Hunting in some areas is also a problem, as are brush fires. Tourism, while increasing local awareness, also means increased development to house and feed tourists. There are captive breeding programs and protected national parks, but as habitat loss continues, extinction of several species is predicted.

FOR MORE INFORMATION

Books:

Alden, Peter C. *National Audubon Society Field Guide to African Wildlife*. New York: Alfred A. Knopf, 1995.

Coppard, Kit. *Africa's Animal Kingdom*. London: PRC Publishing Ltd., 2001.

Fink Martin, Patricia A. *Lemurs, Lorises and Other Lower Primates*. Danbury, CT: Children's Press, 2000.

Maynard, Thane. *Primates: Apes, Monkeys, and Prosimians.* Danbury, CT. Franklin Watts, 1999.

Sleeper, Barbara. *Primates.* San Francisco: Chronicle Books, 1997.

Periodicals:

"New Primate Faces Appear in Brazil." *National Geographic* (December 1998): Earth Almanac section.

Schleichert, Elizabeth. "Can We Save the Lemurs?" *Ranger Rick* (December 2000): 18–22.

Stewart, Doug. "Prosimians Find a Home Far From Home." *National Wildlife* (Feb/Mar 1998): 33–35.

Web sites:

Holder, M. K. "See and Hear." African Primates at Home. http://www .indiana.edu/~primate/primates.html (accessed on July 5, 2004).

Conservation International press release. *Eastern Lowland Gorilla Population Plummets 70 Percent since 1994.* http://conservation .org/xp/news/press_releases/2004/033004.xml (accessed on July 5, 2004).

LORISES AND POTTOS
Lorisidae

Class: Mammalia

Order: Primates

Family: Lorisidae

Number of species: 9 species

PHYSICAL CHARACTERISTICS

Lorises and pottos have short heads covered with hair. Snouts, or nose areas, are small. Their C-shaped ears are close to the scalp, and they have large, round, dark eyes. Arms and legs are long and about equal length. All ten fingers and ten toes have a claw, but the claw is longest on the second toe. This is called a grooming claw, and lorises and pottos use it to comb through and clean their fur. The index finger is quite small compared to the rest of the fingers, and their thumbs and big toes are located far from the other four fingers and toes. When these animals wrap their hands or feet around a tree branch, their grasping hold is very strong, allowing them to hold onto a branch for a long time.

Lorises and pottos are very small animals. The tiniest loris is the gray slender loris. It is only 8.5 inches (21.5 centimeters) long from head to the start of its tail. It weighs only 9 ounces (255 grams). The potto is the largest member of the Lorisidae. Tail length varies in the lorises and the pottos. Some, such as the slender loris, have no tail. Others may have a tail length of up to 2.5 inches (6.5 cm). Their color varies; pottos and lorises can be cream colored, pale brown, grayish brown, reddish brown, orange-brown, or dark brown. Some have mixed fur colors. Some lorises have contrasting markings or striped areas. The color contrast may be especially visible when it forms a ringed area around the large eyes, as it does in the pygmy slow loris.

GEOGRAPHIC RANGE

The slow lorises live throughout tropical rainforests in Southeast Asia. The slender lorises are found in the tropical forests of India and Sri Lanka. Pottos occur only in the tropical and subtropical forests of West and Central Africa.

HABITAT

Lorises and pottos live only in thickly forested areas. Most often, they live in the trees of tropical rainforests, forests where the trees are evergreen and there is a lot of rain.

DIET

Lorises are omnivores, eating both plants and very small animals. They are nocturnal, feeding at night. They locate food with their keen sense of smell. Diet includes insects, lizards, fruits, leaves, birds' eggs, and gum, the liquid from plants. Each species, or type, of Lorisidae, may have a food preference. When feeding, they hang by their feet from a branch.

LORISID COMMUNICATION

When Asian lorisids want to communicate with each other, they make specific noises, or vocalizations. Sounds vary by species, and include panting, hissing, growling, soft and loud whistles, rapid clicking, and chirping. The clicking sound made by infants when separated from their mother is a series of short, sharp, rapid clicks called a "zic" call.

BEHAVIOR AND REPRODUCTION

Lorisids (species in the family Lorisidae) are usually solitary animals, each having a specific range for its food searches. However, the home range (place where an animal feeds and lives) of males may overlap that of females. During the day, lorisids may sleep on a tree branch, in a hollow tree trunk, or in the fork of a tree. They typically sleep while curled up, with head and arms tucked between their thighs. While they see well in daylight and dark, they search for food at night. The animals move very slowly and carefully. Sometimes they don't even disturb tree leaves as they pass through. This careful behavior helps them to avoid predators, animals that hunt them for food. While moving through tree branches, they tend to drag their bottoms to mark their trail with urine. If a lorisid hears even the slightest sound that might mean a predator is nearby, it just stops and hangs on to a branch. With strong arms and legs, it can stay that way for hours, until it feels it can safely move again.

Lorisids may have more than one mate. Pregnancy is from about four to six months, depending on the species. Lorisids usually have just one baby at a time. Babies weigh from 1 to 2 ounces (28.4 to 56.7 grams). After a baby is born, it hangs on to the front fur of its mother's body for a few weeks. Sometimes, as she searches for food at night, the mother may place her infant on a small branch. The infant holds onto the branch until the mother returns. At night, while the mother sleeps, the baby holds onto her belly. As the infant grows, it begins to travel on its mother's back. Then it follows her. As the mother looks for food, she also is teaching her young how to look for, and recognize, suitable food. Young lorisids stay with their mother until they are about a year old, then go off on their own.

LORISES, POTTOS, AND PEOPLE

Large zoos may have special exhibits of lorisids and pottos. In their native homes, in some areas, they are trapped and kept as pets. Occasionally the larger species are used as food.

CONSERVATION STATUS

While no Lorisidae are considered Endangered, two are Vulnerable (facing a high risk of extinction, or dying out, in the wild) due to habitat loss. Two are Near Threatened (not currently threatened with extinction), and four species are fairly common.

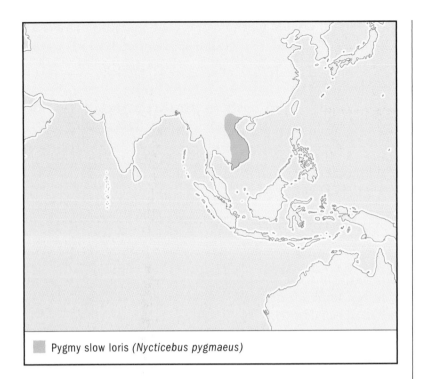

Pygmy slow loris (*Nycticebus pygmaeus*)

PYGMY SLOW LORIS
Nycticebus pygmaeus

Physical characteristics: This small loris is only 10 inches long (25.5 cm). It has no tail. Weight is just 11 ounces (310 grams), with males and females about the same size. The pygmy loris is colorful. It has bright orange-brown fur on its upper back and a light orange-gray area on its upper chest. Its face is gray, with a dark orange-brown eye mask, and a white stripe between its eyes.

Geographic range: The pygmy slow loris is found in China, Laos, and Vietnam.

Habitat: Pygmy slow lorises thrive in evergreen tropical rainforests.

Diet: Pygmy slow lorises eat fruit, insects, and gums (plant juices). Some scientists believe this species prefers to eat gum, because in captivity they have been seen making holes in tree wood to get plant sap.

Behavior and reproduction: Pygmy slow lorises usually travel and feed alone. Each has a preferred territory where it lives. During the

Young pygmy slow lorises stay with their mother until they are about a year old, then go off on their own. (Rod Williams/ Naturepl.com. Reproduced by permission.)

day, the pygmy slow loris sleeps holding on to branches in the midst of thick leaves and branches. At night, they use their strong arms and legs to move slowly and carefully, hand-over-hand, through trees. Like other lorisids, they mark their trails with urine.

Their mating system is not currently known. Females are pregnant for 192 days, a little more than six months. They may have one offspring (baby), or twins. Babies stay with the mother for a few weeks, hanging on to her belly. As the infant grows, it clings to its mother's back while she travels. Then it follows her. Young pygmy lorises stay with their mother until they are about a year old, then go off on their own.

Pygmy slow lorises and people: Because they move around mostly at night, and are quite small, few people see them. However, some pygmy slow lorises are kept as pets in their native areas. Large zoos may include them in special exhibits.

Conservation status: The pygmy slow loris is listed as Vulnerable due to habitat loss from deforestation. ■

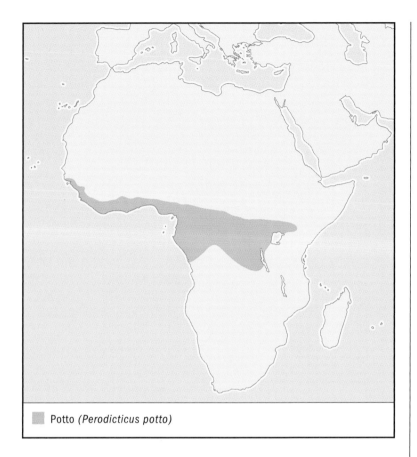

Potto (*Perodicticus potto*)

POTTO
Perodicticus potto

Physical characteristics: Pottos have dark fur on the top of their body, and light brown fur underneath. They have a body length of 15 inches (38.1 centimeters) with a 2.5-inch tail (6.5 centimeters). A grown potto weighs only about 2.75 pounds (1.25 kilograms). Its dark eyes are large and round.

As protection from predators, a potto's upper back has a humped area of thickened skin on top of long vertebral spines. This thickened area, often called a shield, is covered by fur and contains long tactile, or feeler, hairs. These tactile hairs help detect a possible predator attack, and the shield can be turned toward the predator to help protect the potto from the attack.

The potto's upper back has a humped area of thickened skin on top of long vertebral spines. This thickened area, often called a shield, can be turned toward an attacking predator for protection. (Rod Williams/Bruce Coleman Inc. Reproduced by permission.)

Geographic range: Pottos are found in Africa, including Nigeria, Sierra Leone, Ghana, Cameroon, Equatorial Guinea, Gabon, Congo, Democratic Republic of the Congo, Uganda, and Kenya.

Diet: Pottos eat mostly fruit, but they also eat insects and gums (plant juices). They find insects by smell. They will eat insects that other animals might avoid, such as ants, hairy caterpillars, slugs, and stinky beetles.

Behavior and reproduction: Pottos usually live alone. They move about at night in the trees, traveling quite slowly hand over hand. They mark their trails with urine. During the day, pottos sleep in thickly leaved branches.

Female pottos usually have one infant after being pregnant for about 163 days. A potto baby weighs just 2 ounces (56.7 grams). It has a thin layer of fine fur. It eyes are open. From the first day, the infant holds on to the mother's front and travels with her until it becomes more independent. It will leave its mother at about one year old.

Pottos and people: Potto habits of moving slowly and carefully at night, high in the trees, make them difficult to study.

Conservation status: Pottos are listed as Vulnerable. The major problem is habitat, or living site, destruction due to deforestation, cutting down trees. ∎

FOR MORE INFORMATION

Books:

Alterman, Lon, Gerald A. Doyle, and M. Kay Izard, eds. *Creatures of the Dark: The Nocturnal Prosimians.* New York: Kluwer Academic Publishers, 1995.

Ankel-Simons, Friderun. *Primate Anatomy: An Introduction.* San Diego, CA: Academic Press, 1999.

Konstant, William R., and Ronald M. Nowak. *Walker's Primates of the World.* Baltimore: Johns Hopkins University Press, 2000.

Martin, Patricia A. Fink. *Lemurs, Lorises, and Other Lower Primates.* Danbury, CT: Children's Press, 2000.

Nowak, Ronald M. *Walker's Mammals of the World.* Baltimore: Johns Hopkins University Press, 1999.

Nowak, Ronald M. "Lorises, Potto, and Galagos." In *Walker's Mammals of the World Online.* Baltimore: Johns Hopkins University Press, 1997. http://www.press.jhu.edu/books/walkers_mammals_of_the_world/primates/primates.lorisidae.html (accessed on July 5, 2004).

Rowe, Noel. *The Pictorial Guide to the Living Primates.* East Hampton, NY: Pogonias Press, 1996.

Periodicals:

Churchman, Deborah. "Meet the Primates!" *Ranger Rick* 31, no. 10 (October 1997): 8.

Stewart, Doug. "Prosimians Find a Home Far From Home." *National Wildlife* (Feb/Mar 1998): 33–35.

"Super Slow, Super Fast." *Ranger Rick* (August 1995): 3.

"Wildlife of Tropical Rain Forests." *National Geographic World* (January 2000): 22–25.

Web sites:

"Loridae." Wisconsin Regional Primate Research Center. http://www.primates.com/primate/loridae.html (accessed on July 5, 2004).

Schulze, Helga. "Loris and Potto Conservation Database." Loris Conservation Project. http://www.loris-conservation.org/database/info.html (accessed on July 5, 2004).

Schulze, Helga. "Acoustic Communication in Northern Ceylonese Slender Lorises and Some Information about Vocalization by Other Forms or Species of Lorisidae." Loris Conservation Project. http://www.loris-conservation.org/database/vocalization/Loris_voices_with_figures.html (accessed on July 5, 2004).

BUSHBABIES
Galagidae

Class: Mammalia

Order: Primates

Family: Galagidae

Number of species: 20 species

PHYSICAL CHARACTERISTICS

The largest bushbaby is the brown greater bushbaby. An adult male weighs 3.1 pounds (1.4 kilograms). Body length is 12.5 inches (31.5 centimeters) with a 16.5-inch (41-centimeter) tail. The smallest bushbaby is the mouse-size Demidoff's bushbaby. An adult male weighs 2.5 ounces (65 grams). Its body is 5 inches (13 centimeters) long, with a 7-inch (18-centimeter) tail. Females are somewhat smaller than males.

Bushbabies are usually gray, reddish, or brown with lighter underparts, having gray or dark eye patches. Their fur is thick and soft, and larger bushbabies have quite long bushy tails that help them balance. All bushbabies have rounded heads, short pointed faces with forward-facing eyes, and a pointed snout, or nose area. They can rotate their head in a full circle. Their ears individually bend backward or wrinkle forward, enabling them to better locate sounds. Bushbabies have a special reflective, or mirror-like layer at the back of their retina, or light-receiving, part of the eye. This lets them see in extremely dim light. It also makes their eyes shine in the dark, like a cat's eye.

Bushbabies have larger hindlegs, or back legs, than forelimbs, or front legs. Very strong hindlegs and very long anklebones enable most species to move extremely quickly and accurately. A bushbaby's hands and feet have five long slim fingers, or digits, on each forelimb and five long, slim toes on each hindlimb. Their fingertips have round flat pads of thickened skin that help them grip firmly onto branches. All digits have nails, except the second digit of the hind foot, which has a long curved claw for grooming or cleaning. For grooming, bushbabies also use their lower incisors, or front teeth, and pointed canine teeth as a toothcomb. Underneath the tongue is a false-tongue, which is used to clean the toothcomb.

GEOGRAPHIC RANGE

Bushbabies are found in many parts of Africa, from sea level to 6,000 feet (1,800 meters).

HABITAT

Bushbabies live in many areas, from dry, thorny scrub to evergreen tropical rainforests.

DIET

Depending on the species, bushbabies usually eat fruit, gum or plant fluids, and insects. They can find insects by sound alone and snatch them from the air as they fly past.

BEHAVIOR AND REPRODUCTION

Bushbabies are nocturnal, searching for food at night. They usually remain in trees, but occasionally travel on the ground. Most leap from branch to branch. Some can leap long distances from one branch to another. Others hop on their strong hind legs between branch supports. Some can hang onto vertical supports, such as tree trunks. While most move quickly, the thick-tailed bushbaby sometimes moves very slowly and quietly.

Bushbabies usually sleep in social groups of eight to twenty members. During the day, they rest in hollow trees, tree forks, or old bird nests. Some make sleeping nests from leaves. In a few species, a mated pair and their young may sleep together. In other groups, the adult male does not sleep in the group-sleeping nest. He keeps in contact with females when they are outside the sleeping nest.

Bushbabies forage, or search for food, by themselves. Males have larger territories, or feeding areas, than females. These often overlap those of several female groups. Scent, sounds, and facial expressions all play a role in bushbaby communication.

SOUNDING OFF

The common name bushbaby comes from their loud wailing territorial sound, which sounds somewhat like a human baby crying. Bushbabies make a variety of different sounds, as well. The Senegal bushbaby makes a high-pitched scream when upset, has an alarm call which includes grunting, clucking, whistling, wailing, and sneezing, as well as grunts when it is ready to fight. Infants call to their mothers with a "tsic" sound, and mothers reply with a cooing or soft hooting sound.

An adult male bushbaby may mate with several females. Twice a year, one to three infants are born. The young are fully furred with their eyes open at birth. Bushbaby young spend a week or longer in a hidden tree nest. The mother may leave them there while searching for food, or she may travel, carrying her young in her mouth. When she eats, these babies are placed to cling onto branches. Later, bushbaby young may ride on their mother's back as she searches for food. A baby is weaned, or stops feeding on breastmilk, at about two months of age. It becomes independent at about four months of age. Females may remain in their birth area or travel to new areas.

BUSHBABIES AND PEOPLE

Bushbabies are often captured by local people as pets. The larger species may be used as food or killed for their fur. Bushbabies may also be taken for zoo exhibits. Bushbabies can be carriers for the yellow fever virus. Mosquitoes feeding on them can transmit the disease to humans.

CONSERVATION STATUS

Most species are common in Africa. However one species is Endangered, facing a very high risk of extinction, and six are Near Threatened, not threatened, but could become so, due to habitat, or living area, destruction.

Senegal bushbaby (*Galago senegalensis*)

SENEGAL BUSHBABY
Galago senegalensis

Physical characteristics: The Senegal bushbaby is also known as a lesser galago or lesser bushbaby. It is gray with yellowish highlights. It has soft, thick fur. Its large eyes are surrounded by thick dark eyerings. It has very large, moveable ears. A bushbaby can rotate its head in a circle, like an owl. The Senegal bushbaby is 6.5 inches long (16.5 centimeters) with a 10.5-inch (26-centimeter) tail. Adult males weigh 11 ounces (315 grams), with adult females being slightly smaller.

Geographic range: Senegal bushbabies are found in sub-Saharan Africa, from Senegal to Kenya.

Habitat: Senegal bushbabies live in dry forests, thorny scrublands, and grasslands with some trees.

Senegal bushbabies move around at night, usually staying up in the trees and moving from branch to branch. (© Gallo Images/Corbis. Reproduced by permission.)

Diet: Senegal bushbabies usually feed on the gum, or liquid, from acacia (uh-KAY-shah) trees and insects.

Behavior and reproduction: Senegal bushbabies are nocturnal, moving about at night. They usually stay in trees, hanging vertically, or up and down, on tree trunks. They move by making long leaps from branch to branch, up to 10 to 13 feet (about 4 meters). They also can kangaroo-hop on the ground.

A Senegal bushbaby adult male may mate with several females. Females give birth twice a year and are pregnant for about four months. The pregnant mother prepares a leafy birthing nest. Babies weigh about 0.42 ounces (12 grams) at birth. Mothers nurse babies for about three months. For the first few weeks, the infants cling to the mother's fur as she travels. Young males leave their parents at about ten months of age, but females may stay longer. They are ready to have a litter by twelve months of age.

Senegal bushbabies and people: Senegal bushbabies play a small part in the lives of local people.

Conservation status: Senegal bushbabies are not currently endangered, but may become threatened by habitat loss due to land clearing for farming purposes. ■

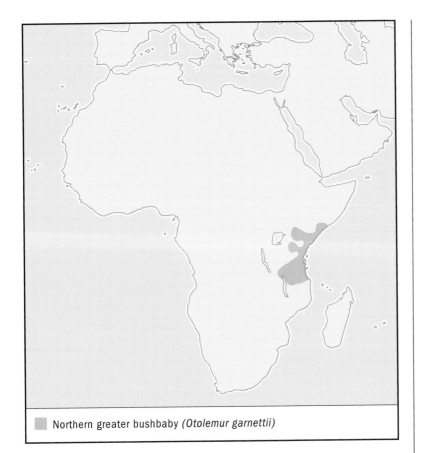

Northern greater bushbaby (*Otolemur garnettii*)

NORTHERN GREATER BUSHBABY
Otolemur garnettii

Physical characteristics: The northern greater bushbaby, also known as Garnett's bushbaby, Garnett's galago, small-eared galago, or greater bushbaby, has reddish to grayish brown fur. It lacks facial markings and has very large, light-sensitive eyes. At night, the pupil opens into a complete circle to allow for better vision in the dark. Adult males weigh 1.75 pounds (795 grams) with females slightly smaller. Body length, including the head, is 10.5 inches (26.5 centimeters), and they have a 14.5-inch (36.5-centimeter) long bushy tail.

Geographic range: Northern greater bushbabies are found in northeastern Africa.

The northern greater bushbaby eats fruit and insects. (© Tom & Pat Leeson/Photo Researchers, Inc. Reproduced by permission.)

Habitat: Northern greater bushbabies live in coastal and highland forests.

Diet: The northern greater bushbaby usually feeds on fruits and insects.

Behavior and reproduction: The northern greater bushbaby adult male may mate with several females. Adult females give birth to one or two infants at a time. They are pregnant for eighteen weeks. Until two weeks of age, the babies stay in a leafy nest. They then cling to the mother's fur as she travels searching for food.

The northern greater bushbaby runs and walks on all four limbs along tree branches, following regular pathways. Occasionally it searches for food on the ground, where it may hop like a kangaroo, or jump-run, hopping first on hind legs, then on forelegs. It hides during the day to avoid predators, such as large snakes.

Northern greater bushbaby males and females often share feeding territories as well as nests. However they usually feed alone at night. Adult males will tolerate younger or lesser males within their feeding range. During the day, these bushbabies return to tree hollows or vine tangles to sleep as a group.

Northern greater bushbabies and people: Northern greater bushbabies have no known interaction with people.

Conservation status: These bushbabies are rather common and not immediately threatened. ■

FOR MORE INFORMATION

Books:

Alden, Peter C. *National Audubon Society Field Guide to African Wildlife.* New York: Alfred A. Knopf, 1995.

Coppard, Kit. *Africa's Animal Kingdom.* London: PRC Publishing Ltd, 2001.

Kennaway, Adrienne. *Bushbaby.* Manningtree, U.K.: Happy Cat Books, 2002.

Maynard, Thane. *Primates: Apes, Monkeys, and Prosimians.* Danbury, CT: Franklin Watts, 1999.

Ricciuti, Edward R., and Bruce S. Glassman. *What on Earth is a Galago?* Woodbridge, CT: Blackbirch Press, 1995.

Sleeper, Barbara. *Primates.* San Francisco, CA: Chronicle Books, 1997.

Stevenson, William. *Bushbabies.* Boston: Houghton Mifflin Co., 1980.

Periodicals:

Bearder, Simon K. "Calls of the Wild." *Natural History* (August 1995): 48–58.

Churchman, Deborah. "Meet the Primates!" *Ranger Rick* 31, no. 10 (October 1997).

"Monkeyshines on the Primates." *Monkeyshines Publications* (1994): 39.

Stewart, Doug. "Prosimians Find a Home Far From Home." *National Wildlife* (Feb/Mar 1998): 33–35.

"Wildlife of Tropical Rain Forests." *National Geographic World* (January 2000): 22–25.

Web sites:

Animal Diversity Web. "Galagonidae." http://www.primates.com/primate/galagonidae.html (accessed on June 23, 2004).

The Chaffee Zoo. "Lesser Bush Baby." http://www.chaffeezoo.org/animals/bushbaby.html (accessed on June 23, 2004).

Singapore Zoo Docent. "Galagos or Bushbabies." http://www.szgdocent.org/pp/p-galago.htm (accessed on June 23, 2004).

DWARF LEMURS AND MOUSE LEMURS
Cheirogaleidae

Class: Mammalia

Order: Primates

Family: Cheirogaleidae

Number of species: 17 species

phylum

class

subclass

order

monotypic order

suborder

▲ **family**

PHYSICAL CHARACTERISTICS

Dwarf lemurs and mouse lemurs are the smallest lemurs. The pygmy mouse lemur weighs just one ounce (30 grams). The largest of these lemurs is the fork-crowned lemur, weighing 16.5 ounces (460 grams), or about a pound. The head and body length of dwarf and mouse lemurs ranges from 4.9 to 10.8 inches (12.5 to 27.4 centimeters), depending on species. Tail length is about as long as total body length.

Dwarf and mouse lemurs have large ears and large, mirror-like eyes set close together. They have excellent night vision. Depending on where they live, these lemurs may have grayish hair or reddish brown hair. Their underbody hair is much lighter, sometimes whitish or yellowish brown. Body hair is soft, thick, and woolly.

GEOGRAPHIC RANGE

Dwarf and mouse lemurs live in Madagascar, an island off the southeast coast of Africa.

HABITAT

Dwarf and mouse lemurs live in a variety of forested habitats, including evergreen rainforest, deciduous forest where trees lose their leaves each year, and semiarid forest, which doesn't get rain part of the year. Mouse lemurs are also found in patches of scrub vegetation where there are small bushes, and in people's gardens in settled areas.

DIET

Dwarf and mouse lemurs usually eat fruit and insects, but some species prefer other foods too. Coquerel's mouse lemur licks the sweet body liquids that are the waste matter produced by some planthopper insects. Fork-crowned lemurs primarily feed on plant gums, or sticky plant liquids. Many of the dwarf and mouse lemurs slow down in the dry season when plants and insects are not as readily available. They survive on stored body fat in their tail until the plentiful rainy season starts, when they become active again.

BEHAVIOR AND REPRODUCTION

Dwarf and mouse lemurs are nocturnal, or active at night. They search for food by themselves, usually in the smaller branches of trees and shrubs.

Dwarf and mouse lemurs are quite social. They have group nests, which they share during the day. The nests can be within tree hollows or tree branches. Five of the little fat-tailed dwarf lemurs may share a tree hole. Mouse lemur nests may have two to nine residents. These nests may have female dwellers, with the males nesting alone or in pairs, or both male and female dwellers. Dwarf lemurs have male-only or female-only nests. Communication is with scent and a variety of calls. Calls include those for keeping contact, mating, alarm, and distress.

Mouse and dwarf lemurs usually travel along branches on all four legs, leaping at times. They can use their tail for balance. Some species can take long leaps from one branch to another. A gray mouse lemur may also move on the ground with froglike hops. Each species, or type, of dwarf or mouse lemur marks its trail with scent while traveling. These markings, deposited by scent or smell glands, or from urine, give information about the traveler's age, sex, and whether it is ready for mating.

After mating, mouse and dwarf lemur females have a two- to three-month pregnancy, depending on species. They may have one to three infants each birth. Births usually take place

MATING COMPETITION

Female mouse lemurs are all ready to mate at one time. Male mouse lemurs can defend only one female at a time. So it's very difficult to keep a group of females all to themselves for mating. Rather than do a lot of fighting, dominant males have a way to put other males out of action. The urine of stronger male mouse lemurs contains chemicals producing a smell that makes weaker males sterile, or unable to reproduce. In addition, these weaker males can't even make the special trills, or calls, used to attract females for mating.

during the rainy season, when food is plentiful. The smaller mouse lemur infants weigh about 0.175 ounces (5 grams) each. The larger Coquerel's mouse lemur infants can have a birth weight of 0.42 ounces (12 grams) each. Mouse and dwarf lemur infants are raised in a nest made of twigs and leaves.

DWARF AND MOUSE LEMURS AND PEOPLE

Dwarf and mouse lemurs are not often hunted for food because of their small size.

CONSERVATION STATUS

Dwarf, red, and gray mouse lemurs are still fairly common. However, they and other small lemur species are at risk due to destruction of their forest habitats, or dwelling places, by human logging, farming, and cattle and goat grazing. It is estimated that only 10 percent of Madagascar's forests remain. The World Conservation Union (IUCN) lists three species as Endangered, facing a very high risk of extinction; one as Vulnerable, facing a high risk of extinction; and one as Near Threatened, not currently threatened, but could become so.

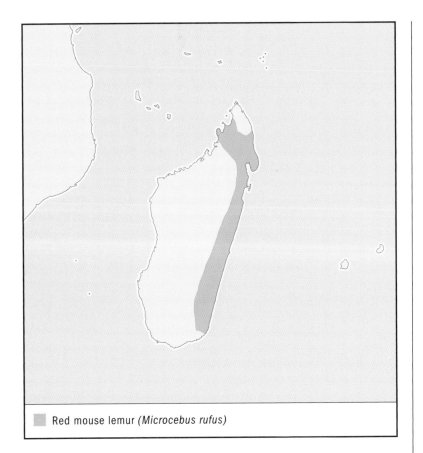

Red mouse lemur (Microcebus rufus)

RED MOUSE LEMUR
Microcebus rufus

Physical characteristics: The red mouse lemur, also called the russet mouse lemur and the brown mouse lemur, is reddish brown on its back and light gray or whitish underneath. It has a whitish stripe between its large round eyes. Its moveable ears are rounded, thin, and hairless. Red mouse lemurs are among the smallest primates. An adult is 5 inches long (12.5 centimeters) with a 5.6-inch tail (14 centimeters). A full-grown red mouse lemur weighs 1.5 ounces (43 grams). Females are about the same size as males.

Geographic range: Red mouse lemurs are found in eastern Madagascar.

A red mouse lemur marks its territory. These markings give information about the mouse lemur's age, sex, and whether it is ready for mating. (Photograph by Harald Schütz. Reproduced by permission.)

Habitat: Red mouse lemurs live in coastal rainforests.

Diet: The red mouse lemur eats a lot of fruit, preferring fruit from plants in the mistletoe family. It also eats insects, spiders, flowers, and gum, or plant juices, and occasionally small frogs and lizards. These lemurs have been seen eating millipedes and scarab beetles as big as they are.

Behavior and reproduction: The red mouse lemur lives in trees and travels through all forests heights. It makes round, leafy nests in hollow trees or among branches. It sleeps during the day, and is nocturnal, active and feeding at night. Each red mouse lemur searches for food by itself. From July to September, fat is stored in its tail. A tail with stored fat may increase this mouse lemur's weight by 1.6 to 2.6 ounces (50 to 80 grams). Then, during the harsh dry season, June to September, it slows down considerably for short periods, becoming almost motionless, utilizing its stored fat as food.

From two to nine male and female red mouse lemurs usually share a sleeping nest. Males may also nest by themselves or in pairs. Home ranges vary with food availability. Males usually have a larger home range than females.

The red mouse lemur has several ways of moving. It runs along branches on all four limbs, like a squirrel. It also may leap as far as 9.8 feet (3 meters) from one tree branch to another, landing on all four limbs. Its long tail helps with balance.

The mating season of the red mouse lemur is from September to October. The female is pregnant about two months, and gives birth to one to three infants. A newborn weighs about 0.18 ounces (5 grams). The infants stay in their nest for three weeks, with the mother leaving only briefly to seek food and water. Weaning, or taking the young off breastmilk, occurs in February when there is the greatest amount of food available.

Red mouse lemurs and people: These lemurs are not considered important by local people.

Conservation status: The red mouse lemur is common in some areas, but could become threatened due to losing habitat through logging and grazing by cattle and goats. ■

FOR MORE INFORMATION

Books:

Boitani, Luigi, and Stefania Bartoli. *Simon & Schuster's Guide to Mammals.* New York: Simon & Schuster, 1983.

Darling, Kathy. *Lemurs on Location.* New York: HarperCollins, 1998.

Dunbar, Robin, and Louise Barrett. *Cousins: Our Primate Relatives.* London: Dorling Kindersley, 2000.

Kavanagh, Michael. *A Complete Guide to Monkeys, Apes and other Primates.* New York: The Viking Press, 1983.

Lasky, Kathryn. *Shadows in the Dawn: The Lemurs of Madagascar.* New York: Gulliver Books, 1998.

Powzyk, Joyce A. *In Search of Lemurs.* Washington, D.C.: National Geographic, 1998.

Sleeper, Barbara. *Primates.* San Francisco: Chronicle Books, 1997.

Periodicals:

Banks, Joan. "Living on the Edge: On the Verge of Extinction, Do Lemurs Have a Fighting Chance?" *National Geographic World* (Jan–Feb 2002): 12–17.

Hubbard, Kim. "For the Love of Lemurs." *Audubon* (September 2000): 60–67.

Mitchell, Meghan. "Securing Madagascar's Rare Wildlife." *Science News* (November 1, 1997): 287.

"Tiny Lemur: Big Find." *National Geographic Explorer* (October 2003): 22–24.

"Wildlife of Tropical Rain Forests." *National Geographic World* (January 2000): 22–25.

Web sites:

"Cheirogaleidae: Dwarf Lemurs, Mouse Lemurs." Animal Diversity Web. http://www.Primates.com/primate/cheirogaleidae.html (accessed on July 5, 2004).

"*Microcebus rufus:* Brown Mouse Lemur." http://info.bio.sunysb.edu/rano.biodiv/Mammals/Microcebus-rufus (accessed on July 5, 2004).

"The Mouse Lemur." http://bibliofile.mc.duke.edu/gww/Berenty/Mammals/Microcebus-murinus/ (accessed on July 5, 2004).

phylum

class

subclass

order

monotypic order

suborder

▲ **family**

PHYSICAL CHARACTERISTICS

Lemur males and females are about the same size. Lemurs weigh 4.4 to 10 pounds (2 to 4.5 kilograms), depending on species, with the mongoose lemur being the smallest. Adult head and body length is 11 to 22 inches (28 to 56 centimeters). Thickly furred lemur tails are from 11 to 22.5 inches (28 to 65 centimeters) long.

For jumping ease, lemurs have strong hind or back limbs which are longer than their forelimbs, or front legs. For better branch hold, thumbs and big toes are set at an angle to the other digits, or fingers and small toes. The palms of the hands and soles of the feet are deeply ridged, or creased, adding to strong branch grip. A clawlike grooming nail is present on the second toe of each hind foot. It is used to clean their fur.

Lemurs have foxlike heads with long muzzles, or nose areas. Large, round, owl-like eyes can be bright red, orange, yellow, or blue. Ears are medium size. Special comb-shaped front teeth are used for grooming in addition to the grooming nail. Lemurs lick their noses to keep them clean and damp. This helps with odor sensing.

Lemurs can be brown, gray, black, and reddish, often with mixed colors. For example, the ruffed lemur is black and white, and the red ruffed lemur is flame-red with a black face and a white neck patch. Lemur fur is thick and soft. Males and females may look alike, or quite different, depending on the species.

GEOGRAPHIC RANGE

Lemurs are found in Madagascar and the Comoros Islands.

HABITAT

Lemurs live in tropical forests, or warm damp forested areas, plus subtropical areas located near tropical areas. These include dry scrub, dry tropical deciduous forests where leaves fall off during winter months, and occasionally grassy areas.

DIET

Lemurs eat plant foods, including flowers, plant juices, fruits, leaves, seeds, and seedpods. Occasionally some feed on insects, small vertebrates such as lizards, and bird's eggs. Bamboo lemurs prefer young bamboo shoots and leaves.

STINK FIGHTS

When ringtailed lemur mating occurs in April, males begin fighting over females. These fights involve lots of loud noises, and "stink fights." The wrists of male ringtailed lemur have scent or stink glands. Males pull their long tail between their wrists, picking up the smell. Males then stand face-to-face, shaking their stinky tail in the direction of their enemy. As yet, no one is sure how a winner is declared.

BEHAVIOR AND REPRODUCTION

All lemurs are arboreal, living in trees. Some species also spend time on the ground. When in trees, lemurs walk and run on all fours. They also leap between trees. Their tail helps in balancing and steering during these leaps.

Lemurs are social, living in groups of two to twenty members, depending on species. Large groups break up into smaller groups to look for food, then rejoin at night. Within each group, lemurs groom each other. This is a very important lemur activity, reinforcing group bonding.

Most lemurs search for food during the day, although some species, like the mongoose lemur, may feed in the day or evening. They are territorial, each group claiming a certain feeding area. When groups meet at territory boundaries, or edges, they get quite upset. Alarm calls and branch shaking are used to get another group to move away. Besides different alarm calls, there are sounds for greeting, meeting other lemurs, and threat calls.

Females often supervise lemur groups. A dominant, or stronger, female in each group leads males and other females in searching for food and shelter. Females have first food choices, with males waiting their turn. Females also choose their mating partners. Females are ready to have young at two to three years old.

After mating, females are pregnant about four months. They usually give birth when the monsoon, or rainy season, starts. There are usually one or two infants each birth, although the ruffed lemur may have up to six infants.

At first, a newborn lemur rides under its mother's body, clinging onto her fur. At a month old, it begins riding on its mother's back. Shortly after, the young lemur starts wandering on its own. It is weaned, or taken off breastmilk, by five months.

LEMURS AND PEOPLE

People hunt and trap lemurs for food. Some lemurs are kept as pets. Others are shipped overseas for the illegal pet trade. Sometimes lemurs are killed if they're blamed for feeding on food crops. However, ecotourism (travelers coming from abroad to see local wildlife) is helping lemurs to survive. Ecotourism brings in a lot of money, so it is hoped that local people will benefit and aid world efforts to keep lemurs from becoming extinct, dying out.

CONSERVATION STATUS

Madagascar is the only place where lemurs are found. Animal grazing, farming, tree cutting for fuel and brush fires decrease habitat, or living areas. Since only 10 to 15 percent of Madagascar's forests remain, all lemur species are threatened or could become threatened. Two species are Critically Endangered, facing an extremely high risk of extinction in the wild; one species is Endangered, facing a very high risk of extinction; and five species are Vulnerable, facing high risk of extinction.

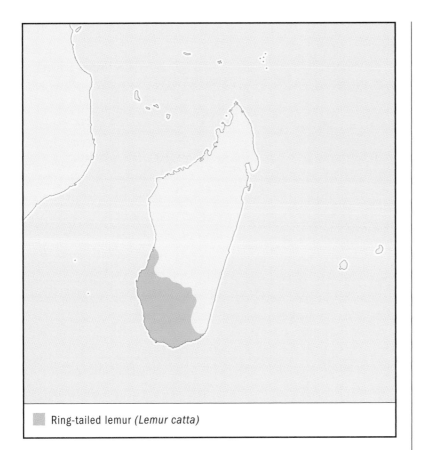

Ring-tailed lemur (*Lemur catta*)

RINGTAILED LEMUR
Lemur catta

Physical characteristics: Ringtailed lemurs are about the size of a cat. Males and females look alike. Adult weight is 6.5 to 7.75 pounds (3 to 3.5 kilograms). Head and body length is 15 to 18 inches long (39 to 46 centimeters). These lemurs are gray with white undersides. Black eye-rings in a white fox-like face surround bright orange eyes. They have a very long, black-and-white ringed tail, which is held straight up in the air as they walk.

Ringtailed lemurs have scent glands on their inner wrists and armpits. These glands give off a stinky substance, or liquid. Ringtailed lemurs use this to mark their feeding areas.

The female ringtailed lemur gives birth to one or two young. The mother carries them around for a few months. (John Giustina/Bruce Coleman Inc. Reproduced by permission.)

Geographic range: Ringtailed lemurs are found in Madagascar.

Habitat: Ringtailed lemurs live in dry brush forests and dense forests near riversides. There is a separate ringtailed lemur population living on rocky areas and cliffs within in a national Madagascar park.

Diet: Ringtailed lemurs eat flowers, leaves, some tree sap, and fruit. Tamarind tree seedpods are a favorite food.

Behavior and reproduction: Ringtailed lemurs live in groups of fifteen to twenty-five members. There are males and females in each group. The strongest female leads each group. Female ringtailed lemurs have first food choice, and may slap males on the nose and take food from them.

Ringtailed lemurs are diurnal, searching for food during the day. They spend half their food-seeking time on the ground, walking on all four limbs. Powerful hind legs permit easy leaps into nearby trees.

When ringtailed lemurs meet, they tap noses. At night, groups go to sleep under big trees. Before falling asleep, there is often a shrill group whoop-like call. Group members huddle together for warmth, sometimes making a purring sound. In the morning, before food searching, ringtailed lemurs sit upright on the ground. The sunlight warms them up. Ringtailed lemurs also like to sunbathe during the day.

Mating occurs in April. The female gives birth to one or two young. At first they are carried everywhere by the mother. By three months old, while still carried about, they are playing with other young ringtailed lemurs. Youngsters are weaned, or stop nursing, by six months old. Females in ringtailed lemur groups often have "aunt behavior." They help take care of infants and watch over the young when they play.

Ringtailed lemurs and people: Ringtailed lemurs are hunted for food and sold in the illegal pet trade. However, they are increasingly important in ecotourism.

Conservation status: The ringtailed lemur is considered Vulnerable due to hunting, fires, and tree removal for farm land, all of which destroy lemur habitat.   ■

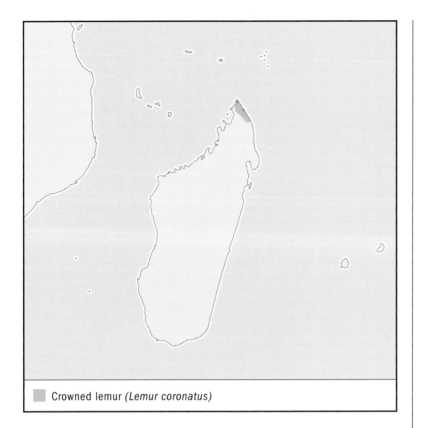

Crowned lemur (*Lemur coronatus*)

CROWNED LEMUR
Lemur coronatus

Physical characteristics: The crowned lemur has a contrasting color, or "crown," on the top of its head. Males have brownish fur with orange fur encircling a whitish face. Their crown is a black fur patch between the ears. Females have short, gray-brown body hair with a red-orange patch on their crown. Both males and females have round orange eyes.

Adult crowned lemurs weigh 4.5 pounds (2 kilograms). Head plus body length is 13.4 inches (34 centimeters) long, with a 17.7-inch (45-centimeter) tail. They have scent glands on various parts of their body.

Geographic range: Crowned lemurs are found in Madagascar.

Crowned lemur males (on the left) and females (on the right) live together in social sleeping groups. (Photograph by Harald Schütz. Reproduced by permission.)

Habitat: Crowned lemurs live in dry to moist forests.

Diet: Crowned lemurs prefer fruit, but also eat flowers, flower pollen, and leaves.

Behavior and reproduction: Crowned lemurs live in groups of about six members. Within a group, communication is by various vocalizations, or sounds, as well as bonding through mutual grooming, or fur cleaning. Crowned lemurs are mainly diurnal, feeding in the daytime, with an afternoon rest. However they may feed for a few hours at night. They search for food at all tree levels, as well as on the ground.

Crowned lemur males and females live together in social sleeping groups. Females are in charge, with the strongest one leading the entire group. Mating takes place at twenty months old. One to two offspring are born each time.

Crowned lemurs and people: Poachers, or illegal hunters, kill crowned lemurs for food, and local people may kill them if lemurs take food from their farms.

Conservation status: Crowned lemurs are considered Vulnerable due to poaching, brush fires, farming, and logging.   ■

FOR MORE INFORMATION

Books:

Darling, Kathy. *Lemurs on Location.* New York: HarperCollins, 1998.

Dunbar, Robin, and Louise Barrett. *Cousins: Our Primate Relatives.* London: Dorling Kindersley: 2000.

Lasky, Kathryn. *Shadows in the Dawn: The Lemurs of Madagascar.* New York: Gulliver Books, 1998.

Powzyk, Joyce A. *In Search of Lemurs.* Washington, D.C.: National Geographic, 1998.

Sleeper, Barbara. *Primates.* San Francisco: Chronicle Books, 1997.

Periodicals:

Banks, Joan. "Living On the Edge Lemurs: On the Verge of Extinction, Do Lemurs Have a Fighting Chance?" *National Geographic World* (January–February 2002): 12–17.

Hubbard, Kim. "For the Love of Lemurs." *Audubon* (September 2000): 60–67.

Mitchell, Meghan. "Securing Madagascar's Rare Wildlife." *Science News* (November 1, 1997): 287.

Schleichert, Elizabeth. "Can We Save the Lemurs?" *Ranger Rick* (December 2000): 18–24.

"Wildlife of Tropical Rain Forests." *National Geographic World* (January 2000): 22–25.

Web sites:

Animal Facts. "Ring-tailed Lemur." http://www.chaffeezoo.org/animals/ringTailedLemur.html (accessed on July 5, 2004).

The Lemur Database. "Crowned Lemur." http://www.stormloader.com/lemur/crowned.html (accessed on July 5, 2004).

The Lemur Database. "Ring-Tailed Lemur." http://www.stormloader.com/lemur/ringtailed.html (accessed on July 5, 2004).

Lemurs. "*Lemur catta.*" http://bibliofile.mc.duke.edu/gww/Berenty/Mammals/Lemur-catta/index.html (accessed on July 6, 2004).

Class: Mammalia

Order: Primates

Family: Indriidae

Number of species: 8 to 10 species

family
CHAPTER

phylum

class

subclass

order

monotypic order

suborder

▲ **family**

PHYSICAL CHARACTERISTICS

This family (also spelled Indridae) includes the indris (IN-dreez), sifakas (suh-FAH-kuhz), and the avahis (ah-VAH-heez) or woolly lemurs. Head and body length is 10.4 to 20.5 inches (26.4 to 52 centimeters). Weight ranges from 2.2 to 16.1 pounds (1 to 7.3 kilograms). The sifakas and avahis have rather long tails, while the indris have just a stump.

Indriids (members of the Indriidae family) fur color varies. Avahis can be whitish, brownish, or reddish. Indris are black and white. Sifakas are mostly black or dark brown. Fur can be woolly or silky. Contrasting fur colors occur on their backs, eyebrows, top of head, and head ruffs (a fringe of long hairs around the neck). Eye colors include golden brown, orange, and yellow. Indriid eyes are reflective, like mirrors, increasing their ability to see in dim light.

Indriids' hind limbs are longer than forelimbs. There are five fingers on each of two forefeet and five toes on each of two hind feet. All toes have nails except the second digit, or toe. This digit has a grooming (or cleaning) claw. Indriids also have a dental toothcomb, or special front teeth, used for fur cleaning.

GEOGRAPHIC RANGE

Indriids are found in Madagascar.

HABITAT

Indriids live in a wide range of environments, including original forests, disturbed forest fragments, and desert areas with spiny plants.

DIET

Indriids feed on fruit, leaves, bark, and flowers.

BEHAVIOR AND REPRODUCTION

Groups of avahis and indris have two to six members, usually an adult male and female and their young offspring. Sifakas have groups of up to ten members. Females are dominant, or in charge, in both the sifakas and indris. Little is known about avahis.

Indris and sifakas mate at three to five years old. Little is known about avahis, or woolly lemurs, although they usually have one offspring each time.

Sifakis and indris are diurnal, or active during the day. Avahis are nocturnal, or active at night.

All indriids are vertical clingers, able to climb up and down trees. They can leap long distances between trees. Indris usually stay in trees, while sifakas occasionally travel on the ground.

ONCE UPON A TIME: SLOTH LEMURS AND BABOON LEMURS

The family Indriidae has lost over half of its species in the last 1,000 years. Lost species include the sloth lemurs and the baboon lemurs. Sloth and baboon lemurs were large. Sloth lemurs might have weighed up to 441 pounds (200 kilograms). They climbed slowly and hung from tree branches. Baboon lemurs weighed up to 49 pounds (22 kilograms). They probably traveled on the ground and within trees. Sloth and baboon lemurs became extinct, not one exists anymore, anyplace, primarily due to forest destruction and human hunting.

Scent marking and facial expressions are important means of communication for all the indriids. Vocalizations, or sounds, are also important. Among other sounds, avahis make shrill whistles, sifakas bark, honk, and making sneezing noises, and indris can sound somewhat like a loud clarinet.

INDRIIDS AND PEOPLE

Sifakas and indris are protected in some areas by taboos, or forbidden deeds. Due to their human-like hands and faces, they may be thought of as ancestor spirits, and so should not be harmed.

CONSERVATION STATUS

Six indriids are considered threatened due to loss of habitat occurring from deforestation (tree removal), fire, poaching, and encroaching human populations. The golden-crowned sifaka is considered Critically Endangered, or at an extremely high risk of extinction, dying out.

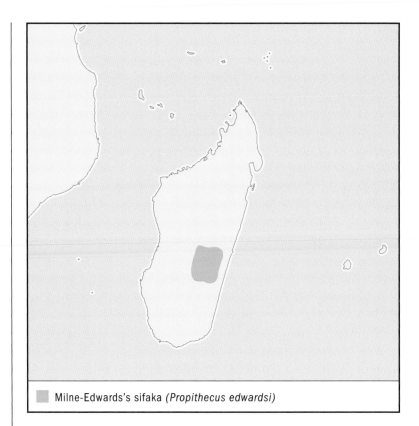

Milne-Edwards's sifaka (*Propithecus edwardsi*)

MILNE-EDWARDS'S SIFAKA
Propithecus edwardsi

Physical characteristics: The Milne-Edwards's sifaka is black or dark brown with a large whitish patch on its lower back. Its fur is long and soft, and its face is hairless and black. Front legs are short, and hind limbs large and strong. Eye color may be orange. Males and females look alike. Adult weight is 12.3 pounds (5.6 kilograms). Head and body length is 18.9 inches (48 centimeters), with a long tail used for balancing. Sifaka males and females have scent glands for marking territory.

Geographic range: These sifakas live on the southeastern coast of Madagascar.

Habitat: Milne-Edwards's sifaka is found in moist, humid mountain rainforests.

Diet: Milne-Edwards's sifaka eats fruits, fruit seeds, leaves, and flowers.

Behavior and reproduction: The Milne-Edwards's sifaka is diurnal, or active during daylight hours. It travels by leaping and clinging onto trees. It usually feeds within large trees, but may food search on the ground. On the ground, sifakas hop on their hind legs in an upright position, holding arms above their heads for balance. At night they sleep with a social group high in the trees. Sleeping locations can change each night to avoid predators.

Social groups have up to ten members. These groups may be all male, all female, or mixed. Females are dominant, leading their group and demanding first choice of food. However, males defend the group against large raptors, such as hawks and eagles.

Sifakas are mature at four to five years old. Females may mate with several males. One infant is born every two years. Newborns weigh 4.4 ounces (125 grams). They cling to the mother's underside for their first month, then ride on her back for the next four months. Infant mortality, or death rate, is high.

Milne-Edwards's sifakas have several vocalizations, or sounds. The loud alarm barking sound warning about bird predators may last up to fifteen minutes. A short, quick "zusss" call warns of ground predators, or enemies. Quiet "moos" tell of a group's current location. Lost sifakas give a long, warbling whistle to announce where they are.

Milne-Edwards's sifakas and people: In some areas, it is forbidden by local custom to hunt sifakas because they resemble humans.

Conservation status: Though not listed as Threatened, Milne-Edwards's sifakas may become threatened due to hunting, logging, firewood use, land clearing to provide pasture for livestock, and slash-and-burn agriculture. It has so far been impossible to keep and breed this sifaka in captivity. ■

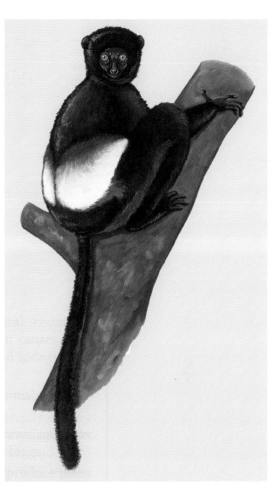

Milne-Edwards's sifakas sleep high in the trees at night. When they're on the ground, they hop in an upright position, holding their arms over their heads for balance. (Illustration by Gillian Harris. Reproduced by permission.)

Indri (*Indri indri*)

INDRI
Indri indri

Physical characteristics: The indris are the largest living prosimians (or "before apes"). They weigh 13.2 to 16.5 pounds (6 to 7.5 kilograms). Head and body length is about 23.6 inches (60 centimeters). The tail is stubby.

An indri is mostly black with white areas. A black hairless face has large tufted ears and a pointed nose area. Large eyes are yellow. Body hair is long and silky. Feet have strong big toes, and long hands have strong thumbs, creating a very powerful tree branch grasp. A special throat sac enables indris to make loud sounds.

Geographic range: Indris are found in northeastern Madagascar.

Habitat: Indris live in humid moist forests from sea level to 6,000 feet (1,830 meters).

Diet: Indris eat leaves, flowers, and fruits. When these foods are hard to find, the indri uses its tooth comb to scrape tree bark and dead wood as food.

Behavior and reproduction: Indris are diurnal, moving about only in the daytime. They live in social groups of two to six members, usually a male and female pair and their young. Female indris are dominant, or in charge. However, males are responsible for defending group feeding territory, which they mark with scent glands.

Indris are arboreal, living in trees. They leap between tree trunks. Leaps can be as long as 33 feet (10 meters). Indris seldom move on the ground; when they do, they walk upright, moving forward by hopping and holding their somewhat short arms above their body. At night, before going to sleep, indris have a group grooming session.

Indris begin mating at seven to nine years old. There are two to three years between births. Only one offspring is born each time. Tiny babies cling to the mother's underside until four months of age, then begin riding on her back. Leaping practice begins at this time. By eight months of age, young move about by themselves, although they stay with the parents for about two years.

Indris sound like a clarinet, a musical instrument, early in the morning. These calls can be heard up to 2 miles (3 kilometers) away. The indris are very territorial, making shrill cries warning other groups to stay away. There are also loud howling or singing sessions by group members. These howling songs can last up to four minutes. Other sounds made by indris include hooting and barking to warn of nearby predators, and grunts and wheezes when frightened.

Indris and people: In many areas there are local taboos against people harming indris, however hunting does occur.

Conservation status: Indris are considered Endangered, facing a very high risk of extinction, due to logging, hunting, and slash-and-burn agriculture (cutting down trees and burning remnants to clear land for farming). ■

FOR MORE INFORMATION

Books:

Dunbar, Robin, and Louise Barrett. *Cousins: Our Primate Relatives.* London: Dorling Kindersley, 2000.

Kavanagh, Michael. *A Complete Guide to Monkeys, Apes and Other Primates.* New York: The Viking Press, 1983.

Nowak, Ronald M., and John L. Paradiso. *Walker's Mammals of the World.* Baltimore and London: The Johns Hopkins University Press, 1983.

Sleeper, Barbara. *Primates.* San Francisco: Chronicle Books, 1997.

Periodicals:

Banks, Joan. "Lemurs: Living on the Edge: On the Verge of Extinction, Do Lemurs Have a Fighting Chance?" *National Geographic World* (January–February 2002): 12–16.

Mitchell, Meghan. "Securing Madagascar's Rare Wildlife." *Science News* (November 1, 1997): 287.

"Sifaka." *Ranger Rick* (August 1999): 37–38.

Web sites:

Animal Diversity Web. "Indridae." http://primates.com/primate/indriidae.html (accessed on June 21, 2004).

Animal Info. "Diademed Sifaka." http://www.animalinfo.org/species/primate/propdiad.htm (accessed on June 21, 2004).

Animal Info. "Indri." http://www.animalinfo.org/ species/primate/indrindr.htm (accessed on June 21, 2004).

"Indri." http://members.tripod.com/uakari/indri_indri. html (accessed on June 21, 2004).

Science & Nature: Animals. "Indri." http://www.bbc.co.uk/nature/wildfacts/factfiles/335.shtml (accessed on June 21, 2004).

SPORTIVE LEMURS
Lepilemuridae

Class: Mammalia
Order: Primates
Family: Lepilemuridae
Number of species: 7 species

PHYSICAL CHARACTERISTICS

Sportive lemurs, also called weasel lemurs, have a head and body length of 9.8 to 13.8 inches (25.0 to 35.0 centimeters). Tail length is 9.8 to 12 inches (25 to 30.5 centimeters). The tail may be shorter or longer than the body, depending on species. Body weight is 1.1 to 2.2 pounds (0.5 to 1 kilograms).

Sportive lemurs have short, pointed heads with large round ears. They have binocular vision, they're are able to see with both eyes at the same time. In the mouth, lower front teeth are joined and tilted forward. This dental-comb is a grooming, or fur-cleaning aid. Sportive fur is woolly and dense. All sportive lemurs have very long, strong hind limbs. They are much longer than the forelimbs, or front legs.

GEOGRAPHIC RANGE

Sportive lemurs live only on the island of Madagascar, which is off the east coast of Africa.

BIOMES

Evergreen forests, where the trees stay green all year, and hot, dry forests.

HABITAT

Most sportive lemurs live in forested areas, ranging from evergreen rainforests to hot dry forests.

DIET

Sportive lemurs feed mostly on leaves. Sportive lemurs may also eat flowers, bark, and fruit. They are different from other lemurs in being able to feed on difficult-to-digest food, such as cactus-like leaves. When these partially digested leaves are eliminated as waste, in order not to waste any nutrition remaining, the sportive lemurs will eat this waste. Basically, they digest everything twice. This process is called cecotrophy (SEE-cuh-troh-fee), and is present in other animals, but not in other lemurs.

BEHAVIOR AND REPRODUCTION

Sportive lemurs are nocturnal, moving about at night. They often gather in groups between the hours of twilight and darkness before moving on to their separate feeding territories, or areas. During the day, they sleep curled up in a ball within a hollow tree, in thick leafy areas, or among vines. They may use the same nesting area for several years. In the afternoon, they tend to stick their heads out of their hiding place, either watching their surroundings or napping.

Sportive lemurs have powerful, long, hind legs. They move by leaping from tree trunk to tree trunk, then clinging onto the tree trunk. Sportive lemurs may leap as far as 13 feet (4 meters) at a time. Large pads on their hands and feet help with holding on to tree trunks. They are also able to run on all four limbs, or hop on their two hind limbs. They can do this on tree branches or on the ground.

Male sportive lemurs often live alone. A mother and her children stay together. A male's territory includes that of several females. Males, and sometimes females, defend their territories from other sportive lemurs of the same sex by vocalizations, or sounds, body actions, chasing, or, if that doesn't succeed, fighting.

Mating occurs at about eighteen months. Males will visit several females for mating purposes. Females are pregnant for four and a half months. One infant is born each year. Mothers may

ONCE THERE WERE MORE

The koala lemur doesn't exist anymore—it is extinct. It weighed 88 to 176 pounds (40 to 80 kilograms) and had a quite large head and a short body, with front legs longer than the hind legs. All legs were somewhat curved, and hands and feet were quite long. The koala lemur would hold onto tree trunks, moving upward with short hops. When humans came to Madagascar, koala lemurs and their living areas were destroyed. They disappeared entirely by the 1500s.

carry their young in their mouth as they leap from tree to tree, or leave them clinging onto branches while the mother hunts for food. At about one month the young start seeking food on their own. The young remain with the mother for about a year, until the next baby is born.

SPORTIVE LEMURS AND PEOPLE

Sportive lemurs are hunted for food.

CONSERVATION STATUS

All seven species of sportive lemur are listed by the World Conservation Union (IUCN) due to loss of forest habitat, or living spaces. This is due to slash-and-burn agriculture, where forests are burned to clear land for people's homes and farms. Cattle and goat overgrazing also destroys habitat. Two species are Vulnerable, facing a high risk of extinction, and five are Near Threatened, not currently threatened, but could become so.

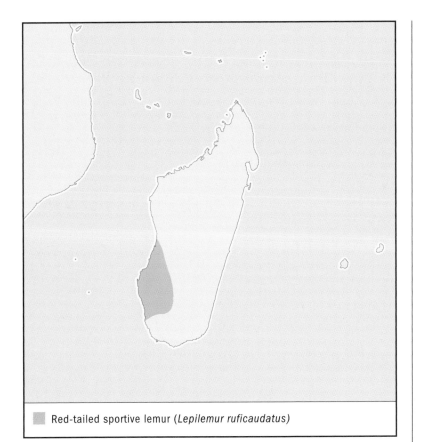

Red-tailed sportive lemur (*Lepilemur ruficaudatus*)

RED-TAILED SPORTIVE LEMUR
Lepilemur ruficaudatus

Physical characteristics: Red-tailed sportive lemurs, also called lesser weasel lemurs, measure about 11 inches (28.0 centimeters) long, including head and body. Their tail is 9.8 to 10.2 inches (25 to 26 centimeters), slightly shorter than body length. Weight is about 1.3 to 2.0 pounds (0.6 to 0.9 kilograms). Eyes are yellow. Upper fur is light gray-brown, with front fur reddish brown. Undersides are whitish.

Geographic range: Red-tailed sportive lemurs are found in southwestern Madagascar.

Habitat: Red-tailed sportive lemurs live in dry forests.

Diet: Red-tailed sportive lemurs usually eat leaves, but they also eat fruit. Because tough leaves are difficult to fully digest, these lemurs re-digest some of their waste matter, so they can obtain all the nutrition from their food.

Behavior and reproduction: Mating occurs about eighteen months of age. Male red-tailed sportive lemurs mate with several females during the mating season. Females are pregnant about four and a half months, giving birth to one baby per year. The young stay with their mother and follow her about until they are about one year old.

Red-tailed sportive lemurs are arboreal, living in trees. A female and her young live in individual tree hollows and tree nests. Males live alone, having home ranges, or activity areas, that overlap that of several females. During the first few weeks of a red-tailed sportive lemur's life, the mother carries it about in her mouth. Later, an infant clings to her fur. However, when she goes food searching, she often leaves her young clinging to a branch or in a tree hollow.

Red-tailed sportive lemurs are nocturnal, active at night. They are very territorial, protecting their feeding areas. Males make loud crow-like calls to tell other males that an area is already taken. Males, and sometimes females, defend their feeding territory with noise, threatening body movements, chases, and even fighting.

Red-tailed sportive lemurs and people: Red-tailed sportive lemurs are hunted for food.

Conservation status: Red-tailed sportive lemurs are Near Threatened due to habitat destruction by fire and overgrazing of cattle and goats as well as hunting. ■

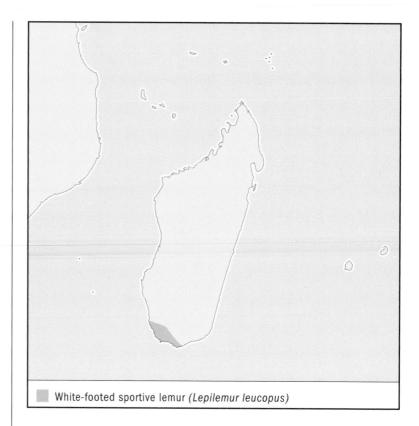

White-footed sportive lemur (*Lepilemur leucopus*)

WHITE-FOOTED SPORTIVE LEMUR
Lepilemur leucopus

Physical characteristics: The white-footed sportive lemur, also called the white-footed weasel lemur, weighs 1.2 to 1.3 pounds (0.5 to 0.6 kilograms). Body and head length measures about 9.8 inches (25.0 centimeters). Their tail is the same length. This lemur has large ears and whitish circles around large orange eyes. Its upper-body fur is gray-beige with brown shoulders. It has white on its forelegs and hindlegs.

Geographic range: The white-footed sportive lemur lives in southern Madagascar.

Habitat: The white-footed sportive lemur lives in trees, bushes, and grass in deserts with spiny plants and forests near streams and rivers.

Diet: The white-footed sportive lemur prefers to feed on thick, juicy leaves. However these may be rare in the dry areas it lives, so it eats tough, fibrous leaves. Because these leaves are hard to digest completely, it will eat some of its waste matter to extract, or get out, any remaining food value.

Behavior and reproduction: The white-footed sportive lemur is arboreal, living in trees. It has very strong, long hind limbs and travels by leaping between trees, then clinging onto tree trunks while climbing.

The basic family group of a white-footed sportive lemur is a mother and her young children. They sleep in tree holes, on branches, or in nests within thick vines. Each female group has its own small feeding territory. Males live alone in tree holes or vine bunches. Each male's feeding territory, or area, overlaps that of several females. During the mating season, a male will mate with more than one female.

White-footed sportive lemurs are arboreal, meaning they spend most of their time in the trees. They move from tree to tree by leaping. (© Nigel J. Dennis/Photo Researchers, Inc. Reproduced by permission.)

White-footed sportive lemurs mate between May and July. Females are pregnant for about four and a half months. Females have one baby at a time. It is very tiny, weighing about 1.8 ounces (50 grams). Babies feed on mother's milk for about four months. When the females go out to search for food, babies are left clinging to a tree branch. Mothers make special noises, which sound like a kiss, to keep in contact with them. The young are mature, or adult, at eighteen months.

White-footed sportive lemurs are nocturnal, or active at night. They are highly territorial, protective of their feeding areas. Males, and sometimes females, threaten intruders with noises and physical displays. Intruders may be chased or even injured.

White-footed sportive lemurs and people: People hunt white-footed sportive lemurs for food.

Conservation status: White-footed sportive lemurs are Near Threatened due to forest fires, overgrazing by livestock, hunting, and poor land use. They are found in two Nature Reserves, a Special Reserve, and the Berenty private reserve. ■

FOR MORE INFORMATION

Books:

Darling, Kathy. *Lemurs on Location.* New York: HarperCollins, 1998.

Dunbar, Robin, and Louise Barrett. *Cousins: Our Primate Relatives.* London: Dorling Kindersley, 2000.

Lasky, Kathryn. *Shadows in the Dawn: The Lemurs of Madagascar.* New York: Gulliver Books, 1998.

Powzyk, Joyce A. *In Search of Lemurs.* Washington, D.C.: National Geographic, 1998.

Sleeper, Barbara. *Primates.* San Francisco, CA: Chronicle Books, 1997.

Periodicals:

Banks, Joan. "Living On the Edge Lemurs: On the Verge of Extinction, Do Lemurs Have a Fighting Chance?" *National Geographic World* (Jan–Feb 2002): 12–17.

Hubbard, Kim. "For the Love of Lemurs." *Audubon* (September 2000): 60–67.

Mitchell, Meghan. "Securing Madagascar's Rare Wildlife." *Science News* (November 1, 1997): 287.

Schleichert, Elizabeth. "Can We Save the Lemurs?" *Ranger Rick* (December 2000): 18–24.

"Wildlife of Tropical Rain Forests." *National Geographic World* (January 2000): 22–25.

Web sites:

Animal Diversity Web. "Family Megaladapidae (Sportive Lemurs)." http://animaldiversity.ummz.umich.edu/site/accounts/information/Megaladapidae.html (accessed on July 6, 2004).

Lemurs. *"Lepilemur leucopus."* http://bibliofile.mc.duke.edu/gww/Berenty/Mammals/Lepilemur-leucopus/index.html (accessed on July 6, 2004).

Lemurs. "Red-tailed Sportive Lemur." http://members.tripod.com/uakari/leilmur_ruficaudatus.html (accessed on July 6, 2004).

Lemurs. "White-footed Sportive Lemur." http://members.tripod.com/uakari/lepilemur_leucopus.html (accessed on July 6, 2004).

Class: Mammalia

Order: Primates

Family: Daubentoniidae

One species: Aye-aye (*Daubentonia madagascariensis*)

family

C H A P T E R

PHYSICAL CHARACTERISTICS

An aye-aye (EYE-eye) has long, woolly, black or dark brown hair tipped with white. Its head is rounded with a short face. Large, hairless black ears are 4 inches (10 centimeters) long and 2.8 inches (7 centimeters) wide. Large eyes are golden brown. The aye-aye has white around its nose and above its eyes. Front teeth, or incisors, are quite large. The incisors grow continuously, and keep growing back as they are worn down by the aye-aye gnawing on trees.

The aye-aye is about 16 inches (40 centimeters) long, including head and body. It has a bushy tail, which, at 22 inches (55 centimeters), is longer than its body. An aye-eye weighs about 6 pounds (2.7 kilograms). Males and females are about the same size.

An aye-aye's arms and legs are about the same size, enabling it to move easily on all fours. Especially unique, or different, are the aye-aye's forefeet or hands. Its hands have five long thin fingers, with an extremely long thin bony middle finger. There is a pointed, clawlike nail on every finger and toe, except for the big toes, which have flat nails. The aye-aye uses its hands for feeding or cleaning itself.

Another unusual feature is the aye-aye's two nipples, for nursing or breastfeeding, which are placed on the lower abdomen rather than on the chest. Aye-ayes are the only primates with this body arrangement.

phylum

class

subclass

order

monotypic order

suborder

▲ **family**

GEOGRAPHIC RANGE

Aye-ayes are found in Madagascar.

HABITAT

Aye-ayes live in several habitats, including rainforests where the weather is damp or wet throughout the year, dry forests that get little rain, mangroves or riverbank tree areas, and bamboo thickets or groups.

DIET

An aye-aye's diet consists of fruits, fungi, seeds including coconuts, nectar (sweet liquid) from palm tree flowers, and wood-boring beetle larvae (LAR-vee) or young. To get at the soft larvae feeding within trees, the aye-aye walks along tree branches, its nose pressed against the bark. The aye-aye has excellent hearing. It may tap on a branch, listening for hollow spaces created by larval feeding. When a larva is located, the aye-aye gnaws quickly through the wood with its long incisors, or front teeth. Larvae are squashed with the aye-aye's unique long, thin middle finger. Squashed remains are scooped out, bit-by-bit, and licked off the tip of this middle finger. Larvae add protein and fat to the aye-aye's diet.

The aye-aye also uses its strong incisors to tear through the outer surface of hard-shelled nuts. Unripe coconuts are a favorite. The aye-aye chews on them until it makes a hole. Then, it uses its long middle finger to scrape out the thick coconut milk and the softer interior, eating both.

BEHAVIOR AND REPRODUCTION

Aye-ayes are nocturnal, or active at night. Each spends most of the day in an individual nest hidden among thick vines that are within a high fork of a tall tree. Each round nest, about 20 inches (50 centimeters) wide, is constructed of leaves and twigs woven together. Each nest takes about twenty-four hours to build. It has a closed top, a side entrance, and a bottom layer

Aye-aye (*Daubentonia madagascariensis*)

of shredded leaves. An aye-aye may build up to twenty nests in its home range. Aye-ayes often change their daytime sleeping nest. Many different aye-ayes may individually occupy a nest over a period of time.

Each aye-aye usually lives alone, however young may stay with the mother for quite a while. Little is known about their social behavior. Female home ranges, or feeding areas, are not usually shared. Male home ranges are larger, and may overlap female home ranges. Range boundaries are marked with urine and with a special scent gland. Some scientists believe that aye-ayes may search for food in male-female or male-male pairs.

When moving upward, the aye-aye climbs with a series of rapid leaps, one after another. It also walks on four limbs on the ground, but more slowly.

A female aye-aye is ready to mate at three to four years old. Mating can occur during several months of the year. Several males fight over who will be the one to mate with a female. However, after this mating, the female may mate again with a different male. Pregnancy is about five months. Females only

The aye-aye taps on tree bark to find grubs and insects burrowing within the bark of a tree. (Photograph by Harald Schütz. Reproduced by permission.)

give birth every two to three years. Births can occur at any time of the year. There is only one infant each time. Babies are weaned, or stop nursing, at about seven months old.

When moving about in the trees, aye-ayes are usually quiet. But they can make many different vocalizations, or sounds. These include an "eep" call when meeting another aye-aye, a "hai-hai" alarm call when fighting over food, and a begging "bird call" given by young aye-ayes that want to feed with older animals.

AYE-AYES AND PEOPLE

In many unprotected areas, aye-ayes are destroyed by the local people, either due to superstition, or because of aye-aye crop raiding on coconut plantations—large coconut growing areas. This problem began when their normal feeding areas were destroyed.

CONSERVATION STATUS

Aye-ayes are considered Endangered, facing a very high risk of extinction, or dying out, due to superstition-related killing, loss of habitat due to logging, and use of former tree land for crop growing. At one time they were considered to be extinct, however some were later found and moved to safer sites. Currently there are aye-ayes in about sixteen reserves, or semi-protected areas, and some other places.

FOR MORE INFORMATION

Books:

Dunbar, Robin, and Louise Barrett. *Cousins: Our Primate Relatives.* London, New York, and Sydney: Dorling Kindersley, 2001.

Kavanagh, Michael *A Complete Guide to Monkeys, Apes and Other Primates.* New York: The Viking Press, 1984.

Maynard, Thane. *Primates: Apes, Monkeys, and Prosimians.* Danbury, CT: Franklin Watts, 1999.

Nowak, Ronald M., and John L. Paradiso, eds. *Walker's Mammals of the World.* Baltimore and London: Johns Hopkins University Press, 1983.

Sleeper, Barbara. *Primates.* San Francisco: Chronicle Books, 1997.

Periodicals:

"Aye-aye." *Ranger Rick* (April 1999): 36–38.

Erickson, Carl. "Aye-aye, Sir: There's Food in These Timbers." *National Geographic* (March 1992).

Skelton, Renee. "Creature of the Night." *National Geographic World Magazine* (1994): 18–31.

Web sites:

Animal Diversity Web. "Daubentoniidae: Aye-aye." http://www.primates.com/primate/daubentoniidae.html (accessed on June 22, 2004).

Animal Info. "Aye-aye." http://www.animalinfo.org/species/primate/daubmada.htm (accessed on June 22, 2004).

ARKive. "Aye-aye." http://www.arkive.org/species/GES/mammals/Daubentonia_madagascariensis/more_info.html (accessed on June 22, 2004).

Docent. "Aye aye." http://www.szgdocent.org/pp/p-aye.htm (accessed on June 22, 2004).

Science & Nature: Animals. "Aye aye." http://www.bbc.co.uk/nature/wildfacts/factfiles/327.shtml (accessed on June 22, 2004).

UNEP, WCMC, WWF. "Aye-aye—*Daubentonia madagascariensis.*" http://www.unep-wcmc.org/species/data/species_sheets/ayeaye.htm (accessed on June 22, 2004).

TARSIERS
Tarsiidae

Class: Mammalia
Order: Primates
Family: Tarsiidae
Number of species: 6 species

phylum

class

subclass

order

monotypic order

suborder

▲ family

PHYSICAL CHARACTERISTICS

Tarsiers (TAR-see-urz) weigh 2.8 to 5.8 ounces (80 to 165 grams). Body length is 3 to 6 inches (8 to 15 centimeters), and tail length is 5 to 11 inches (13 to 28 centimeters). They range in color from sandy to grayish brown to reddish brown. The undersides may be yellowish beige, grayish, or bluish gray. Relative to their body size, tarsiers have the largest eyes of all mammals. Their goggle-like eyes cannot move within the sockets, but a flexible neck can rotate the head 180 degrees for a backward look.

The tarsier is named for its powerful, extended tarsals (TAR-sullz), or ankle bones. The tarsals, together with the merging at the ankles of the two lower-leg bones, the tibia and fibula, allow for remarkable leaps. Fingers and toes are enlarged at the tip, with adhesive pads for gripping vertical branches. The tail is nearly naked, except for a tuft of hair on the tip.

GEOGRAPHIC RANGE

Tarsiers are found in the Philippines, Indonesia, and Borneo.

HABITAT

Tarsiers live in a variety of habitats. They occupy mainly secondary forests with enough canopies that provide vertical branches for clinging, usually about 3 to 6 feet (0.9 to 1.8 meters) above the ground. Tarsiers also inhabit shrublands, bamboo thickets, mangroves, grasslands, and plantations. They also live in primary forests with their characteristic dense canopies and thinner lower vegetation.

DIET

Tarsiers are carnivores, feeding mainly on live animals, including cockroaches, beetles, moths, lizards, snakes, and roosting birds. They consume almost every part of their prey, including the feathers, beaks, and feet of birds.

BEHAVIOR AND REPRODUCTION

Tarsiers are arboreal, spending most of their time in trees. They forage alone at night, although some species may be active at dawn or dusk. When catching large insects, the tarsier closes its eyes, opening them only after putting the prey into its mouth. An insect's sharp body parts could do damage to the tarsier's big, exposed eyes. Tarsiers leap and cling to vertical branches. They communicate through high-pitched calls. When they get together to sleep during the day, tarsier pairs may perform duets, or a group may vocalize together as if in greeting.

Tarsiers have just one partner, mating year round or seasonally, depending on the species. After a pregnancy of about six months, the mother gives birth to a single, well-developed infant, about one quarter of her weight.

TARSIERS AND PEOPLE

Some people take tarsiers for pets. Some farmers mistakenly believe tarsiers eat crops and may kill the tarsiers. Actually, tarsiers help control some harmful insects, including grasshoppers, caterpillars, and moths.

CONSERVATION STATUS

The World Conservation Union (IUCN) lists the Dian's tarsier as Lower Risk/Conservation Dependent, meaning its survival depends on conservation efforts. The Eastern tarsier is listed as Near Threatened, not currently threatened, but could become so, because of habitat loss and degradation due to human activities. The Philippine tarsier and three other species found in Indonesia are listed as Data Deficient, meaning the species may be well-studied but information about distribution is lacking.

FLYING ACROBAT

When preparing to leap from one tree branch to another, the tarsier rotates its head 180° toward the intended landing spot. Then pushing off from its perch using its powerful hind legs, it leaps backward. The body takes off like an acrobat's, twists around in mid-air, and aligns with the forward direction of the head. The tarsier then lands vertically, grasping the branch with its fingers and toes.

Philippine tarsier *(Tarsius syrichta)*

PHILIPPINE TARSIER
Tarsius syrichta

Physical characteristics: The Philippine tarsier has soft gray fur, a body length of about 5 inches (13 centimeters), and a tail length that is twice as long (9 inches, or 23 centimeters). It weighs about 4 to 5 ounces (113 to 142 grams). The head is round and the snout is short. The enormous eyes that seem too big for the sockets are immobile. For side and back vision, the tarsier swivels its head, sometimes almost a full circle. The large, thinly textured ears move like giant antennas to track sounds made by crawling insects and other prey. Long fingers and toes have suction pads at the tips for gripping tree branches. All nails are flattened, except for the second and third toes, which are grooming claws used for removing dead skin and parasites from the fur. The nearly naked tail has a sandy coloration, with a tuft of hair at the tip. The inside part of the tail has ridges that help prop the tarsier against a tree trunk or branch, especially while it sleeps.

Geographic range: The Philippine tarsiers are found in the Philippine Islands.

Habitat: Philippine tarsiers inhabit small trees found under the canopy of less mature forests. They also occupy coastal rainforests. They live in tree hollows close to the ground and are also found in thick bushes and bamboo roots.

Diet: Philippine tarsiers prey on live crickets, beetles, termites, lizards, spiders, scorpions, frogs, and birds.

Behavior and reproduction: Philippine tarsiers mostly live in trees and shrubs, moving from branch to branch by leaping and clinging to vertical branches with their padded fingers and toes. The average jump covers about 5 feet (1.4 meters), with the greatest leaps recorded at 20 feet (6 meters). They also sleep while clinging to vertical branches, supported by their tail. Individuals sleep alone in dense vegetation close to the ground. On the forest floor, they hop, holding the long tail straight. They are nocturnal (active at night), preferring to forage alone. They are usually quiet, but call out to one another by squeaking in a high note, trilling, or chirping. Tarsiers scent mark tree branches, using urine and secretions from skin glands found within the lips, on the chest, and in genital areas.

The Philippine tarsier is usually quiet, but calls out to others by squeaking in a high note, trilling, or chirping. (© Tom McHugh/ Photo Researchers, Inc. Reproduced by permission.)

A male Philippine tarsier may form a family group with one or two females and their offspring. Due to a long pregnancy (about six months), the newborn is well developed, having a full coat and open eyes. The mother carries the infant in her mouth while she forages in trees, resting the infant on branches while she feeds. The newborn is able to cling to branches and can jump after a month.

Philippine tarsiers and people: Some Filipinos believe it is bad luck to touch a tarsier. Others take tarsiers for pets. However, tarsiers do not make good pets. They dislike being handled and will inflict serious bites. They do not thrive in zoos, dying soon after captivity.

Conservation status: IUCN lists the Philippine tarsier as Data Deficient, a category that does not refer to a threatened species. This means that the species may be well studied, but information about its population status is lacking. Nevertheless, tarsiers have experienced habitat loss because of the clearing of land for agriculture and timber. ■

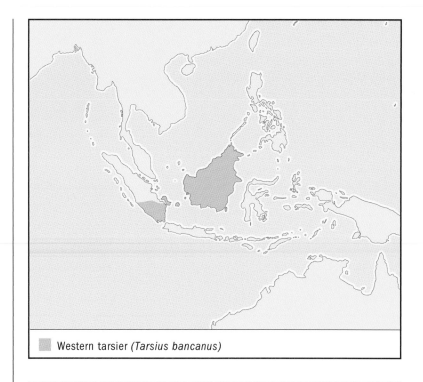

Western tarsier *(Tarsius bancanus)*

WESTERN TARSIER
Tarsius bancanus

Physical characteristics: The western tarsier is yellowish beige or sand-colored. Enormous, goggled eyes take up most of its face. The eyes cannot move within the sockets, so a flexible neck turns the head around almost 180° for a backward look. Large ears are in constant motion as they follow the sounds of possible prey. The fingers and toes are very long and have suction pads at the tips for gripping tree branches. Fingernails and toenails are flattened, except for those on the second and third toes. These two toes have grooming claws, used for cleaning the fur of dead skin and parasites and for scratching. The long, rod-like tail is bare with a small clump of hair at the end. Ridges on the inside part of the tail support the tarsier when it clings to tree trunks or branches.

Geographic range: Western tarsiers are found in Indonesia.

Habitat: Western tarsiers favor secondary forests, with their dense ground vegetation and small trees. They also inhabit primary forests,

A western tarsier eats a cicada. These tarsiers feed mainly on large insects. (Frans Lanting/Minden Pictures. Reproduced by permission.)

characterized by a full-ceiling canopy and trees of different heights. They are found in human settlements and plantations.

Diet: Western tarsiers eat primarily large insects, including beetles, cockroaches, praying mantis, cicadas, butterflies, and grasshoppers. They also feed on birds, bats, and snakes. They even eat poisonous snakes.

Behavior and reproduction: The western tarsier forages for food alone at night and at dawn and dusk, listening for sounds made by insects on the ground and catching them with its hands. It closes its eyes when attacking insects to protect its eyes. During the day, males and females sleep separately, either among vines and tangled vegetation or while clinging to vertical tree trunks or branches. Using urine and scent gland secretions, tarsiers scent mark tree branches to advertise territory ownership. They are rather quiet, although females vocalize when ready to mate.

Western tarsiers may be monogamous (muh-NAH-guh-mus), having just one partner, or polygynous (puh-LIH-juh-nus), with males having several partners. Births occur throughout the year, although more births occur between February and June at the end of the rainy season. Females give birth to a single infant that weighs about one quarter of its mother's weight. The well-developed infant is born with a full coat and open eyes. It can climb right away after birth.

Western tarsiers and people: The Ibans, the indigenous people of Sarawak, Borneo, who were once head-hunters, considered the western tarsier as an omen animal. They had seen the tarsier rotate its head full circle and thought the tarsier had a loose head. A head-hunter who encountered a tarsier would turn around right away so as not to incur the spirits' spell on him and his people. Today, tarsiers are taken for pets but do not survive in captivity.

Conservation status: The IUCN lists the western tarsier as Data Deficient, a category that does not refer to a threatened species. This means that the species may be well-studied, but there is not enough information about its population status.   ■

FOR MORE INFORMATION

Books:

Kavanagh, Michael. *A Complete Guide to Monkeys, Apes and Other Primates.* New York: The Viking Press, 1983.

Napier, John R., and Prue H. Napier. *The Natural History of the Primates.* Cambridge, MA: The MIT Press, 1986.

Nowak, Ronald M. *Walker's Primates of the World.* Baltimore: The Johns Hopkins University Press, 1999.

Preston-Mafham, Rod, and Ken Preston-Mafham. *Primates of the World.* New York: Facts on File, Inc., 1992.

Web sites:

"Philippine Tarsier: *Tarsius syrichta.*" The Philippine Tarsier Foundation, Inc. http://www.bohol.net/PTFI/tarsier.htm (accessed July 6, 2004).

Ramos, Serafin N. Jr. "The Tarsiers of Sarangani." Sarangani, Mindanao, Philippines Website. http://www.sarangani.gov.ph/news/tarsier/m04tarsier.html (accessed July 6, 2004).

"Tarsiers (Tarsiidae)." Singapore Zoological Garden Docents. http://www.szgdocent.org/pp/p-tarsir.htm (accessed July 6, 2004).

SQUIRREL MONKEYS AND CAPUCHINS
Cebidae

Class: Mammalia

Order: Primates

Family: Cebidae

Number of species: 12 species

family

CHAPTER

PHYSICAL CHARACTERISTICS

Cebids (members of the family Cebidae, including squirrel monkeys and capuchins) have round heads, forward-facing eyes, rounded snouts, and small ears. Squirrel monkeys are the smallest cebids. They have a slim body with a dense, soft fur that is gray to black on the crown of the head. The body may be yellow, golden, or reddish. The shoulders are gray to olive, and the underparts are white to yellow. The forearms, hands, and feet are yellow to golden. The furry tail has a black tip.

Capuchins have a heavy body build. The face is covered with short fur, while the rest of the body has longer fur. Color ranges from black to brown to yellowish beige. The chest and shoulders have patches of white, and the underparts are light-colored. The tail is usually coiled at the tip, earning it the nickname ringtail monkey.

GEOGRAPHIC RANGE

Squirrel monkeys are found in most of South America and in Central America (just Costa Rica and Panama). Capuchins are found in most of South America and Central America and the Caribbean islands of Trinidad and Tobago.

HABITAT

Cebids are found in the spreading forest canopy and in smaller understory trees. Squirrel monkeys also inhabit swamps, while capuchins thrive in dry forests.

phylum

class

subclass

order

monotypic order

suborder

▲ **family**

DIET

Squirrel monkeys eat predominantly fruits and insects, but also feed on flowers, shoots, buds, leaves, spiders, frogs, bats, and crabs. Capuchins consume mainly fruits, but also eat insects, snails, lizards, small birds, baby squirrels, crabs, and oysters.

BEHAVIOR AND REPRODUCTION

Cebids are arboreal (tree-dwelling) and diurnal (active during the day). They form large groups headed by a dominant male. Capuchin groups have a dominant female that submits only to the dominant male. The dominant male defends his group but does not try to control the members. Squirrel monkey groups, on the other hand, may or may not have dominant females, depending on the species. However, only the dominant male mates with the receptive females. Nevertheless, all cebids, males and females, have several partners. Females have a single infant, which keeps a close relationship to its mother. Fathers do not share in childrearing. Cebids use vocalizations to communicate. They urinate on their hands, then rub them on their fur and feet to scent mark territory. This behavior is called urine washing.

CEBIDS AND PEOPLE

Cebids are popular as pets and zoo exhibit animals. They are used in medical research. They have been used in the space program to test the effects of space travel. Capuchins are trained to help disabled persons, using their human-like hands to perform daily tasks, such as feeding people.

CONSERVATION STATUS

IUCN lists the yellow-breasted capuchin as Critically Endangered, facing an extremely high risk of extinction, because of habitat loss and degradation, and hunting for food. It classifies the red-backed squirrel monkey as Endangered, facing a very high risk of extinction, and the black squirrel monkey and the crested capuchin as Vulnerable, facing a high risk of extinction, due to habitat loss and degradation.

Common squirrel monkey (*Saimiri sciureus*)

COMMON SQUIRREL MONKEY
Saimiri sciureus

Physical characteristics: Common squirrel monkeys weigh 1.5 to 2.75 pounds (0.6 to 1.2 kilograms), with the males being larger than the females. They measure about 12 inches (30 centimeters), with a tail length of about 16 inches (41 centimeters). The fur is short and dense. The round head is gray to black on top, with a white face mask and a black snout surrounded by black fur. Eyes are large and ears are small. The back is olive-gray, and the underparts are light yellow. The forearms, hands, and feet are yellow-orange. The long tail tipped with black is non-prehensile, or incapable of grasping things such as tree branches.

Geographic range: Common squirrel monkeys are found in Brazil, Colombia, French Guiana, Guyana, Suriname, and Venezuela.

Habitat: Common squirrel monkeys occupy the middle layers of the forest with abundant vines and other vegetation. They also inhabit mangroves and forests along rivers and streams.

Diet: Common squirrel monkeys feed mainly on soft fruits and insects. They also eat frogs, spiders, snails, crabs, and occasionally bats.

Behavior and reproduction: Depending on available habitat, common squirrel monkeys live in groups of twenty to 300. Subgroups of males, mothers with offspring, and juveniles are formed within the main group. They are active during the day, foraging together in small groups. They are mostly arboreal but are sometimes found on the ground. They normally walk on all fours, but can move on their hind legs.

Males and females have several partners. Before the mating season, adult males gain weight on the upper body and in the genital organs in what is known as the "fatted male" condition. They also fight with one another to determine who will mate with the females. One large offspring is born during the rainfall season when food is plentiful. The young stay with the mother for about a year. Males do not share in parenting.

Common squirrel monkeys feed mainly on soft fruits and insects. (Norman Owen Tomalin/Bruce Coleman Inc. Reproduced by permission.)

Common squirrel monkeys and people: Common squirrel monkeys are sometimes hunted for food. They are sold as pets and used for medical research.

Conservation status: Common squirrel monkeys are not considered a threatened species. ∎

White-throated capuchin (Cebus capucinus)

WHITE-THROATED CAPUCHIN
Cebus capucinus

Physical characteristics: White-throated capuchins weigh 5.9 to
8.6 pounds (2.7 to 3.9 kilograms), with males being larger than females. They measure about 18 inches (46 centimeters) with a tail that
is just as long. The robust body is fully furred, with white to yellowish coloration on the throat, head, and shoulders. The back, arms,
and legs are black. The long, black, hairy tail is semiprehensile, able
to wrap around tree branches, but unable to function as a fifth limb
for holding objects.

White-throated capuchins are in the trees for all of their activities, including sleeping. (J-C Carton/ Bruce Coleman Inc. Reproduced by permission.)

Geographic range: White-throated capuchins are found in Colombia, Costa Rica, Honduras, Nicaragua, and Panama.

Habitat: White-throated capuchins occupy evergreen forests with full canopies and those with less-developed canopies but dense understory. They also inhabit mangroves and dry deciduous forests.

Diet: White-throated capuchins feed on plants and animals. Fruits are their favorite food, but they also eat shoots, leaves, flowers, buds, berries, and nuts, as well as insects, spiders, crabs, small birds, baby squirrels, and lizards. They eat oysters, using rocks to open the shells.

Behavior and reproduction: White-throated capuchins form groups of ten to twenty individuals, typically with more adult females than males, but ruled by a large, older male. They are arboreal and active during the day. When foraging, they call out to one another, using squeaks, shrieks, and chatters. They groom each other, looking through each other's fur to remove parasites and dirt. Males defend the group's territory, rubbing urine on their fur and feet and distributing that scent among the trees. They have been known to throw branches and fruits at perceived enemies, including humans.

Adults have several partners. Females have single births. The newborn clings to its mother's undersides or across her shoulders. After six weeks, the infant rides on its mother's back. Males do not share in childcare. Young males leave their birthplace as early as age two.

White-throated capuchins and people: White-throated capuchins are the familiar creatures associated with organ-grinders who used to entertain in city streets. They are popular in zoos worldwide. Their intelligence makes them a prime candidate for medical research. Farmers consider them pests for raiding crops.

Conservation status: White-throated capuchins are not considered a threatened species. ■

Weeper capuchin (*Cebus olivaceus*)

WEEPER CAPUCHIN
Cebus olivaceus

Physical characteristics: Weeper capuchins weigh 5.3 to 6.6 pounds (2.4 to 3 kilograms), males being larger than females. They measure about 20 inches (55 centimeters) with a tail that is just as long. They have an orange-brown body and yellowish shoulders and upper arms. A wedge-shaped, dark brown coloration extends from the forehead to the back of the head. The long, brown tail tipped with black is semiprehensile, so it can wrap around a branch.

Geographic range: Weeper capuchins are found in Brazil, French Guiana, Guyana, Suriname, and Venezuela.

Weeper capuchins live in groups of eight to fifty individuals with a dominant male. Young females stay with the group, but young males leave when they are as young as two years old. (Illustration by Barbara Duperron. Reproduced by permission.)

Habitat: Weeper capuchins inhabit the middle and lower layers of evergreen rainforests. They also live in dry forests, mountain forests, gallery forests (woods along streams and rivers), and shrub woodlands.

Diet: Weeper capuchins eat fruits, buds, shoots, and roots of small trees. They also feed on insects, snails, and birds.

Behavior and reproduction: Weeper capuchins form groups of eight to fifty individuals, ruled by a dominant male. They are arboreal and forage during the day. They take breaks to groom each other's fur, removing parasites and dirt. Capuchins claim territory by urine washing. They soak their hands with urine, which they rub on their fur and feet, leaving the scent throughout their forest routes. They show aggression by shaking branches and bouncing up and down. They have about a dozen vocalizations, one of which is a sad sound that earned them the name "weeper."

All receptive females mate with the dominant male at a given time. Females have single births. The newborn is able to cling to its mother's fur right away. The father does not take care of the young but may find food for the mother. Females stay with the group, but males leave home as early as two years of age.

Weeper capuchins and people: Weeper capuchins are hunted for food in some areas. They are also used in medical research.

Conservation status: Weeper capuchins are not considered a threatened species. ■

FOR MORE INFORMATION

Books:

Kavanagh, Michael. *A Complete Guide to Monkeys, Apes and Other Primates.* New York: The Viking Press, 1983.

Kinzey, Warren G., ed. *New World Primates: Ecology, Evolution, and Behavior.* New York: Aldine de Gruyter, 1997.

Napier, John R., and Prue H. Napier. *The Natural History of the Primates.* Cambridge, MA: The MIT Press, 1986.

Nowak, Ronald M. *Walker's Primates of the World.* Baltimore: The Johns Hopkins University Press, 1999.

Periodicals:

Bergman, Charles. "The Peaceful Primates." *Smithsonian* (June 1999): 78–86.

Web sites:

Broekema, Iris. "Natural History of the White-Throated Capuchin (*Cebus capucinus*)." The Primate Foundation of Panama. http://www .primatesofpanama.org/academicresources/articles/capuchin.htm (accessed on July 6, 2004).

Schober, Nathan, and Chris Yahnke. "*Cebus olivaceus* (Weeping Capuchin)." Animal Diversity Web. http://animaldiversity.ummz.umich. edu/site/accounts/information/Cebus_olivaceus.html (accessed on July 6, 2004).

The Squirrel Monkey Breeding and Research Resource. "Saimiri Natural History." University of South Alabama Department of Comparative Medicine. http://www.saimiri.usouthal.edu/saimiri.htm (accessed on July 6, 2004).

MARMOSETS, TAMARINS,
AND GOELDI'S MONKEY
Callitrichidae

Class: Mammalia
Order: Primates
Family: Callitrichidae
Number of species: 41 species

family

phylum

class

subclass

order

monotypic order

suborder

▲ family

PHYSICAL CHARACTERISTICS

Callitrichids (cal-ih-TRICK-ids; members of the family Callitrichidae) are among the smallest primates and include the world's smallest monkey, the pygmy marmoset. They have luxurious, silky fur that ranges from the brightly colored to the more subdued black or brownish black. Some species come in several color combinations. A shock of hair may be worn on top of the head, over the nape and shoulder, or as a beard. All have claws on fingers and toes, except for the big toes. The claws are useful for vertical clinging. Non-prehensile (non-grasping) tails are long, sometimes several inches longer than the body. Most callitrichids have scent glands in different areas of their bodies.

GEOGRAPHIC RANGE

Callitrichids are found in most of South America and in Central America (Panama and Costa Rica).

HABITAT

Callitrichids occupy various habitats, including primary forests with well-developed canopies and secondary forests with dense understories. They live in open woodlands, bamboo thickets, and scrub forests, as well as forests along rivers.

DIET

Fruits, insects, and gum (a sticky substance from tree bark) make up the main diet of all callitrichids. Most also eat nectar (sweet liquid from flowering plants), lizards, tree frogs, baby birds, bird eggs, butterflies, and spiders.

BEHAVIOR AND REPRODUCTION

Callitrichids are very social animals, living in extended family groups made up of a breeding pair, their offspring, and other relatives. They are arboreal (tree-dwelling) and diurnal (active during the day). They perform mutual grooming, or looking through each other's fur to remove parasites and dirt. Only one female breeds in a family, giving birth to twins. Goeldi's monkeys are the exceptions, having single births. The father and other family members share in childrearing, taking turns carrying the infants and sharing food with them. They guard their territories, sending messages through scent marking, loud calls, body language, and facial expressions.

COOPERATIVE PARENTING

In tamarin and marmoset groups, just one female gives birth, producing twins each time. At birth, the twins weigh as much as 25 percent of the mother's weight. Juvenile siblings and other adults help take care of the infants, sharing food after the infants are weaned from milk and guarding them against predators. Family members take turns carrying the twins, especially since there are no places to set the babies down in tree tops.

CALLITRICHIDS AND PEOPLE

Marmosets and tamarins are sold as pets. These animals are commonly used in medical research, especially in the United States.

CONSERVATION STATUS

The World Conservation Union (IUCN) lists the black-faced lion tamarin and the black lion tamarin as Critically Endangered, facing an extremely high risk of extinction, because of habitat loss/degradation from logging and hunting. The pied tamarin is also classified as Critically Endangered due to human expansion into its habitat. Five species are Endangered, facing a very high risk of extinction, because of habitat loss/degradation resulting from deforestation for agriculture: the buffy tufted-ear marmoset, the buffy-headed marmoset, the golden-headed lion tamarin, the golden lion tamarin, and the cotton-top tamarin. The IUCN classifies two other species as Vulnerable, facing a high risk of extinction, due to habitat loss/degradation from logging and hunting.

Cotton-top tamarin (*Saguinus oedipus*)

COTTON-TOP TAMARIN
Saguinus oedipus

Physical characteristics: The cotton-top tamarin gets its name from the long, white hair that starts as a wedge at its forehead and flows all way to the nape of the neck. Black or brown fur covers the back, and white fur covers the undersides. The black face is framed in grayish fur. The arms and legs are grayish white. The long, brownish black tail helps in keeping balance when jumping and climbing. It has claws for vertical climbing, except for the big toe, which has a flat nail. It weighs about 12.4 to 15.9 ounces (350 to 450 grams) and measures 7.9 to 11 inches (20 to 28 centimeters), plus an additional 12.2 to 16.1 inches (31 to 41 centimeters) for the tail.

Cotton-top tamarins prefer the tropical deciduous forests that are typically found on the edges of rainforests. They live in Colombia. (Gail M. Shumway/Bruce Coleman Inc. Reproduced by permission.)

Geographic range: Cotton-top tamarins are found in Colombia.

Habitat: Cotton-top tamarins are found in rainforests, but prefer the tropical deciduous forests that are typically found on the edges of rainforests. They also inhabit open woodlands and dry forests.

Diet: Cotton-top tamarins eat mainly ripe fruits, insects, and spiders. They also feed on flowers, buds, young leaves, nectar, gum, tree frogs, snails, and lizards.

Behavior and reproduction: Cotton-top tamarins live in groups of three to ten individuals, consisting of a dominant pair, their offspring, and several subordinate males and females. During the day, they travel through the forest as a group foraging for food. They take long breaks for grooming sessions to remove parasites and dirt from each other's fur. Cotton-top tamarins are vocal, making long calls to contact group members or to greet other tamarin species. They scent mark territories and use body language to communicate, such as raising their head fur or nape fur when agitated.

Only the dominant pair breeds, usually having twins. Infants travel with their parents by clinging to their fur. Both parents care for the young, although fathers usually carry the young. The parents are assisted by older siblings and other group members, who also share their food with the young. Young females leave home at about eighteen months of age, while young males stay longer until they are about two years old.

Cotton-top tamarins and people: Cotton-top tamarins are popular as pets. They are used in medical research, especially in the study of colon cancer.

Conservation status: The IUCN lists the cotton-top tamarin as Endangered because of habitat loss and degradation due to deforestation for agriculture and ranching. ∎

Goeldi's monkey (Callimico goeldii)

GOELDI'S MONKEY
Callimico goeldii

Physical characteristics: Goeldi's monkeys have long, silky, brownish black fur, with a mane of hair covering the neck and shoulders and longer hairs on the rump. They weigh about 1.1 pounds (500 grams) and measure 8 to 9 inches (20 to 23 centimeters), with a tail length of 10 to 12 inches (25 to 30 centimeters). Unlike other callitrichids, they have thirty-six teeth instead of thirty-two, due to an extra molar on both sides of the jaws. The long tail is used for balance in traveling through the trees. They have claws, except for the large toes that have flat nails.

Geographic range: Goeldi's monkeys are found in Bolivia, Brazil, Colombia, Ecuador, and Peru.

Habitat: Goeldi's monkeys prefer secondary forests with less-developed canopy and dense bamboo grasses and shrubs. They also inhabit deciduous scrub forests.

Diet: The Goeldi's monkey's diet consists predominantly of fruits and insects. It also eats tree frogs and occasionally forages for grasshoppers, crickets, and cockroaches on the forest floor.

Behavior and reproduction: Goeldi's monkeys live in groups of two to nine individuals, made up of one to three adult males and females. During the day they travel through the forest by vertical clinging and leaping, instead of on their four feet. They communicate through a variety of vocalizations, including trills for warning signals and whistles for long-distance calls.

Each group has two breeding females, who may give birth twice a year. Unlike tamarins and marmosets who give birth to twins, Goeldi's monkeys give birth to a single young. The mother alone takes care of the newborn for almost three weeks, after which the father and other family members share in parenting. The infant is carried on the back. However, when escaping predators, animals that hunt them for food, the monkeys do not take their young with them, but hide them among vegetation. They themselves hide in the lower shrubbery. Infants become independent by the eighth week.

Goeldi's monkeys and people: Goeldi's monkeys are trapped for the pet trade.

Conservation status: The IUCN lists Goeldi's monkey as Near Threatened, meaning they are not currently threatened, but could become so, due to habitat loss and degradation from human settlements and logging. It is classified as vulnerable in Colombia because of limited populations. ■

Pygmy marmoset (*Cebuella pygmaea*)

PYGMY MARMOSET
Cebuella pygmaea

Physical characteristics: The smallest of the New World primates, the pygmy marmoset weighs about 4.4 ounces (125 grams) and measures about 5 inches (13 centimeters), with another 8 inches (20 centimeters) for the tail. The fine, soft fur is brown and tinged with yellow, resulting in a grizzled look that makes it blend in with the tree branches. The fur is thicker on the head and chest, giving it a larger appearance. The orange or yellow hands and feet have claws, except for the big toes. The non-prehensile tail maintains balance when the marmoset darts through the forest. The lower jaw has chisel-shaped front teeth for gouging holes in tree barks to extract gum.

The pygmy marmoset is the smallest of the New World primates. (© Art Wolfe/The National Audubon Society Collection/Photo Researchers, Inc. Reproduced by permission.)

Geographic range: Pygmy marmosets are found in Bolivia, Brazil, Colombia, Ecuador, and Peru.

Habitat: Pygmy marmosets prefer forests along rivers, as well as flood-plain forests. They also occupy scrub forests.

Diet: Pygmy marmosets consume mainly tree gum, which they collect by excavating holes on tree barks with their sharp lower incisors

and canines. The gum hardens when exposed to air but can be dis-
lodged for a fresh supply. Marmosets also feed on insects, spiders,
lizards, and grasshoppers.

Behavior and reproduction: Pygmy marmosets live in groups of two
to nine individuals, typically an adult pair and their offspring, which
may include up to four generations. Some groups may have more than
one male and female, but just one breeding pair. Marmosets breed
throughout the year, producing twins. The whole family shares in
child care.

Pygmy marmosets are active during the day, traveling on all fours
and sometimes clinging and leaping vertically. They communicate
through various vocalizations, body postures, and facial expressions.
They are territorial, defending their forest sites using scent gland secretions. Defense of their territory involves calls, threat displays, and
chasing of intruders.

Pygmy marmosets and people: Pygmy marmosets are sometimes
kept as pets.

Conservation status: The pygmy marmoset is not a threatened
species.   ■

FOR MORE INFORMATION

Books:

Angier, Natalie, and Nicholas Wade, eds. "Cotton-Top Tamarins: Coop-
erative, Pacifist and Close to Extinct." In *The Science Times Book of
Mammals.* New York: The Lyons Press, 1999.

Kinzey, Warren G., ed. *New World Primates: Ecology, Evolution, and
Behavior.* New York: Aldine de Gruyter, 1997.

Napier, John R., and Prue H. Napier. *The Natural History of the Primates.*
Cambridge, MA: The MIT Press, 1986.

Nowak, Ronald M. *Walker's Primates of the World.* Baltimore: The Johns
Hopkins University Press, 1999.

Preston-Mafham, Rod, and Ken Preston-Mafham. *Primates of the World.*
New York: Facts on File, Inc., 1992.

Tattersall, Ian. *Primates: Lemurs, Monkeys, and You.* Brookfield, CT: The
Millbrook Press, 1995.

Periodicals:

Richardson, Sarah. "A Monopoly on Maternity." *Discover* (February
1994): 28–29.

Web sites:

Golden Lion Tamarin Conservation Program. "About Lion Tamarins." Smithsonian National Zoological Park. http://nationalzoo.si.edu/ConservationAndScience/EndangeredSpecies/GLTProgram/Tamarins/About.cfm (accessed on July 6, 2004).

Paschka, Nick, and Phil Myers, eds. "*Callimico goeldii.*" Animal Diversity Web. http://animaldiversity.ummz.umich.edu/site/accounts/information/Callimico_goeldii.html (accessed on July 6, 2004).

"Pygmy Marmoset." Smithsonian National Zoological Park. http://natzoo.si.edu/Animals/Primates/Facts/FactSheets/PygmyMarmosets/default.cfm (accessed on July 6, 2004).

NIGHT MONKEYS
Aotidae

Class: Mammalia
Order: Primates
Family: Aotidae
Number of species: 8 species

phylum

class

subclass

order

monotypic order

suborder

▲ **family**

PHYSICAL CHARACTERISTICS

Night monkeys, so named because they are the world's only nocturnal (active at night) monkeys, are medium-sized animals weighing about 2 pounds (0.9 kilograms). They measure about 13.5 inches (34 centimeters), with a tail length of about 14.6 inches (37 centimeters). Forward-facing, large eyes dominate the round face. The large size of the eyes makes up for the lack of a reflective eye layer used by many nocturnal mammals for night vision. Night monkeys are also called owl monkeys because of their round, flat face and eyes that resemble those of an owl.

Night monkeys have a thick, woolly fur that ranges in color from gray to brown, with yellow to orange undersides. An orange stripe runs down the back. Large white or gray patches surround the eyes and the mouth. Three dark stripes extend from the top of the nose and on each side of the head. The stripes vary in darkness and width. Very small rounded ears seem almost absent in the thick fur. A sac under the chin can be inflated to make vocalizations louder. The long, bushy tail is non-prehensile, or incapable of grasping. It is used for balance when traveling through the forest on hands and feet and for leaping.

GEOGRAPHIC RANGE

Night monkeys are found in Argentina, Bolivia, Brazil, Colombia, Nicaragua, Panama, Paraguay, and Venezuela.

HABITAT

Night monkeys inhabit evergreen tropical rainforests and deciduous scrub forests. They also occupy forests along rivers.

They prefer dense middle-level canopies and understories with tangled vines that provide cover for sleeping sites. They also like hollows in old trees.

DIET

Night monkeys eat mainly fruits, but also consume leaves, flowers, insects, tree frogs, spiders, bats, birds, and eggs. They forage, search for food, at all levels of the forest, from the canopy down to the forest floor.

BEHAVIOR AND REPRODUCTION

Night monkeys are arboreal and live in family groups consisting of an adult pair and two or three offspring. During the day, the family sleeps in tree hollows or tangled vines. At night they forage for food throughout the forest levels, sometimes descending to the ground. They are especially active on moonlit nights, when they can see better. Night monkeys are adaptable. In Argentina, when the nights get cold at certain times of the year, the animals sleep at night and look for food during the day.

Night monkeys are monogamous (muh-NAH-guh-mus), having just one partner. The female gives birth to one offspring a year. The mother nurses the infant for up to eight months, but only carries the infant during the first week after birth and when nursing. The father provides almost all the child care. He carries the infant when the family travels through the trees. He also plays with the infant and the older offspring and guards them from predators, animals that hunt them for food. If the father dies, the older sibling, not the mother, assumes infant care. The young leave home at about three years of age.

Night monkeys scent mark territories with a behavior called urine washing. They wet their hands with urine, then rub them on their coats and the soles of their feet. The urine scent is transferred to the leaves and branches during their travels. They also communicate using secretions from scent glands on the chest and on the base of the tail. Conflicts between neighbors tend to occur when the moon is bright, perhaps because they can better see aggressive physical signals that include arching the back, erecting the fur, passing wastes, and urinating. The monkeys emit a variety of calls, including shrill cries, squeaks, and loud owl-like hoots that can be made louder by inflating the throat sac. Young males wishing to attract a mate hoot for long periods of time during a full moon.

NIGHT MONKEYS AND PEOPLE

Night monkeys are hunted for their meat and fur by native people. They are sold as pets and used for medical research.

CONSERVATION STATUS

The IUCN lists the Andean night monkey as Vulnerable, facing a high risk of extinction in the wild, because of small populations and habitat destruction from deforestation. The gray-bellied night monkey is also classified as Vulnerable due to hunting by humans and collection for the pet trade and medical research.

Three-striped night monkey (*Aotus trivirgatus*)

THREE-STRIPED NIGHT MONKEY
Aotus trivirgatus

Physical characteristics: The three-striped night monkey has a woolly, dense fur that varies in coloration from grizzled gray to brown to reddish. Its undersides are orange or yellowish. The ears are small and rounded. Very large eyes are forward-facing and are brown or orange. Large white patches surround the eyes and the mouth, giving the appearance of alertness even when sleeping. Three dark stripes extend from the top of the nose and on each side of the head. The distinctive facial markings may prove helpful for communications among family members, especially on moonless nights. The legs, which are longer than the arms, are used for jumping. An inflatable

sac under the chin is used to produce loud vocalizations. The orange, bushy tail, which is tipped in black, is non-prehensile. It is used for maintaining balance when leaping on branches and moving on hands and feet through the different levels of the forest. Males weigh about 1.8 pounds (0.8 kilograms). Females are slightly smaller. The monkeys measure 9.5 to 18.5 inches (24 to 47 centimeters) with a tail length of 8.7 to 16.5 inches (22 to 42 centimeters).

Geographic range: Three-striped night monkeys are found in Brazil, Colombia, and Venezuela.

Habitat: Three-striped night monkeys inhabit different types of forests, including evergreen forests, wet and dry forests, and forests along rivers. They prefer forests with thick, tangled vines and thickets for cover during sleep or rest. They also thrive near human developments.

Diet: Three-striped night monkeys feed mainly on fruits, supplementing them with insects, tree frogs, nectar, and leaves.

Behavior and reproduction: Three-striped night monkeys live in family groups in forest trees. A typical family consists of the parents and their infant and juvenile offspring. The family forages at night, staying up longer on moonlit nights. They travel through the same areas of the trees, which is especially helpful in finding their way in the dark. They usually move on all fours, but can jump from tree to tree. During the day, they share a sleeping site among tangled vines, dense vegetation, or in a tree hollow.

Mothers give birth to a single infant annually, although they may have twins, but very rarely. Fathers are the principal caregivers, carrying the infant starting from birth. They play with the infant and older offspring, guard them against predators, and also teach them. The infant is given to the mother only during nursing. The mother does not participate in play and gives the infant back to the father immediately after it is fed. The infant is weaned by eight months of age. Older offspring help the father care for the newborn. The young stay with the family for up to three years, leaving peacefully on their own.

Three-striped night monkeys are territorial, advertising their ownership with secretions from scent glands in the chest and the tail base. They also use urine for scent marking. They soak their fur and the soles of their feet with urine, which gets transferred to leaves, branches, and trunks. They are loud creatures, announcing their presence with different types of sounds. They use an owl-like hoot when ready to mate or when separated while foraging in the dark. They whoop and grunt to threaten intruders, and trill when greeting each other. Hostile physical communications include back-arching, fur-raising, defecating, and urinating.

Three-striped night monkeys and people: Three-striped night monkeys are hunted for food by native people. They are also trapped and sold as pets. These monkeys have been found to be carriers of the human malaria parasites. They are especially valued for research in the development of drugs used for treatment and prevention of malaria.

Conservation status: The three-striped night monkey is not a threatened species. ■

FOR MORE INFORMATION

Books:

Kavanagh, Michael. *A Complete Guide to Monkeys, Apes and Other Primates.* New York: The Viking Press, 1983.

Kinzey, Warren G., ed. *New World Primates: Ecology, Evolution, and Behavior.* New York: Aldine de Gruyter, 1997.

Napier, John R., and Prue H. Napier. *The Natural History of the Primates.* Cambridge, MA: The MIT Press, 1986.

Nowak, Ronald M. *Walker's Primates of the World.* Baltimore: The Johns Hopkins University Press, 1999.

Web sites:

"*Aotus trivirgatus* (Northern Gray-Necked Owl Monkey)." The Primate Foundation of Panama. http://www.primatesofpanama.org/academicresources/articles/monoculture/atrivirgatus.htm (accessed on July 6, 2004).

The Squirrel Monkey Breeding and Research Resource. "*Aotus* Natural History." University of South Alabama Department of Comparative Medicine. http://www.saimiri.usouthal.edu/aotus_natural_history.htm (accessed on July 6, 2004).

Class: Mammalia
Order: Primates
Family: Pitheciidae
Number of species: 28 species

family

phylum
class
subclass
order
monotypic order
suborder
▲ **family**

PHYSICAL CHARACTERISTICS

Pitheciids (PITH-uh-sidz; members of the family Pitheciidae) are small- to medium-sized monkeys, ranging from the smallest, the titis, to the largest, the uakaris. Male bearded sakis and uakaris are about 20 percent larger than the females. Male and female white-faced sakis differ in coloration. The bald uakari is easily recognized by its pinkish to bright red naked face. All pitheciid species have long coats, except for the short-furred bearded saki. The bald uakari alone has a short tail, about a third of its body length. The rest of the species have long, non-prehensile (nongrasping) tails.

GEOGRAPHIC RANGE

Pitheciids are found in Bolivia, Brazil, Colombia, Ecuador, French Guiana, Guyana, Peru, and Suriname.

HABITAT

Pitheciids inhabit a variety of rainforest habitats. Sakis prefer the middle and lower layers of the canopy, as well as the understory. They are found in savanna forests, mountain forests, swamps, and forests along rivers, but not flooded forests. Uakaris choose forests that get flooded from seasonal rainfall for about six months. Titis occupy coastal forests, living in the understory.

DIET

Sakis and uakaris feed mainly on seeds, especially from tough-skinned fruits, while titis prefer fruit pulps. All species supplement their diet with flowers, leaves, shoots, and insects.

BEHAVIOR AND REPRODUCTION

Pitheciids differ in the size of their social groups, ranging from small parent-and-offspring groups among titis to the uakari multimale-multifemale groups of up to 100 members. They are mostly arboreal, living in the trees of the forest canopy and understory. Active during the day, these primates take breaks for mutual grooming. Pitheciids are vocal and use body postures to communicate, such as erecting the body hair to show aggression.

All pitheciids give birth to one infant. Some species breed seasonally, while others do not. Saki fathers do not help with child care but do groom infants. Titi fathers are the principal caregivers, even of older offspring. The young are weaned at different ages, with sakis being independent at about age one and titis remaining with the parents until they are two or three years old.

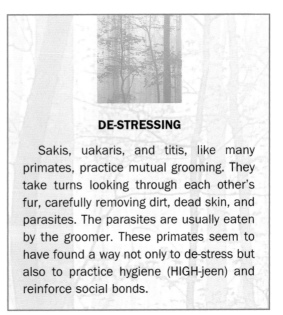

DE-STRESSING

Sakis, uakaris, and titis, like many primates, practice mutual grooming. They take turns looking through each other's fur, carefully removing dirt, dead skin, and parasites. The parasites are usually eaten by the groomer. These primates seem to have found a way not only to de-stress but also to practice hygiene (HIGH-jeen) and reinforce social bonds.

PITHECIIDS AND PEOPLE

Pitheciids are hunted for food and trapped for the pet trade. Sakis are hunted for their long, bushy tails that are made into dusters.

CONSERVATION STATUS

The World Conservation Union (IUCN) lists Barbara Brown's titi and Coimbra's titi as Critically Endangered, facing an extremely high risk of extinction, due to habitat loss or degradation from logging. The bearded saki is classified as Endangered, facing a very high risk of extinction, because of hunting and pet collection, as well as habitat loss from deforestation. Six other species are listed as Vulnerable, facing a high risk of extinction, and two species as Near Threatened, not currently threatened, but could become so, due to several factors, including hunting, capture for the pet trade, and habitat loss from deforestation for timber and agriculture.

White-faced saki (*Pithecia pithecia*)

WHITE-FACED SAKI
Pithecia pithecia

Physical characteristics: The white-faced saki weighs 1.8 to 5.5 pounds (0.8 to 2.5 kilograms). It measures 13.2 to 13.8 inches (33.5 to 35 centimeters), with a tail length of 13.5 to 17.5 inches (34.3 to 44.5 centimeters). The coarse fur is long, thick, and shaggy, making the animal seem larger. The saki is named for its white facial coloration, sometimes tinged with red, which is typical only of males. Females have black or brownish fur, with a pale stripe running down from under the eyes to each side of the face. This marked color difference is unusual in primates. Long nape hair flows forward like a hood. The black nose is very wide, and the nostrils are flat. The long, bushy tail is non-prehensile, or incapable of grasping. It is used for balance when traveling through the forest.

Geographic range: White-faced sakis are found in Bolivia, Brazil, Colombia, Ecuador, French Guiana, Guyana, Peru, and Suriname.

Habitat: White-faced sakis inhabit savanna forests where grassland and forest meet, as well as mountain forests. They live in palm swamps and forests along rivers, although they do not like flooded areas. They prefer the middle and lower levels of the forest canopy but will forage at the tangled vegetation below.

Diet: White-faced sakis feed mainly on seeds, fruits, flowers, shoots, and leaves. They occasionally eat birds, termites, and other insects. They sometimes catch mice and bats, which they skin and tear to pieces before eating.

The white-faced saki is named for the white facial coloration of the males. Males show the white coloration at two months old. (Norman Owen Tomalin/Bruce Coleman Inc. Reproduced by permission.)

Behavior and reproduction: White-faced sakis are active during the day, sleeping at night curled up on branches. They are agile climbers, traveling and climbing on all fours. They are known as the flying monkeys because of their ability to jump downward through forest gaps of up to 33 feet (10 meters). Sakis also travel upright on their hind feet. They show aggression by arching their back, erecting their fur, and shaking their body. Sakis communicate using loud calls, chirps, and high-pitched whistling.

Sakis live in small groups of up to five individuals, typically the parents and their young. Larger groups may get together at abundant food sources. Females give birth to a single infant from December to April. All infants are born with female colorations. Males acquire their striking facial coloration at two months. The mother alone rears the young, who leave home at age one.

White-faced sakis and people: White-faced sakis are hunted for food and collected for the pet trade.

Conservation status: The white-faced saki is not considered a threatened species. ■

Bald uakari (*Cacajao calvus*)

BALD UAKARI
Cacajao calvus

Physical characteristics: The bald uakari has long, coarse, shaggy hair that varies in coloration from white to red to reddish gold to orange. The bald face is pink to bright red. It is thought that the red face is an indication to a potential mate that the individual is healthy. Malaria is a common disease in the Amazon rainforest, and uakaris afflicted with the disease tend to have paler faces. Sharp incisors, canine teeth, and powerful jaws are especially adapted for piercing and cracking the hard shells of fruits and extracting the seeds, their favorite food. Bald uakaris weigh about 6.6 to 7.7 pounds

It is thought that the red face of a bald uakari is an indication to a potential mate that the individual is healthy. Malaria is a common disease in the Amazon rainforest, and uakaris afflicted with the disease tend to have paler faces. (R. A. Mittermeier/ Bruce Coleman Inc. Reproduced by permission.)

(3 to 3.5 kilograms) and measure about 21.3 to 22.4 inches (54 to 57 centimeters), with a tail length of 5.9 to 6.3 inches (15 to 16 centimeters). It is the only South American monkey with a short tail.

Geographic range: Bald uakaris are found in Brazil, Colombia, and Peru.

Habitat: Bald uakaris prefer flooded rainforests along small rivers. Seasonal rainfall, which can last six or more months, causes water to cover as much as 33 feet (10 meters) of tree trunks, so the uakaris remain in the trees during that time.

Diet: Bald uakaris are seed specialists, preferring the seeds found in unripe fruits and those with hard skins that abound in flooded rainforests. They eat young saplings on the ground when the waters dry up. They also feed on flowers, insects, and snails.

Behavior and reproduction: Bald uakaris generally live in groups of ten to thirty individuals. Large groups consisting of up to 100 individuals form smaller groups when foraging. Uakaris sleep at night in the forest canopy. They travel on four limbs and also leap through the forest, although they are not expert leapers. When feeding, they sometimes suspend themselves in the air using their limbs.

Uakaris have several mating partners. Females have single births every two years, caring for the infants themselves. The mother carries the newborn on her front during the first three or four months, after which she carries it on her back. Infants are weaned by twenty-one months.

Bald uakaris and people: Bald uakaris are hunted for food and collected as pets.

Conservation status: The IUCN lists the bald uakari as Near Threatened due to continued hunting for food and trapping for the pet trade. ■

Masked titi (*Callicebus personatus*)

MASKED TITI
Callicebus personatus

Physical characteristics: The masked titi weighs 0.9 to 3.6 pounds (1 to 1.7 kilograms). It measures 12.2 to 16.5 inches (31 to 42 centimeters), with a tail length of 16.5 to 21.7 inches (41.8 to 55 centimeters). The long, soft, hairy coat is grayish to yellowish or orange. The face, hands, and feet are black. The non-prehensile tail is long and bushy.

Geographic range: Masked titis are found in Brazil.

Masked titis mate for life, and the father provides most of the child care for infants as well as for older offspring. (Illustration by Marguette Dongvillo. Reproduced by permission.)

Habitat: Masked titis prefer coastal forests. They are found in dense understory vegetation up to 33 feet (10 meters) high. They also inhabit banana groves.

Diet: Masked titis feed on unripe fruits, leaves, flowers, and insects.

Behavior and reproduction: Masked titis are active during the day. At dawn, neighboring groups emit loud calls, usually initiated by the mated pair, announcing ownership of a certain territory. Titis defend their territory, chasing away intruders. They move through the forest canopy on all fours. They intertwine their tails when sleeping, resting, or sitting on tree branches.

Titis mate for life, producing a single infant annually. The family group consists of two to seven individuals, typically the parents and offspring of different ages. The father almost exclusively rears the infant, carrying it on his back and giving it to the mother just to nurse. The father is known to move the infant to his underside to protect it from the rain. He also rears the older offspring, grooming them, guarding them from predators, and sharing his food with them. The mother does not share her food with the young. The young leave their home at ages two to three.

Masked titis and people: Masked titis are hunted for food and collected as pets.

Conservation status: The IUCN lists the masked titi as Vulnerable due to hunting and trapping by humans, as well as habitat loss and degradation from logging. ∎

FOR MORE INFORMATION

Books:

Kavanagh, Michael. *A Complete Guide to Monkeys, Apes and Other Primates.* New York: The Viking Press, 1983.

Kinzey, Warren G., ed. *New World Primates: Ecology, Evolution, and Behavior.* New York: Aldine de Gruyter, 1997.

Napier, John R., and Prue H. Napier. *The Natural History of the Primates.* Cambridge, MA: The MIT Press, 1986.

Nowak, Ronald M. *Walker's Primates of the World.* Baltimore: The Johns Hopkins University Press, 1999.

Preston-Mafham, Rod, and Ken Preston-Mafham. *Primates of the World.* New York: Facts on File, Inc., 1992.

Periodicals:

Jones, Clyde, and Sydney Anderson. "*Callicebus moloch.*" *Mammalian Species* 112 (December 29, 1978): 1–5.

Web sites:

Heilhecker, Ellen, and Chris Yahnke. "*Callicebus personatus* (Masked Titi)." Animal Diversity Web. http://animaldiversity.ummz.umich.edu/site/accounts/information/Callicebus_personatus.html (accessed July 6, 2004).

"What's Out There in the Primate World?" Investigate Biodiversity. http://investigate.conservation.org/xp/IB/speciesdiversity/ (accessed July 6, 2004).

"White-faced Saki." Como Park Zoo & Conservatory. http://www.comozooconservatory.org/zoo/saki.htm (accessed July 6, 2004).

HOWLER MONKEYS AND SPIDER MONKEYS
Atelidae

Class: Mammalia
Order: Primates
Family: Atelidae
Number of species: 22 to 24 species

phylum

class

subclass

order

monotypic order

suborder

▲ family

PHYSICAL CHARACTERISTICS

The atelids (members of the Atelidae family) are the largest New World primates. They range in color from yellowish beige to dark red to black. Males and females of some howler species differ in color. Many spider monkeys have light-colored masks around their eyes. Howler and woolly monkeys have stocky bodies and shorter limbs, while spider monkeys and muriquis have slimmer bodies and long tails. All tails are prehensile, capable of grasping tree branches, so that the monkeys usually feed while suspended.

GEOGRAPHIC RANGE

Atelids are found in Mexico, all of Central America (Belize, Costa Rica, El Salvador, Guatemala, Honduras, Nicaragua, and Panama), and South America (including Argentina, Bolivia, Brazil, Colombia, Ecuador, French Guiana, Guyana, Paraguay, Peru, and Venezuela).

HABITAT

Howler monkeys and muriquis inhabit secondary forests with open canopies. Spider and woolly monkeys prefer full-canopied primary forests, although spider monkeys are also found in semideciduous and secondary forests.

DIET

Howler monkeys prefer leaves, while other atelids favor ripe fruits. All diets are supplemented with flowers, seeds, and insects.

BEHAVIOR AND REPRODUCTION

All atelids are arboreal (tree-dwelling) but occasionally descend to the ground. They are diurnal (active during the day). Some species have grooming sessions and play time. Atelids do not defend territories. They generally move through the forest on all fours with brachiation (brake-ee-AY-shun; swinging below branches using the arms), usually assisted by the tail.

Adults have several mating partners. Females have single births, which occur at different intervals depending on species. The mother alone tends to the infant. Except for howler monkeys, young males remain with the group, while females leave to join other males. Male howler monkeys form their own group and invade another group, killing the young.

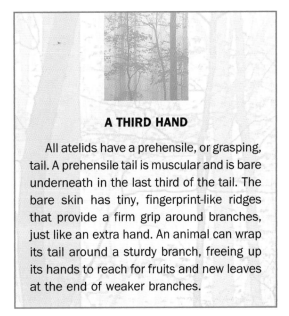

A THIRD HAND

All atelids have a prehensile, or grasping, tail. A prehensile tail is muscular and is bare underneath in the last third of the tail. The bare skin has tiny, fingerprint-like ridges that provide a firm grip around branches, just like an extra hand. An animal can wrap its tail around a sturdy branch, freeing up its hands to reach for fruits and new leaves at the end of weaker branches.

ATELIDS AND PEOPLE

Atelids are valued for their meat. Spider monkeys and muriquis are collected as pets because they are typically good-natured.

CONSERVATION STATUS

The IUCN lists eleven species as threatened because of continued hunting and habitat loss and degradation from human activities. The variegated spider monkey, the northern muriqui, and the yellow-tailed woolly monkey are listed as Critically Endangered, facing an extremely high risk of extinction, dying out, in the wild. The Guatemalan black howler monkey, the white-whiskered spider monkey, and the southern muriqui are listed as Endangered, facing a very high risk of extinction. The Colombian woolly monkey is classified as Vulnerable, facing a high risk of extinction, and two other species are listed as Near Threatened, not currently threatened, but could become so.

Venezuelan red howler monkey (*Alouatta seniculus*)

VENEZUELAN RED HOWLER MONKEY
Alouatta seniculus

Physical characteristics: The Venezuelan red howler monkey has thick, dark red to purplish red fur, with bright orange or gold underparts. The prehensile tail is used as a third hand for picking food. The black face is naked, and the wide jaw is covered with a thick beard. An enlarged hyoid (HYE-oid) bone at the root of the tongue gives the throat a swollen appearance. This bone is responsible for producing the loud howls that gave the monkey its name. Together with the enormous jaw, the swollen throat gives the monkey a grim appearance. It weighs 8 to 25 pounds (3.6 to 11 kilograms) and mea-

At dawn and dusk, Venezuelan red howler monkeys perform deafening howls that can be heard for at least 2 miles (3 kilometers). (Norman Owen Tomalin/Bruce Coleman Inc. Reproduced by permission.)

sures 17.5 to 27 inches (44 to 69 centimeters), with another 21 to 31 inches (54 to 79 centimeters) for the tail.

Geographic range: Venezuelan red howler monkeys are found in Venezuela and Brazil.

Habitat: Red howler monkeys prefer the forest canopy and understory. They inhabit secondary forests where the canopy is less developed but the ground vegetation is dense. They are also found in mountain forests, mangroves, and forests by rivers and streams.

Diet: Leaves make up more than 60 percent of a howler monkey's diet. It prefers the young leaves that are plentiful in the treetops. It also eats fruits, seeds, flowers, and insects.

Behavior and reproduction: Venezuelan red howler monkeys are arboreal and diurnal. Sluggish creatures, these monkeys spend plenty of time resting during the day. At dawn and dusk, they perform deafening howls that can be heard for at least 2 miles (3 kilometers). These calls advertise territory and group size to avoid confrontations with other groups. The monkeys also howl during heavy rainstorms.

Red howlers form groups of three to ten individuals, generally consisting of several unrelated adults. Adults have several mating partners, although the dominant male mates with all the receptive females. Females have single births every eighteen to twenty-four months. Mothers carry infants for about six months, first against the stomach and later on the back. Young howlers leave home by two years of age, although females may stay with the group. Young males leave to form their own all-male groups, which later take over another group, sometimes killing the young.

Venezuelan red howler monkeys and people: Red howler monkeys are hunted for food.

Conservation status: The IUCN does not consider the Venezuelan red howler monkey a threatened species. ■

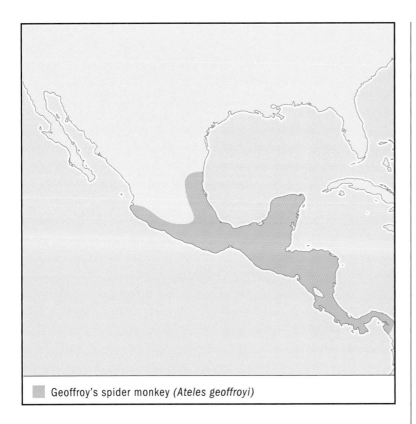

Geoffroy's spider monkey (*Ateles geoffroyi*)

GEOFFROY'S SPIDER MONKEY
Ateles geoffroyi

Physical characteristics: Geoffroy's spider monkeys have a coarse, shaggy coat that comes in yellow, red, or black, turning lighter on the undersides. The black hands and feet are very long and spidery, giving the monkeys their name. The hands have underdeveloped thumbs. White cheek hair is raised, and the eyes are surrounded by pale skin to form a mask. The prehensile tail, at 25 to 33 inches (63.5 to 84 centimeters), is longer than the head and body length of 12 to 24.8 inches (30.5 to 63 centimeters). The prehensile tail enables the large animal to hang from a sturdy branch to pick fruits at the end of thin branches. The monkey weighs 13 to 20 pounds (6 to 9 kilograms).

Geographic range: Geoffroy's spider monkeys are found in Mexico, Belize, Costa Rica, El Salvador, Guatemala, Honduras, Nicaragua, and Panama.

While they usually travel on all fours, or use their arms to swing from branch to branch, Geoffroy's spider monkeys can also jump down through forest gaps of over 33 feet (10 meters). (Erwin and Peggy Bauer/Bruce Coleman Inc. Reproduced by permission.)

Habitat: Geoffroy's spider monkeys prefer the top level of the forest canopy, where ripe fruits and young leaves are abundant. They occasionally descend to the middle layers. They inhabit mountain forests and mangroves.

Diet: Spider monkeys eat mainly ripe fruits. They especially prefer those with big seeds. They also feed on young leaves, flowers, buds, insects, insect larvae, and bird eggs.

Behavior and reproduction: Geoffroy's spider monkeys form groups with over forty individuals. When food is scarce, smaller subgroups and lone monkeys split from the main group when feeding. They forage, search for food, mostly in the early morning, resting the remaining part of the day. Spider monkeys are agile climbers, using their tail as an extra limb to move through the trees. They also travel on all fours and brachiate. They can jump down through forest gaps of over 33 feet (10 meters). The monkeys tend to go back to the same sleeping areas at nightfall.

Adults have several partners. Some males and females are dominant over others, but males competing for the same females are seldom aggressive with one another. A female determines which partner she will take. On average, females give birth to a single infant every three years because infants take that long to be independent. This is the longest period of infant dependency known among monkeys. Young females leave home, while young males remain in their birthplace.

Geoffroy's spider monkeys and people: Humans hunt spider monkeys for food.

Conservation status: The IUCN does not list Geoffroy's spider monkey as a threatened species. ∎

Colombian woolly monkey (*Lagothrix lugens*)

COLOMBIAN WOOLLY MONKEY
Lagothrix lugens

Physical characteristics: Colombian woolly monkeys range in color from black to blackish brown to lighter gray, with darker undersides, head, limbs, and tail. The fur is short, thick, and soft. The head is large and round, with a flat face and a snub nose. The ears are small. The body is stocky, with a protruding belly and a long, thick, muscular tail. The powerful prehensile tail can hold the large animal while suspended from a branch, as well as function as an additional hand. Woolly monkeys measure 20 to 27 inches (50.8 to 68.6 centimeters), with a tail length of 23.6 to 28.4 inches (60 to 72 centimeters). They weigh about 12 to 24 pounds (5.5 to 10.8 kilograms).

During midday, Colombian woolly monkeys rest, groom each other, and play. They greet each other by kissing on the mouth and embracing. (Illustration by Bruce Worden. Reproduced by permission.)

Geographic range: Colombian woolly monkeys are found in Colombia and Venezuela.

Diet: Colombian woolly monkeys feed mainly on fruits, supplemented with leaves, seeds, and occasional insects.

Behavior and reproduction: Colombian woolly monkeys are arboreal, sharing home ranges with other groups of their own species without hostility. They form groups of ten to forty-five individuals. Some males are dominant over other males, and all males are dominant over females, but they have a friendly relationship. They are diurnal, mostly foraging in the early morning and late afternoon, splitting into smaller subgroups when doing so. During midday, they rest, groom each other, and play. They greet each other by kissing on the mouth and embracing. Woolly monkeys travel through the forest on all fours, with some brachiation. They do not jump up but drop down to a branch by as many as 20 feet (6 meters).

Woolly monkeys have several partners, with dominant males mating with all receptive females. Females have single births every two to three years. An infant can cling to its mother's fur right away, first holding on to her stomach and later on to her back or side. Mothers carry the young for six to eight months, but nursing continues for up to twenty months. Young males remain in their birthplace, while females leave home to join other males.

Colombian woolly monkeys and people: Colombian woolly monkeys are hunted for food and trapped for the pet trade.

Conservation status: The IUCN lists the Colombian woolly monkey as Vulnerable due to habitat loss and degradation from logging and human settlement. ∎

FOR MORE INFORMATION

Books:

Emmons, Louise H. *Neotropical Rainforest Mammals: A Field Guide.* Chicago: The University of Chicago Press, 1997.

Kavanagh, Michael. *A Complete Guide to Monkeys, Apes and Other Primates.* New York: The Viking Press, 1983.

Kinzey, Warren G., ed. *New World Primates: Ecology, Evolution, and Behavior.* New York: Aldine de Gruyter, 1997.

Napier, John R., and Prue H. Napier. *The Natural History of the Primates.* Cambridge, MA: The MIT Press, 1986.

Nowak, Ronald M. *Walker's Primates of the World.* Baltimore: The Johns Hopkins University Press, 1999.

Periodicals:

Campbell, Christina J. "Female-Directed Aggression in Free-Ranging *Ateles Geoffroyi.*" *International Journal of Primatology* (April 2003): 223–237.

Wallace, Robert. "Diurnal Activity Budgets of Black Spider Monkeys, *Ateles Chamek* in a Southern Amazonian Tropical Forest." *Neotropical Primates* (December 2001): 101–107.

Web sites:

Broekema, Iris. "Natural History of the Black-Handed Spider Monkey (*Ateles geoffroyi*)." The Primate Foundation of Panama. http://www.primatesofpanama.org/academicresources/articles/spiderblack.htm (accessed on July 6, 2004).

Broekema, Iris. "Natural History of the Mantled Howler Monkey (*Aloutta palliata*)." The Primate Foundation of Panama. http://www.primatesofpanama.org/academicresources/articles/howler.htm (accessed on July 6, 2004).

"Spider Monkey." Honolulu Zoo. http://www.honoluluzoo.org/spider_monkey.htm (accessed on July 6, 2004).

"What is a Woolly Monkey?" The Monkey Sanctuary. http://www.ethicalworks.co.uk/monkeysanctuary/woolly.htm (accessed on July 6, 2004).

Class: Mammalia

Order: Primates

Family: Cercopithecidae

Number of species: 131 species

family

C H A P T E R

PHYSICAL CHARACTERISTICS

Old World monkeys are divided into the leaf-eating monkeys (including langurs [lang-GURZ] and colobus and proboscis monkeys) and the cheek-pouched monkeys (including macaques [muh-KOCKS] and mandrills). Most have subdued dark colorations with lighter undersides. Some, such as mandrills, have spectacular color combinations. All species have forward-facing eyes and short snouts. The buttocks have two hardened pads for prolonged sitting. Most have long tails. Leaf-eaters have a four-chamber stomach for digesting their main diet of plants. The cheek pouches are used for storing food to be safely eaten in trees.

GEOGRAPHIC RANGE

Leaf monkeys are found in Asia and Southeast Asia, except for the colobus monkeys. Cheek-pouched monkeys are found in Africa, including the Barbary macaque. All other macaques are found in Southeast Asia.

HABITAT

Old World monkeys live in virtually all land habitats, including grasslands, open dry forests, dense evergreen forests, mangroves, swamps, and forests along rivers. Some live near humans.

DIET

Leaf monkeys eat mainly leaves. Cheek-pouched monkeys consume fruits, seeds, insects, and occasionally young leaves.

BEHAVIOR AND REPRODUCTION

Old World monkeys are diurnal (active during the day). Most are arboreal (tree-dwelling), traveling on all fours. They can also leap, using the tail for balance. Some species use some brachiation (brake-ee-AY-shun, a type of locomotion in which an animal swings below branches using its arms. Social groups vary in size. Larger groups may split into subgroups when foraging. They are polygynous (puh-LIH-juh-nus), with males having several partners. Females have single births. Young females leave their birthplace, while young males stay with the group.

OLD WORLD MONKEYS AND PEOPLE

Old World monkeys are hunted for food. Some species are used in medical research.

CONSERVATION STATUS

The World Conservation Union (IUCN) lists five species as Critically Endangered, facing an extremely high risk of extinction, due to hunting, as well as habitat loss and degradation from agriculture, logging, and other human activities. These are the eastern red colobus, the Tonkin snub-nosed monkey, the Delacour langur, the white-headed langur, and the Mentawai macaque. Twenty-two species are classified as Endangered, facing a very high risk of extinction in the wild; seventeen are Vulnerable, facing a high risk of extinction in the wild; and twenty are Near Threatened, not currently threatened, but could become so.

POT BELLIES

The western red colobus, the proboscis monkey, and the red-shanked douc langur, all considered leaf monkeys, have evolved a four-chamber stomach that brings about a pot-bellied look. The stomach houses bacteria that break down fibrous leaves, the monkeys' main diet. The bacterial action not only releases nutrients from the leaves but also renders harmless the poisons found in some leaves.

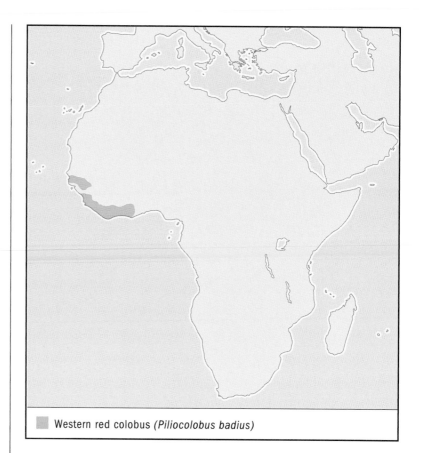

Western red colobus (*Piliocolobus badius*)

WESTERN RED COLOBUS
Piliocolobus badius

Physical characteristics: The western red colobus monkeys are black or dark gray with bright red undersides. The cheeks and the lower parts of the limbs are also bright red. The Greek word *kolobos*, meaning "cut short," describes the missing thumbs, which allow for faster brachiation because thumbs do not get caught in the branches. The long tail maintains balance when leaping. Males measure about 23 inches (57 centimeters), with a tail length of 26.5 inches (66.5 centimeters), and weigh 18.4 pounds (8.36 kilograms). Females are slightly smaller.

Geographic range: The monkeys are found in Cameroon, Ivory Coast, the Democratic Republic of the Congo, Gambia, Ghana, Guinea-Bissau, Liberia, Nigeria, Senegal, and Sierra Leone.

Habitat: Red colobus monkeys prefer rainforests that provide young leaves year round. They inhabit primary and secondary forests, forests along rivers and streams, and wooded grasslands.

Diet: Western red colobus monkeys feed mainly on leaves, especially young leaves, but also eat flowers and shoots. They consume only un-ripe fruits. Ripe fruits contain sugar, which can be broken down by stomach bacteria, causing gas and acid formation that may be fatal.

Behavior and reproduction: Western red colobus monkeys form groups of nineteen to eighty individuals with numerous adult males and females. They do not defend their territory. They are arboreal and diurnal, splitting off into smaller subgroups when foraging. They move through the trees on all fours, with some brachiation. However, they are not agile climbers.

Males have several mating partners. Females give birth to a single infant every two years. The mother alone carries the infant. Young females leave home, transferring from one group to another. Males stay in their birthplace, forming a close association with one another.

Western red colobus monkeys and people: Western red colobus monkeys are hunted for food.

Conservation status: The IUCN lists the western red colobus as Endangered due to hunting for meat, as well as habitat loss and degradation from agriculture, logging, and human settlement.   ■

Proboscis monkey (*Nasalis larvatus*)

PROBOSCIS MONKEY
Nasalis larvatus

Physical characteristics: The proboscis monkey got its name from its bulbous nose, which in the male is long and drooping. It is thought that females are attracted to the large nose. The naked face is pinkish brown. The head and back are reddish orange, while the shoulders, neck, and cheeks are pale orange. The undersides, legs, and tail are grayish white. The webbed feet are useful for swimming. Males weigh about 45 pounds (20.4 kilograms) and measure about 30 inches (74.5 centimeters), with a tail length of 26.5 inches (66.5 centimeters). Females are about half the male size, weighing 21.6 pounds (9.8 kilograms) and measuring 25 inches (62 centimeters), with a tail length of 23 inches (57.5 centimeters).

Geographic range: Proboscis monkeys are found in Borneo.

Habitat: Proboscis monkeys occupy coastal mangrove forests and forests along rivers.

The proboscis monkey is found in mangrove and lowland forests in Borneo. (© Aaron Ferster/Photo Researchers, Inc. Reproduced by permission.)

Diet: Proboscis monkeys feed mainly on leaves, supplemented with flowers and seeds. They eat unripe fruits but not ripe fruits, which, when processed by stomach bacteria, can cause potentially deadly gas and acid formation.

Behavior and reproduction: A proboscis monkey family consists of an adult male and several females and their offspring. Females give birth to a single infant and are assisted by other females with child-care. Young males are usually expelled upon puberty, traveling alone for a while or joining other bachelors. Proboscis monkeys do not defend their territory, but adult males threaten intruders with loud honks using their nose.

They are arboreal and diurnal, foraging in the early morning, then taking a long rest to digest their food. They may eat again before dark. The monkeys move on all fours and brachiate through the trees. They often jump from the trees into the water, from heights of as much as 53 feet (16 meters). They swim well and can stay underwater to escape a predator. They sleep in trees with branches that extend over water, perhaps as a lookout for their main predator, the clouded leopard.

Proboscis monkeys and people: Proboscis monkeys are hunted for meat.

Conservation status: The IUCN lists the proboscis monkey as Endangered due to hunting, as well as habitat loss and degradation from logging. ■

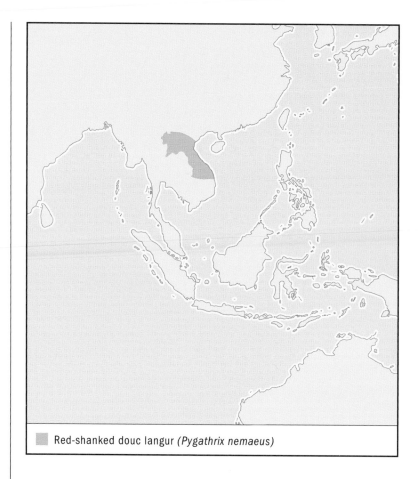

Red-shanked douc langur (*Pygathrix nemaeus*)

RED-SHANKED DOUC LANGUR
Pygathrix nemaeus

Physical characteristics: The red-shanked douc langur is a colorful monkey. The back and upper arms are a grizzled gray, turning to a lighter gray on the undersides. Black hair covers the top of the head, and long, white whiskers frame the golden face. The eyelids are pale blue. The lower arms, wrists, and tail are white, and the hands and feet are black. The thighs are black, and the lower legs are maroon. Males weigh about 24.4 pounds (11 kilograms), and females weigh about 18.6 pounds (8.45 kilograms). Males measure 23.5 inches (58.5 centimeters), plus a tail length of 27 inches (68 centimeters). Females are 24 inches (60 centimeters) long, with a tail of the same length.

Geographic range: Red-shanked douc langurs are found in Vietnam and Laos.

Habitat: Douc langurs inhabit primary and secondary forests. They also live in evergreen forests, as well as in monsoon deciduous forests, characterized by heavy rainfall and dry periods during which leaves drop. They also occupy lowland and mountain forests.

Diet: Red-shanked douc langurs eat leaves, buds, flowers, fruits, and seeds.

Behavior and reproduction: Red-shanked douc langurs form groups of four to fifteen individuals, typically with more females than males. Both sexes have dominant individuals, but males are always dominant over females. The langurs are arboreal and diurnal, moving through the forest canopy on all fours and by leaping from branch to branch, landing on their hind legs. They socialize by grooming, going through each other's fur to remove dirt and parasites. They are vocal, using growls and squeaks to communicate.

Red-shanked douc langurs form groups of four to fifteen individuals, and socialize by grooming, going through each other's fur to remove dirt and parasites. (© Art Wolfe, Inc./Photo Researchers, Inc. Reproduced by permission.)

Males have several mating partners. Every two years, females give birth to a single infant who receives plenty of attention and care from other females. Males sometimes tend to the young. Young males and females leave home when they are ready to start their own families.

Red-shanked douc langurs and people: Red-shanked douc langurs are hunted for meat.

Conservation status: The IUCN lists the red-shanked douc langur as Endangered due to habitat loss and degradation from human activities. ■

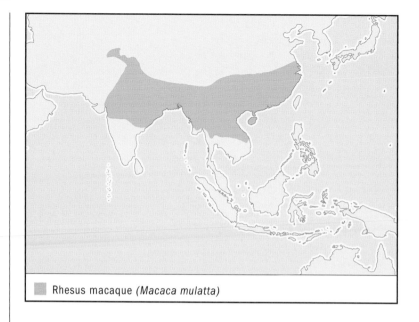

Rhesus macaque (*Macaca mulatta*)

RHESUS MACAQUE
Macaca mulatta

Physical characteristics: Rhesus macaques have long, brown hair with pale brown undersides. The hair at the top of the head is short. Facial skin is pinkish, while the rump is red. Males are slightly bigger than females, weighing about 17 pounds (7.7 kilograms) and measuring 21 inches (53 centimeters), with a tail length of 10 inches (24.5 centimeters). Females are about 11.8 pounds (5.4 kilograms), measuring 18 inches (45 centimeters), with a tail length of 9 inches (22 centimeters).

Geographic range: Rhesus macaques are found in Afghanistan, Pakistan, India, Nepal, Bhutan, Bangladesh, Myanmar, China, Thailand, Laos, and Vietnam.

Habitat: Rhesus macaques are adaptable, able to thrive in mangrove swamps, cedar-oak forests, woodlands, semi-desert scrub forests, forests along rivers, and even human settlements.

Diet: Rhesus macaques eat fruits, seeds, leaves, flowers, grasses, roots, bark, gum, and insects.

Behavior and reproduction: Rhesus macaques live in groups of eight to 180 individuals, although the average size is about twenty, with two to four times as many females as males. There are dominant males and females within a group, with the offspring inheriting the mother's rank. Macaques are arboreal but descend to the ground to forage and to move among human settlements. They prefer to sleep in the trees at night. They communicate through facial expressions, body language, and vocalizations, including barks, squawks, and growls. Adults have several partners. Females give birth to a single infant annually. Females remain with the group, while males may transfer from one group to another.

Rhesus macaques and people: The Rh factor in humans is named after the rhesus macaque, which was discovered to have this substance in its blood. Rhesus macaques are popular zoo animals. Farmers consider them pests for eating crops.

Conservation status: The IUCN lists the rhesus macaque as Near Threatened, meaning it could become threatened, due to hunting and habitat loss and degradation from human activities. ■

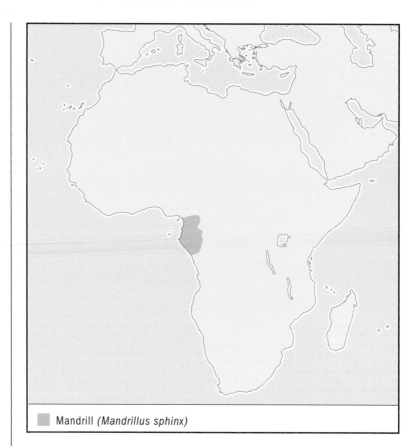

Mandrill (*Mandrillus sphinx*)

MANDRILL
Mandrillus sphinx

Physical characteristics: Mandrills have a grizzled brown coat and gray-white undersides. Males have the most striking coloration of all mammals. The large, bright red nose is enclosed by blue bony bulges. The whiskers are white and the beard is golden. A tuft of hair on top of the head and a mane over the shoulders can be erected for threat displays. The rump has shades of red, blue, and lilac, and is used as a signal when leading the group through the dense forest. Females have almost similar colorations, but are not as striking. They have black faces. The largest of the Old World monkeys, male mandrills weigh about 69.7 pounds (31.6 kilograms), more than twice as heavy as females, who weigh 28.4 pounds (12.9 kilograms). Males measure 27.5 inches (70 centimeters), with a tail length of 3 inches (8 centimeters).

Females measure 22 inches (54.5 centimeter), with a tail length of 3 inches (7.5 centimeters).

Geographic range: Mandrills are found in Cameroon, the Democratic Republic of the Congo, Equatorial Guinea, and Gabon.

Habitat: Mandrills occupy evergreen forests and forests along rivers and coasts.

Diet: Mandrills have a varied diet of fruits, seeds, grains, leaves, bark, mushrooms, tubers, snakes, and insects.

Behavior and reproduction: Although a typical mandrill family consists of a male and several females and their offspring, large groups with as many as 800 members have stayed together year after year, foraging for food, breeding, and fighting. A group having 1,350 individuals had been recorded. However, when not mating, males tend to be loners. Males prefer to forage on the ground, while females and the young climb trees. They may travel as much as 5 miles (8 kilometers) a day while feeding. All sleep in the trees. Mandrills communicate using grunts and crowing sounds. Adults have several partners, and females have single births. Young females stay with the group, but young males leave home, fighting fiercely during mating season, using their large, sharp canines.

Mandrills and people: Mandrills are hunted for meat.

Conservation status: The IUCN lists the mandrill as Vulnerable due to continued hunting, as well as habitat loss and degradation from agriculture, logging, and human settlements. ■

Mandrills are the largest of the Old World monkeys. (© C. K. Lorenz/Photo Researchers, Inc. Reproduced by permission.)

FOR MORE INFORMATION

Books:

Fleagle, John G. *Primate Adaptation and Evolution,* 2nd ed. San Diego, CA: Academic Press, 1999.

Kavanagh, Michael. *A Complete Guide to Monkeys, Apes and Other Primates.* New York: The Viking Press, 1983.

Napier, John R., and Prue H. Napier. *The Natural History of the Primates.* Cambridge, MA: The MIT Press, 1986.

Nowak, Ronald M. *Walker's Primates of the World.* Baltimore: The Johns Hopkins University Press, 1999.

Preston-Mafham, Rod, and Ken Preston-Mafham. *Primates of the World.* New York: Facts on File, Inc., 1992.

Sterry, Paul. *Monkeys & Apes: A Portrait of the Animal World.* New York: Todtri Productions Limited, 1994.

Periodicals:

Angier, Natalie. "In Mandrill Society, Life Is a Girl Thing." *New York Times on the Web.* http://www.nytimes.com/library/national/science/052300 sci-animal-mandrill.html (accessed on July 6, 2004).

Ferrero, Jean-Paul. "Swingers of Borneo." *International Wildlife* (November/December 1999): 53–57.

Laman, Tim. "Borneo's Proboscis Monkeys Smell Trouble." *National Geographic* (August 2002): 100–117.

Web sites:

"Cercopithecids (Cercopithecidae)." Singapore Zoological Garden Docents. http://www.szgdocent.org/pp/p-cercop.htm (accessed on July 6, 2004).

GIBBONS

Hylobatidae

Class: Mammalia

Order: Primates

Family: Hylobatidae

Number of species: 10 to 12 species

PHYSICAL CHARACTERISTICS

Gibbons have a thick coat that ranges in color from black to silvery gray to ash blond. They have a slender body and no tail. The bare face is framed in white fur or other markings. The extremely long arms, with hooklike fingers, are used for brachiating (BRAKE-ee-ate-ing), or swinging from branch to branch. Scientists consider gibbons as the only true brachiators, having powerful shoulder joints for reaching overhead and a wrist that can be rotated 180 degrees for switching position without tiring the arms and upper body. Gibbons are the only apes with skin pads on their buttocks that allow them to sleep comfortably sitting up.

GEOGRAPHIC RANGE

Gibbons are found in Southeast Asia, including China, India, Bangladesh, Myanmar, Thailand, Cambodia, Laos, Vietnam, Malaysia, and Indonesia.

HABITAT

Gibbons prefer the upper forest canopy, where fruits are abundant and spreading branches allow for continuous travel. They also thrive in surviving areas of forests that have been logged.

DIET

Ripe fruits are gibbons' main diet. Figs are their favorite. They also feed on leaves, flowers, buds, shoots, bird eggs, young birds, and insects.

phylum

class

subclass

order

monotypic order

suborder

▲ **family**

SINGING GIBBONS

Gibbons typically begin their day by singing. It is thought that singing serves to advertise territory ownership or readiness to mate. It also reinforces pair bonds and family ties. Songs are loud and long, lasting up to an average of fifteen to thirty minutes. The songs, either solos or duets, follow certain complicated patterns and are specific just to a particular species. Siamangs sing hooting-bark notes made louder by their inflated throat sacs.

BEHAVIOR AND REPRODUCTION

Gibbons are predominantly arboreal (tree-dwelling), defending their territory by chasing intruders and shaking branches. They sing to advertise ownership. Gibbons brachiate by grasping one branch after another or by propelling themselves through the air, loosening their grasp. They walk upright on wide branches or on the ground, arms held overhead to avoid tripping. They are diurnal (active during the day), but go to sleep before dark, sleeping in a sitting position.

The family consists of the parents and one to four juveniles. Females have single births every two or three years. The mother carries the infant around her waist for the first two months. When a juvenile reaches the age of five, the parent of the same sex may start chasing it off. Offspring who refuse to leave home stay in the vicinity of the family, but keep a distance when feeding and sleeping. Most leave home when they become sexually mature, or able to reproduce, at age seven or eight.

GIBBONS AND PEOPLE

Gibbons are popular zoo animals. The Ibans, the native people of Borneo, believe gibbons are human reincarnation, or the reappearance of a loved one's soul in the animal's body. Infants are captured for the pet trade.

CONSERVATION STATUS

The IUCN lists the Moloch gibbon and the eastern black gibbon as Critically Endangered, facing an extremely high risk of extinction in the wild, due to hunting, as well as habitat loss and degradation from logging and human settlement. The hoolock gibbon and the black crested gibbon are listed as Endangered, facing a very high risk of extinction, due to habitat loss and degradation from human activities. The pileated gibbon, the Kloss gibbon, and the golden-cheeked gibbon are classified as Vulnerable, facing a high risk of extinction, due to habitat loss and degradation from human activities.

Pileated gibbon (*Hylobates pileatus*)

PILEATED GIBBON
Hylobates pileatus

Physical characteristics: Pileated gibbons have dense, woolly fur. Males are black, with a black face framed in white. Hands and feet are white. Females are silvery beige or ash blond, with a black face and chest. The top of females' head is also black. The body is slender and the small head is rounded. Very long arms have hook-like fingers for brachiation. Thick skin pads line the rears for prolonged sitting. Males weigh 17 to 23 pounds (7.7 to 10.4 kilograms), and females about 14 to 19 pounds (6.3 to 8.6 kilograms). The average head and body length is 17.5 to 25 inches (44 to 63.5 centimeters).

A pileated gibbon family consists of an adult pair and up to four offspring. The family searches for food together. (© Terry Whittaker/Photo Researchers, Inc. Reproduced by permission.)

Geographic range: Pileated gibbons are found in Thailand, Cambodia, and Laos.

Habitat: Pileated gibbons prefer primary forests with well-developed canopies. They live in evergreen and semi-evergreen forests. They also occupy monsoon deciduous forests that have periods of heavy rainfall and dry spells, causing leaves to fall.

Diet: Pileated gibbons eat predominantly ripe fruits, supplemented with flowers, leaves, and insects.

Behavior and reproduction: The family consists of an adult pair and up to four offspring. The gibbons are arboreal and diurnal. Upon waking, the mated pair sings a duet, in which the offspring may join. The family forages soon after. Gibbons are territorial, defending their home against outsiders. They mostly travel by brachiating, but sometimes walk on two feet or leap through wide forest gaps. The family almost never goes down to the forest floor. They sleep before sundown, sitting on tree branches.

Females give birth to an infant every two or three years. The mother is the principal caregiver. The young tend to stay with the parents until they are ready to start their own family at seven or eight years of age. However, the parents may try to expel them when they reach the age of five.

Pileated gibbons and people: Poachers (illegal hunters) kill gibbons for food and capture the young for pets.

Conservation status: The IUCN lists the pileated gibbon as Vulnerable due to habitat loss from logging and human settlement. ■

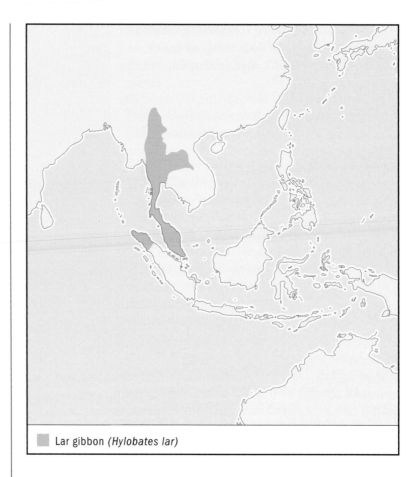

Lar gibbon (Hylobates lar)

LAR GIBBON
Hylobates lar

Physical characteristics: Lar gibbons have thick, shaggy fur that is dark brown, beige, or a combination of both. The hands and feet are white. The black naked face is surrounded by a ring of white hair. Extremely long arms end in slender fingers that hook over branches when brachiating. The buttocks have thickened pads, adapted for prolonged sitting while asleep. Males weigh 11 to 16.8 pounds (5 to 7.6 kilograms), and females about 9.7 to 15 pounds (4.4 to 6.8 kilograms). The average head and body length is 16.5 to 23 inches (42 to 58 centimeters).

Geographic range: Lar gibbons are found in China, Indonesia, Malaysia, Myanmar, and Thailand.

Lar gibbon mother with young. The parents might send their young away by age five, but some females stay with the family until age eight. (Gail Shumway/Bruce Coleman Inc. Reproduced by permission.)

Habitat: Lar gibbons prefer the high forest canopy where plentiful fruits are found. They occupy evergreen and semi-evergreen forests. They also inhabit monsoon deciduous forests, characterized by heavy rainfall and dry periods during which leaves fall.

Diet: Lar gibbons feed mainly on fruits, supplemented with flowers, leaves, and insects.

Behavior and reproduction: Lars gibbons are arboreal and diurnal. Brachiation is their chief means of moving through the forest. On the ground and on wider branches, they walk on two feet, holding their long arms over their heads for balance and to avoid tripping over the arms. They are territorial, chasing neighbors off their home boundaries and advertising ownership by loud singing.

The family consists of the mated pair and their young. However, there have been reports of the adult male or female moving in with the neighbors. Some stay permanently; others eventually return home. Females give birth to one infant every two or three years. When a juvenile reaches the age of five, the parent of the same sex may force it to leave. The young may continue to stay in the vicinity of the family, but keeps a distance when feeding and sleeping. Young females typically leave home by age eight.

Lar gibbons and people: The young are captured for the pet trade, and the mothers are usually killed.

Conservation status: The IUCN lists the lar gibbon as Near Threatened, not threatened, but could become so, due to habitat loss and degradation from agriculture, logging, and capture for the pet trade. ■

Siamang (*Symphalangus syndactylus*)

SIAMANG
Symphalangus syndactylus

Physical characteristics: Siamangs are the largest gibbons, weighing about 18 to 29 pounds (8 to 13 kilograms), with a head and body length of 29.5 to 35.5 inches (75 to 90 centimeters). Their black fur is long and shaggy, making them look larger. The face is reddish brown. Both sexes have a pinkish throat sac that can be inflated to magnify the siamangs' booming and barking calls. Thick skin pads on the rear provide comfort when sleeping in a sitting position. Hooked fingers at the end of long arms allow for brachiation. The second and third toes are fused by a webbing of skin.

Geographic range: Siamangs are found in Indonesia and Malaysia.

Male and female siamangs have a pinkish throat sac that can be inflated to magnify the siamangs' booming and barking calls. (© R. Van Nostrand/Photo Researchers, Inc. Reproduced by permission.)

Habitat: Siamangs are found in the lower canopy of evergreen forests. They also occupy mountain forests and monsoon deciduous forests, characterized by heavy rainfall and dry periods during which leaves fall.

Diet: Siamangs consume ripe fruits, leaves, flowers, shoots, and insects.

Behavior and reproduction: Siamangs are arboreal and diurnal. Upon waking, they sing harsh barking and booming notes, made louder by their inflatable throat sacs. Brachiation is the chief mode of locomotion among siamangs, who are capable of gliding over a forest gap of 25 to 32 feet (8 to 10 meters). They walk upright when on the ground or when branches are too wide for grasping.

The family consists of the parents and up to four offspring of different ages. Females have single births every two or three years. The mother carries the infant around her waist for the first two months. The father may help carry the infant when it stops nursing at two years of age. Offspring who reach sexual maturity at ages seven or eight leave the family to form their own.

Siamangs and people: Some local people revere siamangs for their impressive songs. Poachers hunt them to sell the meat for food and body parts for medicinal use.

Conservation status: The IUCN lists the siamang as Near Threatened due to habitat loss and degradation from human activities. ■

FOR MORE INFORMATION

Books:

Fleagle, John G. *Primate Adaptation and Evolution,* 2nd ed. San Diego, CA: Academic Press, 1999.

Hunt, Patricia. *Gibbons.* New York: Dodd, Mead, & Company, 1983.

Kavanagh, Michael. *A Complete Guide to Monkeys, Apes and Other Primates.* New York: The Viking Press, 1983.

Nowak, Ronald M. *Walker's Primates of the World.* Baltimore: The Johns Hopkins University Press, 1999.

Periodicals:

Brockelman, Walter Y., and Ulrich Reichard. "Dispersal, Pair Formation and Social Structure in Gibbons, (*Hylobates lar*)." *Behavioral Ecology and Sociobiology* (1998): 329–339.

Geissman, Thomas, and Mathias Orgeldinger. "The Relationship between Duet Songs and Pair Bonds in Siamangs, *Hylobates syndactylus.*" *Animal Behaviour* (2000): 805–809.

Gibbons, Ann. "Monogamous Gibbons Really Swing." *Science* (1998): 677–678.

Web sites:

"Gibbon." American Zoo and Aquarium Association Ape Taxon Advisory Group (AZA Ape TAG). http://www.apetag.org/Ape%20Tag/gibbon.html (accessed on July 6, 2004).

"Great Apes & Other Primates: Siamangs." Smithsonian National Zoo-logical Park. http://natzoo.si.edu/Animals/Primates/Facts/FactSheets/Gibbons/Siamang/ (accessed on July 6, 2004).

"White-Handed Gibbon." Honolulu Zoo. http://www.honoluluzoo.org/whitehanded_gibbon.htm (accessed on July 6, 2004).

Other sources:

Gibbon Research Lab and Gibbon Network. http://www.gibbons.de (accessed on July 6, 2004).

Gibbon Conservation Center. http://www.gibboncenter.org (accessed on July 6, 2004).

GREAT APES AND HUMANS
Hominidae

Class: Mammalia
Order: Primates
Family: Hominidae
Number of species: 7 species

PHYSICAL CHARACTERISTICS

Gorillas, chimpanzees, and bonobos are dark-colored, while orangutans are reddish brown. All have arms that are longer than their legs. Gorilla and orangutan males are twice as big as females. Great apes have forward-facing eyes for three-dimensional (height, width, and depth) viewing. They have powerful fingers and toes for gripping branches. They have no tails.

GEOGRAPHIC RANGE

Orangutans are the only great apes residing in Asia, in the countries of Indonesia and Malaysia. Gorillas and chimpanzees live in most countries of Africa, while bonobos are found only in the Democratic Republic of the Congo.

HABITAT

Great apes generally occupy fully developed forest canopies and dense shorter vegetation. They inhabit grasslands, bamboo forests, swamp forests, and mountain forests.

DIET

The diet of great apes includes fruits, leaves, flowers, seeds, barks, insects, and meat.

BEHAVIOR AND REPRODUCTION

African apes are mostly ground-dwellers, walking on their knuckles and feet. The lighter species climb trees, swinging by their arms from branch to branch in a mode of traveling called brachiation (brake-ee-AY-shun). Orangutans are arboreal

phylum

class

subclass

order

monotypic order

suborder

▲ **family**

A CHOREOGRAPHED DISPLAY

A silverback puts on an impressive threat display to protect his family from an intruder. First he hoots, and then throws vegetation around. Standing erect, he beats his chest with cupped hands. He kicks with one leg and shows his sharp canine teeth. Running on all fours, he rips off more vegetation. Standing up again, he slaps the ground with his hands. Finally, he rushes the intruder, stopping just a few feet away to allow the intruder to leave.

(tree-dwelling). On the rare occasions that they descend to the ground, they walk on their clenched fists. All great apes are diurnal, foraging during the day and sleeping in nests at night. Some take long breaks for grooming sessions.

Great apes are not seasonal breeders. Females have single births, caring for the young for a lengthy period with no help from the fathers. Male gorillas and chimpanzees engage in rivalries and takeovers that result in infanticide (killing of the young). Bonobo females are constantly receptive to mating. Orangutan males may commit forceful mating.

GREAT APES AND PEOPLE

Great apes are hunted by humans for meat and trophies. Some people believe apes' body parts have medicinal or magical powers. When infants are collected for the pet trade, the mothers are often killed.

CONSERVATION STATUS

The IUCN lists the Sumatran orangutan as Critically Endangered, facing an extremely high risk of extinction in the wild, due to hunting, as well as habitat loss and degradation from agriculture and logging. The remaining five great ape species are Endangered, facing a very high risk of extinction, for the same reasons.

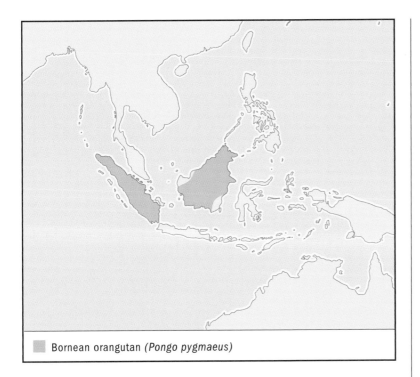

Bornean orangutan (*Pongo pygmaeus*)

BORNEAN ORANGUTAN
Pongo pygmaeus

Physical characteristics: Bornean orangutans have long, shaggy, reddish brown hair. Facial skin color ranges from pink to red to black. Arms, which are longer than the orangutan is tall, are useful for reaching fruits and brachiating. Scooplike hands and feet have powerful grips for grasping branches. Cheek pads in adult males make the face look larger. A throat pouch is inflated to produce loud, long calls to advertise their whereabouts. Males may reach 200 pounds (90.7 kilograms), with a standing height of about 5 feet (1.5 meters). Females are about 100 pounds (45.4 kilograms), standing 3 feet (1 meter) tall.

Geographic range: Bornean orangutans are found in Indonesia and Malaysia.

Habitat: Bornean orangutans prefer mature forests with fruiting trees. They also inhabit mangroves, swamps, mountain forests, and deciduous forests.

Bornean orangutans spend most of their time in the trees, and they feed on fruits there. Males sometimes travel on the ground, and they sleep in nests on the ground. (© B. G. Thomson/Photo Researchers, Inc. Reproduced by permission.)

Diet: Orangutans feed mainly on fruits, supplemented with leaves, flowers, buds, barks, honey, insects, and bird eggs. They use tools, such as sticks, to get honey out of beehives.

Behavior and reproduction: Orangutans are mostly arboreal, although heavy adult males travel on the ground, walking on their clenched fists and feet. They ascend trees to feed. Females and juveniles build sleeping nests in trees, while adult males sleep on ground nests. Orangutans use big leaves as umbrellas for protection from the hot sun and rain.

Orangutans do not form social groups. Adult males avoid one another, using long calls to warn neighbors to stay away. When encounters are unavoidable, fights may end fatally. Females with offspring congregate briefly at abundant feeding sites. Females ready to breed pursue males, who leave soon after mating. Both sexes may have several partners. Some males force themselves on unwilling females. Females have single births every four to eight years, the longest interval between births of any mammal. Orangutan young also have the longest childhood of all animals. After nursing for about four years, they stay close to their mothers for another three (males) to five (females) years.

Bornean orangutans and people: Orangutans are hunted for meat and infants are sold as pets.

Conservation status: The IUCN lists the Bornean orangutan as Endangered due to hunting for food and capture of young for the pet trade. Habitat is lost to agriculture, logging, and human settlements.   ■

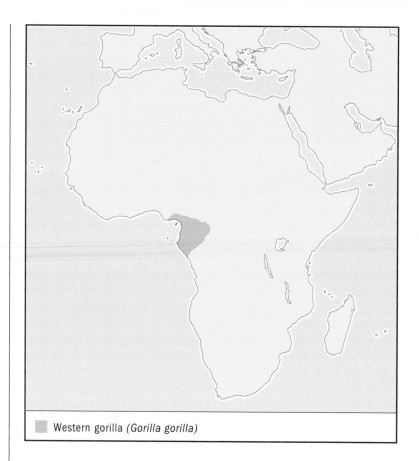

Western gorilla *(Gorilla gorilla)*

WESTERN GORILLA
Gorilla gorilla

Physical characteristics: The western gorilla has short black hair with red or brown coloration on the top of the head. The face is black. The head is elongated, and a brow ridge sits over the eyes. A protruding belly houses a large intestine for processing a plant diet. The arms are very long, and the thick-skinned knuckles are used for walking. Big toes help grasp tree branches. At ages eleven to thirteen, males acquire silver-gray hair on their back, earning the name silverbacks. Males are bigger than females, averaging 352 pounds (160 kilograms) with a standing height of 5 to 6 feet (1.5 to 1.8 meters). Females weigh 150 to 251 pounds (68 to 114 kilograms), standing 5 feet (1.5 meters) tall.

Geographic range: Western gorillas are found in Angola, Cameroon, the Central African Republic, Congo, the Democratic Republic of the Congo, Equatorial Guinea, Gabon, and Nigeria.

Habitat: Western gorillas occupy open canopies and dense understories and forests that have been cultivated or logged. They inhabit swampy clearings, forests along rivers, and full-canopied primary forests.

Diet: Western gorillas prefer fruits but also feed on plants. In swamp forests, they eat water plants. Juveniles also eat termites and ants.

Behavior and reproduction: The gorilla family typically consists of a dominant male (silverback), a younger male, several adult females, and their offspring. The silverback protects the group, settles conflicts, and determines daily activities. The group forages on the ground, climbing trees only for special fruits or leaves. Members communicate using facial expressions, body language, and vocalizations. Females groom the silverback and mothers and infants groom each other, but other adults do not engage in mutual grooming. Gorillas build sleeping nests in trees, although heavier males nest on the ground.

The silverback mates with all receptive females, but adults of both sexes may have several partners. Females have single births every four years, nursing the young for three years. A young female leaves home to join a lone male or another group. She may change groups several times. A young male may inherit his father's position or leave home. When ready to reproduce, he will try to take over a group. If he succeeds, he kills the infants so that the mothers will be receptive to breeding. Scientists have found that males who stay in the neighborhood after leaving home have nonaggressive encounters, because they may be siblings or half-brothers and, therefore, have a familiar relationship.

Western gorillas and people: Western gorillas are popular in zoo exhibits. They are hunted for meat.

Conservation status: The IUCN lists the western gorilla as Endangered due to hunting, as well as habitat loss and degradation from agriculture, logging, and human developments. ■

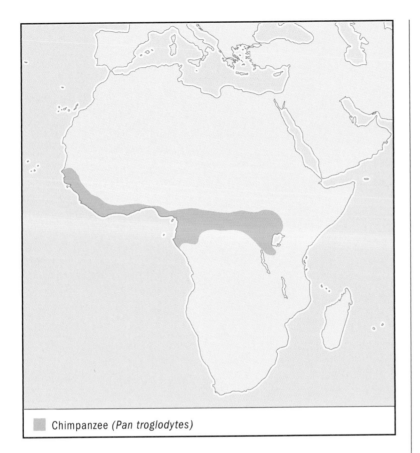

Chimpanzee (Pan troglodytes)

CHIMPANZEE
Pan troglodytes

Physical characteristics: Chimpanzees have black hair, which may turn gray with age, accompanied by partial balding. The naked face varies from pink to black and has a short, white beard. They have a brow ridge, protruding snout, and large ears. The thumbs function like those of humans for handling objects. The large toes are used for a firm grip when climbing trees. Males weigh 80 to 130 pounds (36.3 to 59 kilograms), and females about 70 to 100 pounds (31.8 to 45.4 kilograms). They stand about 3.8 to 5.5 feet (1 to 1.7 meters) tall.

Geographic range: Chimpanzees are found in many African countries, including Senegal, Guinea, Sierra Leone, Ivory Coast, Ghana,

Young chimpanzees play with one another, as these orphaned chimpanzees are doing. (K. and K. Ammann/Bruce Coleman Inc. Reproduced by permission.)

Nigeria, Cameroon, the Central African Republic, the Democratic Republic of the Congo, Rwanda, Tanzania, Uganda, and Sudan.

Habitat: Chimpanzees occupy mountain forests, open woodlands, and grasslands.

Diet: Chimpanzees are omnivorous, eating both plants and animals. They feed on fruits, nuts, flowers, seeds, and bird eggs. Their favorite prey is the red colobus monkey. They also eat termites, small antelopes, and bush pigs.

Behavior and reproduction: Chimpanzees live in communities of as many as eighty individuals, but may form subgroups of just males, mothers and young, or both sexes of different ages. A dominant male rules a group but may be replaced at any time. Adult males dominate all females. Males defend their territory from outside groups, sometimes killing all the members of the outside group. Chimpanzees sleep in tree nests. They are expert tool users, using rocks to open nuts and sticks to get termites. They communicate through facial expressions and a variety of sounds. Group members groom each other to strengthen social bonds.

Adults have several partners. Females have single births every four or five years. The young nurse for about four years, staying close to their mothers for another four years. Adolescent females may join another group.

Chimpanzees and people: Chimpanzees are popular exhibit animals in zoos and have been used in movies and television shows. They are hunted for food. They are used in medical research and were used in the space program.

Conservation status: The IUCN lists the chimpanzee as Endangered due to hunting for food, as well as habitat loss and degradation for agriculture, logging, and human settlements. ■

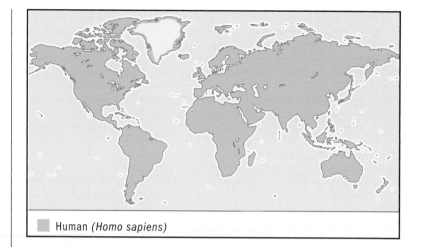

Human (*Homo sapiens*)

HUMAN
Homo sapiens

Physical characteristics: Humans differ in skin color, depending on the amount of the pigment melanin in their skin. The body is hairless, except for the head, armpits, and genital areas. Scientists suggest that early humans had shed their fur to prevent over-heating when chasing their prey, and developed sweat glands on the skin surface to cool the body by perspiring. The subcutaneous fat, or the fatty layer under the skin, preserves body heat when the environment gets cold and serves as an energy source when food is scarce.

Humans possess a distinct trait, bipedalism (bye-PED-ul-ih-zem), or a mode of locomotion on two legs. Strong, muscular legs are adapted for upright walking. The S-shaped curve of the spine keeps an erect human from toppling by distributing the body weight to the lower back and hips. However, the flexible spine, adapted by early humans for running and catching prey, has caused problems to modern humans, especially the weak lower backbone that is not adapted for supporting the heavy head and trunk.

Geographic range: Humans inhabit almost all of Earth's land surfaces. While humans may not be able to live in the very cold regions of Antarctica or in the central Sahara Desert, they are capable of visiting those areas. Modern technology has allowed humans to travel over water, underwater, and through the air. Humans are also able to

live in space, such as in the International Space Station, and have landed on the moon.

Habitat: Humans live in all land habitats.

Diet: Humans are omnivorous, feeding on both plant and animal matter.

Behavior and reproduction: Humans differ from other primates by their use of language, a distinct type of communication that can be manipulated to produce an unlimited number of expressions. Humans use symbols and communicate through symbols, such as art. Another human-specific behavior is their reliance on tools and technology. However, humans' most striking characteristic is their mental ability to create ideas.

Although a monogamous (muh-NAH-guh-mus) family, with a mated male and female, typically represents the human social unit, many cultures practice polygyny (puh-LIH-juh-nee; one male with several mates), polyandry (PAH-lee-an-dree; one female with several mates), and polygamy (puh-LIH-guh-mee; both sexes have several mates). Humans are unique in that they do not generally sever ties with relatives when they move. However, humans are capable of aggressive and violent relationships.

Humans have no breeding seasons. While single births are most common, multiple births occasionally occur. Human young develop slowly, needing care and protection from adults. The young learn social behaviors through imitation. While average life spans can vary around the world, men and women generally live into their sixties and seventies. While males can parent children in old age, females stop reproducing with menopause (generally starting at age fifty), after which they may live many more years.

According to scientists, the human baby, given the big size of its brain, needs about twenty-one months to develop fully in the mother's womb. But, since the female birth canal, through which a baby passes, has evolved to a narrower size to allow for upright locomotion, babies have to be born "prematurely" (after nine months). The brain develops further outside the womb.

FOR MORE INFORMATION

Books:

Arsuaga, Juan Luis. *The Neanderthal's Necklace: In Search of the First Thinkers.* New York: Four Walls Eight Windows, 2001.

Bright, Michael. *Gorillas: The Greatest Apes.* New York: DK Publishing, Inc., 2001.

Dunbar, Robin, and Louise Barrett. *Cousins: Our Primate Relatives.* New York: DK Publishing, Inc., 2001.

Estes, Richard D. *The Behavior Guide to African Mammals: Including Hoofed Mammals, Carnivores, Primates.* Berkeley, CA: The University of California Press, 1991.

Fleagle, John G. *Primate Adaptation and Evolution,* 2nd ed. San Diego, CA: Academic Press, 1999.

Grace, Eric S. *Apes.* San Francisco, CA: Sierra Club Books for Children, 1995.

Kaplan, Gisela, and Lesley J. Rogers. *The Orangutans: Their Evolution, Behavior, and Future.* Cambridge, MA: Perseus Publishing, 2000.

Lindsey, Jennifer *The Great Apes.* New York: MetroBooks, 1999.

Lynch, John, and Louise Barrett. *Walking with Cavemen.* New York: DK Publishing, Inc., 2003.

Nowak, Ronald M. *Walker's Primates of the World.* Baltimore: The Johns Hopkins University Press, 1999.

Povey, Karen. *The Chimpanzee.* San Diego, CA: Lucent Books, 2002.

Russon, Anne E. *Orangutans: Wizards of the Rain Forest.* New York: Firefly Books, 2000.

Tattersall, Ian. *Becoming Human: Evolution and Human Uniqueness.* New York: Harcourt Brace & Company, 1998.

Periodicals:

Bradley, Brenda J., et al. "Dispersed Male Networks in Western Gorilla." *Current Biology* (March 23, 2004): 510–513.

Jones, Clyde, et al. *"Pan troglodytes." Mammalian Species* 529 (May 17, 1996): 1–9.

Stanford, Craig B. "Close Encounters: Mountain Gorillas and Chimpanzees Share the Wealth of Uganda's 'Impenetrable Forest,' Perhaps Offering a Window onto the Early History of Hominids." *Natural History* (June 2003): 46–51.

Web sites:

Friend, Tim. "Chimp Culture." *International Wildlife* (September/October 2000). Online at http:www.nwf.org/internationalwildlife/2000/chimpso.html (accessed on July 7, 2004).

"Great Apes & Other Primates: Gorillas." Smithsonian National Zoological Park. http://natzoo.si.edu/Animals/Primates/Facts/FactSheets/Gorillas/default.cfm (accessed on July 7, 2004).

Gunung Palung Orangutan Project. http://www.fas.harvard.edu/gporang/index.html (accessed on July 7, 2004).

"Orangutans: Just Hangin' On." Public Broadcasting Service (PBS) Nature. http://pbs.org/wnet/nature/orangutans/index.html (accessed on July 7, 2004).

Sea World Education Department. "Gorillas." Sea World/Busch Gardens ANIMALS. http://www.seaworld.org/animal-info/info-books/gorilla/index.htm (accessed on July 7, 2004).

Stanford, Craig B. "Chimpanzee Hunting Behavior and Human Evolution." *American Scientist Online* http://www.americanscientist.org/template/AssetDetail/assetid/24543?fulltext=true&print=yes (accessed on July 7, 2004).

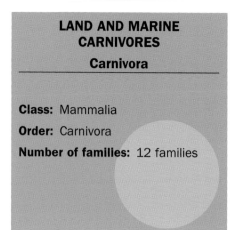

**LAND AND MARINE
CARNIVORES**

Carnivora

Class: Mammalia
Order: Carnivora
Number of families: 12 families

order

PHYSICAL CHARACTERISTICS

The order Carnivora (kar-NIH-vuh-ruh) refers to a group of mammals whose evolutionary ancestors were carnivores, or meat-eaters. Over several millions of years, these ancestors had adapted to the rise of bigger and more powerful herbivores, their main prey, by developing carnassials (kar-NAH-see-uls), bladelike teeth that slice through flesh. Powerful jaws that move up and down were especially useful for stabbing and holding prey and the incisors for biting off pieces of food.

Although the 264 species in the order Carnivora come from the same ancestors, not all species eat only meat. Therefore, while the carnassials are very pronounced in species that eat large prey (cats, for example), those that are not purely carnivorous have less developed carnassials (bears). Some, like the aardwolf that feeds on termites, and the giant panda that eat mainly bamboo, have no carnassials at all.

Carnivores come in a wide range of sizes. The smallest carnivore, the least weasel, weighs about 1.76 ounces (50 grams). In contrast, the southern elephant seal, the largest carnivore, weighs about 5,300 pounds (2,400 kilograms). Some carnivores are terrestrial (land-dwelling) mammals, including the familiar dogs, cats, bears, raccoons, hyenas, mongooses, and skunks. Land carnivores either walk on the soles and heels of their feet (plantigrade) or on their toes (digitigrade). A combination of strong bones in the feet and bendable wrists allow these mammals to climb, run, jump, and overcome their prey. An undeveloped collarbone allows for increased movements of the arms when pursuing prey. The long baculum (penis bone) enables prolonged mating and is especially important in species in which mating brings on ovulation (the formation and release of eggs from the ovary). Anal glands release substances used as scent marks for various types of communication.

Other carnivores are marine (sea-dwelling) mammals, including eared seals, true seals, and walruses. Marine mammals, also called pinnipeds (fin-footed mammals), have a torpedo-shaped body that allows for easy movement through water. The thick layer of blubber, or fat under their skin, not only provides insulation but also contributes to streamlining (smoothing out) their bodies.

GEOGRAPHIC RANGE

Carnivores are found throughout the world. Some, however, are not naturally occurring but have been introduced to some areas.

HABITAT

Carnivores are found both on land and sea. Although most terrestrial carnivores live on land, the polar bear spends most of its time on sea ice, while the palm civet is arboreal (a tree-dweller). The sea otter lives exclusively in the water, as opposed to other marine carnivores who forage in the sea and breed on land.

DIET

The term carnivore literally means meat-eater, but not all species in the order Carnivora live on a strict diet of meat. Among the true carnivores are cats. Although lions in the Kalahari Desert have been known to eat melons, they only do so for the moisture content, not for sustenance. Some mustelids (weasels, martens, and otters) are also pure carnivores. The rest of the mustelids (skunks, badgers, and tayras) are omnivores, supplementing their meat diet with fruits, roots, and seeds. The bears are generally omnivores, although most prefer a larger proportion of plant food, including fruits, grasses, and roots. The exceptions in the bear family are the giant panda that lives exclusively on bamboo and the polar bear that consumes mainly ringed seals.

Procyonids (raccoon family) are omnivores, with several food specialists. Ringtails prefer meat, red pandas eat mainly bamboo leaves, and kinkajous and olingos live off fruits. The civets and genets (viverrids) eat a mixture of animals and fruits, although palm civets are primarily frugivores (fruit-eaters). The mongoose family, while generally favoring insects, also lives on a mixed diet of rodents, worms, reptiles, and plant matter. Canids (dogs) are also omnivores, eating all sizes of mammals, as well as insects, berries, carrion (dead and decaying flesh), and garbage.

The smallest carnivore family consists of three hyena species and the aardwolf. While the aardwolf eats termites almost exclusively, hyenas have a varied diet, ranging from large antelopes and reptiles to wildebeest feces and human garbage. Hyenas are often described as scavengers who feed off the leftover kills of other animals. However, they often hunt their own prey. In fact, lions have been known to scavenge hyena kills.

The marine carnivores eat various marine mammals, including fish, crustaceans (shrimps, crabs, and lobsters), mollusks (clams, mussels, squid, and octopus), and penguins. Some marine carnivores have specialized diets. The crab-eater seal feeds almost exclusively on krill (a small shrimplike animal), while the walrus feeds almost entirely on mollusks.

BEHAVIOR AND REPRODUCTION

Many carnivores are solitary creatures, except for mating pairs and mother-offspring groups. The majority are not antisocial, as they share overlapping territories and congregate at abundant food sources. Some belong to social groups, in which strict rules are observed. For example, carnivores "talk" to one another through scent marking, or the depositing of anal secretions, urine, and feces. They also use a variety of vocalizations. Some use body postures to show dominance or submission.

The typical mating system among carnivores is polygyny (puh-LIH-juh-nee) in which a male has two or more partners. Some, like canids, are monogamous (muh-NAH-guh-mus), with a male and a female mating with just with each other. Pinnipeds usually breed on land. Males arrive on land to stake out a territory. Females arrive later to give birth to the previous year's pup before mating. The father departs for the sea soon after mating, leaving the mother to raise the pup. When the pup is able to survive on its own, mother and pup leave land for the water, going their separate ways.

CARNIVORES AND PEOPLE

The relationship between carnivores and humans is complex. Humans have domesticated the wolf and wild cats and made them house pets. In addition, humans have trained dogs to perform certain tasks. Collies help herd sheep, German shepherds serve as seeing-eye dogs, beagles sniff for drugs at airports, and bloodhounds help locate missing people.

Humans and carnivores have historically had conflicting interests. Thousands of years ago, early humans and carnivores competed for food. Today, carnivores in the wild continue to prey on domesticated animals, even attacking and killing some humans. Humans who feel threatened by carnivores resort to poisoning, trapping, and shooting, leading to the extinction of certain species. Some carnivores are also hunted for their fur, meat, and body parts, resulting in declining populations.

IT'S ALL IN THE TEETH

The feature that differentiates the order Carnivora from other orders is a set of scissor-like carnassial teeth, specifically the upper last premolar and the lower first molar on both sides of the jaw. These are shearing teeth that slice animal flesh and crush bones. Each carnassial has ridges that grip meat, much like a fork that holds a piece of steak in place, so it does not slide around.

Certain government agencies and private organizations around the world have established programs to try to save the threatened species. Millions of dollars and plenty of human effort have been devoted to the conservation and protection of endangered species.

CONSERVATION STATUS

The World Conservation Union (IUCN) promotes the conservation of species, assesses their conservation status worldwide, and publishes an annual list of threatened species. The 2003 IUCN Red List of Threatened Species lists 125 carnivores as threatened. Five are listed as Extinct, no longer living: the Falkland Island wolf, the Caribbean monk seal, the sea mink, the Barbados raccoon, and the Japanese sea lion. The black-footed ferret is classified as Extinct in the Wild. The five Critically Endangered species, facing an extremely high risk of extinction, are the red wolf, the Ethiopian wolf, the Iberian lynx, the Mediterranean monk seal, and the Malabar civet.

The Endangered list of carnivores, facing a very high risk of extinction, consists of thirty-one species, made up of one dog, one eared seal, one true seal, two bears, four cats, four mongooses, four viverrids, seven mustelids, and seven procyonids. Of these species, three are classified as endangered species in the United States. These are the sea otter, the northern sea lion, and the Hawaiian monk seal.

FOR MORE INFORMATION

Books:

Attenborough, David. *The Life of Mammals.* Princeton, NJ: Princeton University Press, 2002.

Ewer, R. F. *The Carnivores.* Ithaca, NY: Comstock Publishing Associates, 1998.

Kruuk, Hans. *Hunter and Hunted: Relationships between Carnivores and People.* Cambridge, U.K.: Cambridge University Press, 2002.

McLoughlin, John C. "The Rise of the Carnivores" and "The World of Mammalian Carnivores." *The Canine Clan.* New York: The Viking Press, 1983.

Wade, Nicholas, ed. *The Science Times Book of Mammals.* New York: The Lyons Press, 1999.

Whitaker, John O. Jr., and William J. Hamilton Jr. *Mammals of the Eastern United States,* 3rd ed. Ithaca, NY: Comstock Publishing Associates, 1998.

Periodicals:

Tedford, Richard H. "Key to the Carnivores." *Natural History* (April 1994): 74–77.

Web sites:

American Society of Mammalogists. *Why Species Become Threatened or Endangered: A Mammalogist's Perspective.* http://www.mammal-society.org/committees/commconslandmammals/whyendangered.pdf(accessed on June 23, 2004).

World Conservation Union. The IUCN Red List Collection. http://www.iucn.org/redlistcollection/english/index.html (accessed on June 23, 2004).

DOGS, WOLVES, COYOTES, JACKALS, AND FOXES

Canidae

Class: Mammalia

Order: Carnivora

Family: Canidae

Number of species: 35 species

family
C H A P T E R

PHYSICAL CHARACTERISTICS

Canids (members of the dog family) have a uniform body color with markings on the head and tail tip. Dogs typically come in black, black and white, brown, or red. The only exception is the African wild dog that has patches of black, white, and yellow. The canid's coat consists of a dense underfur and an overcoat of waterproof guard hairs, which retain a large amount of body heat for survival in very cold climates. Canids range in weight from the fennec fox, at about 3 pounds (1.3 kilograms), to the gray wolf, which can be as heavy as 175 pounds (80 kilograms). They are digitigrade, walking on their toes. This enables them to make quick stops and turns. A keen sense of smell comes from more than 200 million scent cells in the nose (humans have about five million scent cells).

GEOGRAPHIC RANGE

Canids live on every continent except Antarctica.

HABITAT

Most canids favor areas where forests meet open country. Some live in deserts. The Arctic fox and some gray wolves occupy the tundra. The bush dog and raccoon dog prefer thick forests near water. Canids have also adapted to human environments.

DIET

Canids primarily prey on other mammals. Large prey include elk and caribou, and small animals include rodents and rabbits.

phylum

class

subclass

order

monotypic order

suborder

▲ **family**

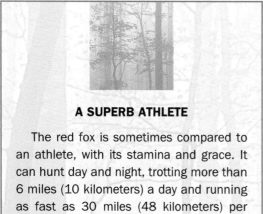

A SUPERB ATHLETE

The red fox is sometimes compared to an athlete, with its stamina and grace. It can hunt day and night, trotting more than 6 miles (10 kilometers) a day and running as fast as 30 miles (48 kilometers) per hour. When attacking prey, the fox uses a lunge-and-pounce move, first crouching very low, then jumping as far as 17 feet (5 meters) over ground to pounce on the surprised prey.

They also eat insects, berries, carrion (dead and decaying flesh), and garbage.

BEHAVIOR AND REPRODUCTION

Canids live in packs, or social groups, ruled by a male and his partner. They communicate through vocalization, including barks, growls, and howls. They also use body language, such as erecting the fur, to show dominance. Canids mate for life, with the whole pack parenting the young.

CANIDS AND PEOPLE

Many canids are hunted for their fur. Humans have always felt threatened by certain canids, such as wolves and foxes. Canids sometimes prey on pets and livestock.

CONSERVATION STATUS

The United States lists the red wolf as Endangered, facing a very high risk of extinction in the wild, because of habitat loss due to deforestation and hunting. The IUCN classifies the African hunting wolf and the Ethiopian wolf as Endangered because of habitat loss resulting from human settlement and killing.

Gray wolf (*Canis lupus*)

GRAY WOLF
Canis lupus

Physical characteristics: The gray wolf, ancestor to the domestic dog, is the largest of the wild dogs. Males weigh up to 175 pounds (80 kilograms). The smoky gray fur is tipped with brown or red hair. The long, bushy tail helps the wolf keep its balance when running, while large, padded paws provide traction (resistance to slipping), especially in snow.

Geographic range: Gray wolves, although sparsely populated, occur in more than fifty countries, including the United States, Canada, Russia, Spain, Portugal, and Italy.

Habitat: Gray wolves live in deciduous forests inhabited by their main prey, herbivores (plant-eaters), such as deer, elk, and moose. They also thrive in the tundra and desert, where they prey on small animals.

Diet: Packs hunt large ungulates, or hoofed animals, such as elk and deer, but lone wolves usually hunt smaller animals, including rabbits,

beavers, and mice. Wolves also eat carrion and prey on domestic livestock, insects, fish, and berries. In the Arctic, they eat birds, seals, and caribou. An adult eats an average of 5.5 to 13 pounds (2.5 to 6 kilograms) of food per day. If food is unavailable, it can fast for two or more weeks.

Behavior and reproduction: Gray wolves live in packs of as many as thirty individuals, consisting of parents, offspring, and relatives. The top dogs are the dominant male and female, called the alpha pair. They alone breed and feed first. However, younger and more powerful members may replace the leaders at any time. Sometimes, couples pair off and leave the pack.

The pack uses facial expressions, body postures, and vocalizations to communicate. Members show submission by licking the leader's face or rolling on their back. Howling is used to warn other packs that a certain territory is taken, to announce the start of a hunting expedition, or to summon members to help defend a kill. The pack hunts together, traveling for up to 30 miles (about 48 kilometers) a day.

Gray wolves mate for life, producing six or seven pups a year. Pack members care for the young when the mother goes hunting. Adults feed weaned pups regurgitated (re-GER-jih-tate-ed) food, partly digested food kept in the stomach and brought up to the mouth.

Gray wolves and people: Although humans have always felt threatened by wolves, no attack has ever been reported. In fact, wolves avoid human contact. Some hunters regard wolves as competitors for big game (wild animals hunted for sport).

Conservation status: In 1973, on the brink of extinction from extensive killing, gray wolves were placed under the protection of the newly enacted U.S. Endangered Species Act. They were subsequently reintroduced to the Yellowstone National Park. Some states established programs to protect them. Since then, the gray wolf populations have increased. In 2003, gray wolves (except those in the Southwest) were reclassified as Threatened, or likely to become extinct in the foreseeable future. The IUCN does not list the gray wolf as a threatened species worldwide.   ■

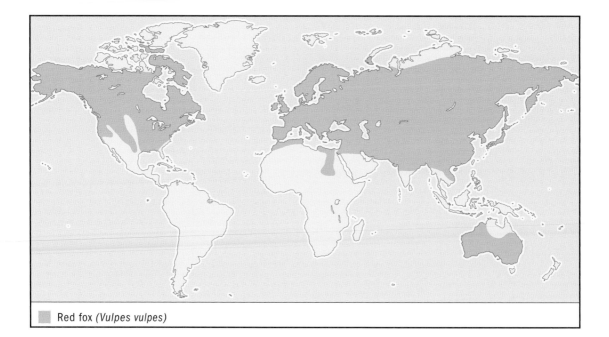

 Red fox (*Vulpes vulpes*)

RED FOX
Vulpes vulpes

Physical characteristics: The largest of all foxes, the red fox is reddish brown with a white- or black-tipped bushy tail. It weighs 6 to 15 pounds (2.7 to 6.8 kilograms). The snout, backs of the ears, and the lower legs and feet are black. Sensitive, pointed ears can detect prey from 150 feet (45 meters) away. Sensitive whiskers guide the fox in inflicting a killing bite on the prey's body.

Geographic range: The most widely distributed of all canids, the red fox is found in the United States, Canada, Australia, Europe (except Iceland), and Asia.

Habitat: Red foxes prefer a mixture of woodlands and open areas. They thrive in the tundra and desert, where they prey on animals foraging for food at night. They live close to humans in farmlands, the suburbs, and cities, where rabbits, rodents, and garbage pits abound.

Diet: Red foxes prefer rodents but also feed on rabbits, squirrels, insects, earthworms, birds, and carrion. They eat fruits and human

leftovers. Foxes eat about 1 to 3 pounds (0.5 to 1.5 kilograms) of food a day. When full, they continue to hunt for prey, but unlike wolves who gorge themselves, foxes cache (store in a hidden place) excess food. They bury the food in a hole, occasionally digging it up, then reburying it.

Behavior and reproduction: Red foxes are crepuscular (kri-PUS-kyuh-lur; active at dawn and dusk) and nocturnal (active at night), timing their foraging habits with those of their prey. They live alone, except when breeding. Males and females pair off in late winter or early spring, producing five to thirteen kits. Fathers provide food to the family, and nonbreeding daughters or sisters may share the den and help in child rearing. Red foxes are playful creatures, engaging in games of chasing and mock fighting.

Red foxes and people: Red foxes are prized for their fur and for the sport of fox hunting. However, a love-hate relationship exists between foxes and humans. Some suburbanites treat them as pets, putting out food for them. Others detest them for stealing house pets and livestock.

Conservation status: The red fox is not a threatened species. ■

Dogs, Wolves, Coyotes, Jackals, and Foxes |

Maned wolf (*Chrysocyon brachyurus*)

MANED WOLF
Chrysocyon brachyurus

Physical characteristics: The maned wolf has a long, black mane on its neck down to the middle of its back. The body is golden-red, and the snout and legs are black. The throat, tail tip, and ears have white markings. Very long legs allow for a better view over the tall grasses of its habitat and for high leaps to catch prey and hold it down. It covers great distances, moving the legs of each side of its body together, unlike other canids that move their legs alternately. It weighs 44 to 51 pounds (20 to 23 kilograms) with a shoulder height of 29 to 34 inches (74 to 87 centimeters).

Geographic range: Maned wolves are found in Argentina, Bolivia, Brazil, Paraguay, Peru, and Uruguay.

Habitat: Maned wolves live in grassland that supports small mammals, reptiles, and insects. They also occupy scrub forests, home to a tomato-like fruit that makes up half of their diet.

Diet: A tomato-like fruit, *Solanum lycocarpum*, which comprises 50 percent of the wolf's diet, protects it against giant kidney worm infestation. Although known for preying on domestic chickens, maned wolves prefer rodents, rabbits, and armadillos. Occasionally, they eat birds, lizards, and seasonal fruits, such as guavas and bananas.

Behavior and reproduction: Maned wolves are the most solitary of the canids. Males and females only get together to breed, producing a litter of two to six pups. They normally hunt at night. White markings on the throat, tail tip, and on the large, erect ears serve as visual signals at a distance. They further communicate using harsh barks. Quite territorial, they use urine and feces as boundary markings.

Maned wolves usually live alone. They meet up with other wolves only at breeding time. (Illustration by Wendy Baker. Reproduced by permission.)

Maned wolves and people: The fur of the maned wolf is worn in South America as a good luck charm. Native Brazilians harvest the right eye from live wolves, believed to bring luck with women and gambling.

Conservation status: The maned wolf is listed as Endangered in its native countries due to habitat loss to overgrazing by cattle and deforestation, particularly for soybean farming. The IUCN classifies the maned wolf as Near Threatened. ■

FOR MORE INFORMATION

Books:

Alderton, David. *Foxes, Wolves and Wild Dogs of the World.* New York: Facts on File, 2004.

Gibson, Nancy. *Wolves.* Stillwater, MN: Voyageur Press, 2002.

Greenaway, Theresa. *The Secret World of Wolves, Wild Dogs, and Foxes.* Austin, TX: Raintree Steck-Vaughn Publishers, 2001.

Rogers, Lesley J., and Gisela Kaplan. *Spirit of the Wild Dog: The World of Wolves, Coyotes, Foxes, Jackals, & Dingoes.* Crows Nest, Australia: Allen & Unwin, 2003.

Sillero-Zubiri, Claudio, David W. Macdonald, and the IUCN/SSC Canid Specialist Group. "Portrait of an Endangered Species." In *The Ethiopian Wolf—Status Survey and Conservation Action Plan.* Gland, Switzerland: IUCN, 1997.

Periodicals:

Henry, J. David. "Spirit of the Tundra (Arctic and Red Foxes)." *Natural History* (December 1998): 60–65.

Larivière, Serge, and Maria Pasitschniak-Arts. "*Vulpes vulpes.*" *Mammalian Species* 537 (December 27, 1996): 1–11.

Robbins, Jim. "Weaving a New Web: Wolves Change an Ecosystem." 27, no. 3 (1998). Online at http://nationalzoo.si.edu/Publications/ZooGoer/1998/3/weavingwolfweb.cfm (accessed on July 6, 2004)

Stewart, Doug. "Caught in a Dog Fight." *National Wildlife* (June–July 1999): 34–39.

Walker, Tom. "The Shadow Knows (In Alaska's Far North, the Arctic Fox Shares its Secrets of Survival)." *National Wildlife* (February/March 2002): 46–53.

Web sites:

"Canid Species Accounts." IUCN/SSC Canid Specialist Group. http://www.canids.org/SPPACCTS/sppaccts.htm (accessed July 6, 2004).

"Delisting a Species." U.S. Fish & Wildlife Services. http://endangered.fws.gov/recovery/delisting.pdf (accessed July 6, 2004).

Gorog, Antonia. "*Chrysocyon brachyurus* (Maned Wolf)." Animal Diversity Web. http://animaldiversity.ummz.umich.edu/site/accounts/information/Chrysocyon_brachyurus.html (accessed July 6, 2004).

Hinrichsen, Don. "Wolves Around the World: The Global Status of the Gray Wolf." Defenders of Wildlife. http://www.defenders.org/publications/wolvesarworld.pdf (accessed July 6, 2004).

Ives. Sarah. "Wolves Reshape Yellowstone National Park." *National Geographic Kids News.* http://news.nationalgeographic.com/kids/2004/03/wolvesyellowstone.html (accessed July 6, 2004).

BEARS
Ursidae

Class: Mammalia
Order: Carnivora
Family: Ursidae
Number of species: 8 species

phylum

class

subclass

order

monotypic order

suborder

▲ **family**

PHYSICAL CHARACTERISTICS

Bears have big heads, round ears, small eyes that face forward, very short tails, and stocky legs. They are plantigrade, walking on the heels and soles of their feet like humans do. Each paw has five curved claws that are not retractable, or cannot be pulled back.

Bears come in many colors, from the familiar black, brown, and white to blonde, cinnamon, and blue-gray. Some have a yellow, orange, or white chest marking in the form of a patch, a letter V or U, or a short horizontal line. Spectacled bears are called "spectacled" because of the light markings around their eyes. Among Malayan sun bears, the smallest species, males are 4 to 5 feet (1.2 to 1.5 meters) long and weigh between 60 and 150 pounds (27 and 70 kilograms). In comparison, male polar bears on average are 8 to 9 feet (2.4 to 2.7 meters) long and weigh 900 to 1,300 pounds (400 to 590 kilograms). Females, or sows, of all species are usually smaller than males, or boars.

GEOGRAPHIC RANGE

Spectacled bears are found in Bolivia, Colombia, Ecuador, Peru, and Venezuela. Brown bears live in the United States, Canada, Europe, and Asia. American black bears inhabit the United States, Mexico, and Canada. Malayan sun bears, sloth bears, and Asiatic black bears thrive in Asia. Giant pandas live in China, while polar bears occupy the Arctic regions.

SURVIVING IN THE ARCTIC

The polar bear has a dense underfur next to its skin and a water-repellent outer fur, called guard hairs. The hairs are clear, hollow tubes that conduct sunlight to the black skin, where heat is absorbed. The clear tubes reflect sunlight, making the outer coat appear white. Blending in with the whiteness of the ice and snow, the polar bear can easily sneak up on its prey. The hollow hairs also keep the bear afloat when swimming. A thick layer of blubber, or fat, further insulates the body from the cold. Compact ears also prevent heat loss. Fur-covered feet serve as snowshoes, while thickly padded soles provide traction against slippage on ice.

HABITAT

Bears live in a variety of habitats. For example, spectacled bears can be found in the dense rainforests of South America, and Malayan sun bears thrive in tropical rainforests in Southeast Asia, while polar bears live on the Arctic tundra.

DIET

Bears are generally omnivores, eating both plants and animals. However, the polar bear is almost entirely carnivorous, eating mainly ringed seals, while the giant panda lives exclusively on bamboo. The sloth bear favors termites and ants. The other species, while preferring plant sources, also eat young animals and fish.

BEHAVIOR AND REPRODUCTION

Bears maintain a solitary lifestyle, living alone, except when mating and rearing their young. When food is plentiful, they share but keep their personal space. Bears are usually crepuscular (active at dawn and dusk). Their excellent memory enables them return to past food sources. They are agile tree climbers and fast runners, reaching speeds of up to 30 miles per hour (48 kilometers per hour). Polar bears and Asiatic black bears are expert swimmers.

Most bears mate during spring or summer, but the fertilized egg undergoes delayed implantation, during which it takes up to six months to attach to the uterus and start developing. As a result, cubs are born tiny, ranging in weight from about 11 ounces (325 grams) in sun bears to 21 ounces (600 grams) in polar and brown bears. Most sows have two cubs, although some have as many as five. Depending on the species, cubs may stay with their mothers for one to more than four years.

BEARS AND PEOPLE

People hunt some bear species for meat and trophies. Some Asian cultures use bear parts to treat diseases. In addition, many zoos house bears as exhibit animals.

CONSERVATION STATUS

The giant panda is considered Endangered, facing a very high risk of extinction, or dying out, in the wild. The spectacled, sloth, and Asiatic black bears are considered Vulnerable, facing a high risk of extinction in the wild. These and other bear species are threatened by declining populations due to losing habitat, as humans clear more land for agriculture, mining, and other activities.

American black bear (*Ursus americanus*)

AMERICAN BLACK BEAR
Ursus americanus

Physical characteristics: Although most American black bears are black, some are brown, cinnamon, blue-gray, or even white. Siblings (brothers and sisters) may have different colors. Some bears have a white chest marking. They stand about 5 feet (1.5 meters) tall. Males weigh about 250 to 350 pounds (110 to 160 kilograms), almost twice as much as females (150 to 175 pounds, or 70 to 80 kilograms).

Geographic range: American black bears are found in the United States, Mexico, and Canada.

Habitat: American black bears thrive in forested regions, wetlands, and meadows. They range in the frozen tundra (treeless plain) of

Alaska and Labrador, Canada. They are also found around campsites and other places where human food and garbage are available.

Diet: American black bears are mostly herbivores, preferring berries, fruits, grasses, and roots. With strong claws, they dig up insects in the ground and pry open honeycombs. In the absence of plant food, they eat fish, young birds, and small mammals. They also feed on carrion (dead and decaying flesh) and campsite leftovers.

Behavior and reproduction: American black bears are active at dawn and dusk, sleeping or resting most of the day and night. They are, however, adaptable, adjusting their schedule to mate or to avoid humans or predators (animals that hunt them for food). Skillful tree climbers, they scale tree trunks with their curved claws to escape predators, such as timber wolves and grizzly bears. Except for mothers and cubs, these bears are loners, although they may feed close together at an abundant food source. From late spring to early summer, adults breed for a few days, then go their separate ways. On average, two cubs are born in mid-winter. They remain with their mothers for up to two years.

American black bears and people: People hunt American black bears for meat and trophies. Poachers, or illegal hunters, kill the animals for body parts believed to have healing powers. The bears very rarely attack humans, although they may become aggressive in places where human food is found. Some bears damage cornfields and beehives.

Conservation status: American black bears are not in danger of extinction (dying out). ■

Giant panda (*Ailuropoda melanoleuca*)

GIANT PANDA
Ailuropoda melanoleuca

Physical characteristics: Giant pandas are white, with black fur around the eyes and on the ears, shoulders, chest, and legs. Each front paw has six toes, the last toe functioning as a thumb. Actually an extension of the wrist bone, the oversized thumb helps the panda grasp bamboo stems. Powerful jaws and large molar teeth help grind the tough bamboo.

Giant pandas have bigger heads and shorter legs than other bears. Adults are about 5.5 to 6 feet (1.7 to 1.8 meters) in body length. Males weigh about 175 to 280 pounds (80 to 125 kilograms), and females weigh about 155 to 220 pounds (70 to 100 kilograms).

Geographic range: Pandas are found in southwestern China.

Habitat: Giant pandas live in mountainous bamboo forests.

Giant pandas live in bamboo forests in China. They are an important symbol for conservation. (© Keren Su/Corbis. Reproduced by permission.)

Diet: The giant pandas' diet consists almost entirely of bamboo. Occasionally they eat bulbs and small animals, such as bamboo rats and musk deer fawns.

Behavior and reproduction: Although giant pandas mostly live alone, they communicate through different sounds, including squeals, honks, and snorts. They share community scent-marking areas, sending messages through anal-genital secretions rubbed on surfaces. They also use urine to mark tree trunks, with the males doing so on handstands for higher markings. Giant pandas mate during spring. Sows give birth to twins half of the time, but usually only one cub survives when two are born.

Giant pandas and people: Giant pandas are major attractions in zoos around the world. In addition, their endangered status has made them symbols for conservation.

Conservation status: The giant panda is Endangered, driven from its habitat by human activities, such as deforestation, or the clearing of land, for farming. The panda cannot reproduce fast enough to recover its losses. Females mate only in the spring and within just a two-to-three-day period. Only one cub survives, and the mother waits up to three years to mate again. ■

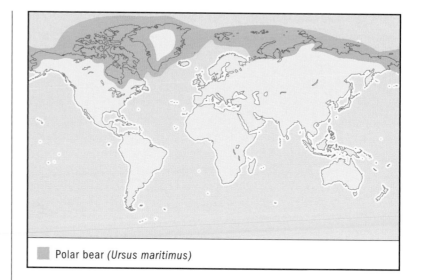

Polar bear (*Ursus maritimus*)

POLAR BEAR
Ursus maritimus

Physical characteristics: Polar bears, the largest land carnivores, have a thick white or yellowish coat, a long body and neck, black nose, and small eyes and ears. The front paws, webbed like a duck's feet, function as paddles for swimming. The long, sharp claws are used for grasping and killing prey. On average, adult males weigh about 900 to 1,300 pounds (400 to 590 kilograms) and stand 8 to 9 feet (2.4 to 2.7 meters). Adult females weigh about 450 to 600 pounds (200 to 270 kilograms) and stand 6 to 7 feet (1.8 to 2.1 meter).

Geographic range: Polar bears live in the icy Arctic Ocean and in the countries that extend into the ocean: United States (Alaska), Canada, Russia, Norway, and Greenland (a territory of Denmark).

Habitat: Polar bears prefer the Arctic pack ice, formed when big pieces of thick ice are frozen together. In summer, when the ice melts, they live on land, staying close to the water.

Diet: Polar bears eat mainly ringed seals and occasionally bearded seals. They also prey on walruses and belugas. In warmer months, they hunt ducks and rabbits, as well as feed on mussels, berries, and kelp, a brown seaweed.

Behavior and reproduction: Polar bears mostly keep to themselves but do not defend a particular home territory. They gather on shore to share beached whales and walruses. A bear may share its food with another if the latter begs submissively through body language, such as nodding its head. Polar bears are very tidy, washing themselves in the ocean after meals.

Polar bears mate in the spring. In the fall, after stuffing herself with food, the pregnant sow digs a den in deep snow and hibernates while awaiting childbirth. Cubs that are born in winter nurse until spring, with the mother living off the fat storage in her body. Cubs stay with their mothers for at least two and a half years.

Polar bears and people: Once hunted as trophies and for their fur and meat, polar bears are now protected by the laws of the five countries where they live.

Conservation status: Some scientists believe that, within a hundred years, polar bears may become extinct if Earth's temperature continues to rise. Warmer temperatures cause more arctic ice to melt, preventing

Polar bears give birth to one or two cubs at a time. The cubs stay with their mothers for at least two and a half years. (John Swedberg/Bruce Coleman Inc. Reproduced by permission.)

the bears from hunting their primary food source, the ringed seals, on the sea ice. ■

FOR MORE INFORMATION

Books:

Busch, Robert H. *The Grizzly Almanac.* New York: The Lyons Press, 2000.

Craighead, Lance. *Bears of the World.* New York: Voyageur Press, 2000.

Lumpkin, Susan, and John Seidensticker. *Smithsonian Book of Giant Pandas.* Washington, D.C. and London, England: Smithsonian Institution Press, 2002.

Patent, Dorothy Hinshaw. *A Polar Bear Biologist at Work.* New York: Grolier Publishing, 2001.

Periodicals:

Conover, Adele. "Sloth Bears: They Eat Ants, but Take On Tigers." *Smithsonian* (January 2000): 88–95.

Fair, Jeff. "When Bears Go Fishing." *Ranger Rick* (June 2001): 38–39.

Kleiman, Devra G. "Giant Pandas: Bamboo Bears." *ZooGoer* 21, no. 2 (1992) Online at http://nationalzoo.si.edu/Publications/ZooGoer/1992/2/giantpandasbamboobears.cfm (accessed on June 15, 2004).

Morrison, Jim. "The Incredible Shrinking Polar Bears." *National Wildlife* 42, no. 2 (2004) Online at http://www.nwf.org/nationalwildlife/article.cfm?articleId=880&issueId=66 (accessed on June 15, 2004)

Zoffka, Kennda. "Sleeping with the Bears." *Odyssey* (January 2002): 38–39.

Web sites:

American Zoo and Aquarium Association Bear Advisory Group. "Bear species." *The Bear Den.* http://www.bearden.org/species.html (accessed on June 15, 2004).

"Black Bears." National Park Service, Big Bend National Park. http://www.nps.gov/bibe/teachers/factsheets/blackbear.htm (accessed on June 15, 2004).

Sea World Education Department. "Polar Bears." SeaWorld/Busch Gardens Animal Information Database. http://www.seaworld.org/infobooks/PolarBears/home.html (accessed on June 15, 2004).

Class: Mammalia
Order: Carnivora
Family: Procyonidae
Number of species: 16 species

family
CHAPTER

PHYSICAL CHARACTERISTICS

Procyonids (members of the Procyonidae family) range in size from the ringtail, at 2 pounds (1 kilogram), to the northern raccoon, at 35 pounds (16 kilograms). Most have a rounded head. The erect ears may be rounded or pointed. The snout may be short or long. Except for kinkajous, procyonids have long tails with alternating dark and light rings. In the kinkajou, the ringless tail is prehensile, able to grab on to tree branches. Fur coloration ranges from pale yellowish gray (ringtail) to reddish brown (red panda) to grayish black (white-nosed coati [kuh-WAH-tee]). Most have facial markings. Each paw has five toes with short, recurved claws, or claws that curve back. Procyonids are generally plantigrade, walking on the heels and soles of their feet instead of on their toes.

GEOGRAPHIC RANGE

Except for red pandas, procyonids are found throughout Central America (including Costa Rica and Panama), South America (including Argentina, Bolivia, Brazil, Colombia, Ecuador, Peru, and Venezuela), the United States, Canada, Mexico, Germany, and Russia. Red pandas live in Asia, including China, India, Nepal, and Tibet.

HABITAT

Some procyonids prefer forested areas close to streams and rivers where they can fish for food. Many inhabit a mixed coniferous-deciduous forest, with rich vegetation and canopies (uppermost forest layers made up of the spreading branches of

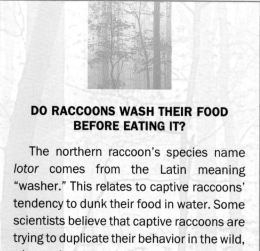

DO RACCOONS WASH THEIR FOOD BEFORE EATING IT?

The northern raccoon's species name *lotor* comes from the Latin meaning "washer." This relates to captive raccoons' tendency to dunk their food in water. Some scientists believe that captive raccoons are trying to duplicate their behavior in the wild, where they search for and grasp food underwater using their sensitive forepaws. In captivity, when raccoons dip their food in water, they give the impression of washing the food before eating it.

trees) that provide sleeping and resting sites. Some have established residence in farmlands, cities, and suburban areas.

DIET

Procyonids are omnivorous, consuming both meat and plant food. However, ringtails prefer animal matter (rodents, insects, and birds), while red pandas eat mainly bamboo leaves. Fruits are the favorite food of kinkajous and olingos.

BEHAVIOR AND REPRODUCTION

Procyonids are adept climbers and usually live in trees. Of all the species, the kinkajou rarely leaves the forest canopy. Groups of kinkajous usually feed together in fruit trees. Some species are solitary, while others live in pairs or in family groups. They are nocturnal (active at night), except for the coatis, which are diurnal (active during the day). Some communicate through vocalizations, including chirps, screams, hisses, and barks. Only the red panda is territorial, claiming an area of land for its own and defending it against intruders.

Most procyonids do not mate for life. Breeding occurs commonly in the spring. In warmer climates, breeding may occur throughout the year. Females give birth to one to seven cubs and raise the cubs by themselves.

PROCYONIDS AND PEOPLE

Procyonids are hunted for their meat and fur. Raccoons and coatis are considered pests for attacking chickens and damaging crops. The northern raccoon is a carrier of rabies, an often deadly disease affecting the central nervous system and transmitted through the raccoon's saliva.

CONSERVATION STATUS

The IUCN lists the red panda as Endangered, facing a very high risk of extinction in the wild, due to habitat loss and fragmentation (division of a habitat into small areas, resulting in insufficient food sources and home range) as a result of forest clearing. They are hunted by humans for their fur and preyed on by domestic dogs. Seven other procyonid species are considered Endangered as well.

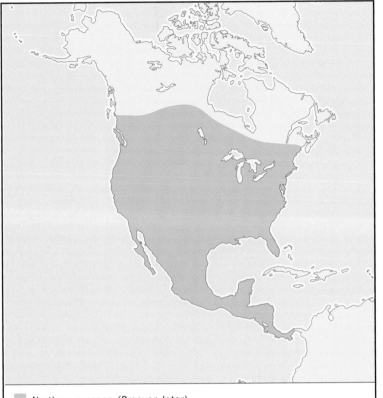

Northern raccoon (Procyon lotor)

NORTHERN RACCOON
Procyon lotor

Physical characteristics: The northern raccoon wears a black "bandit" face mask, has a large rounded head, rounded ears, and a pointed snout. The tan underfur topped with gray to black guard hairs gives it a grizzled appearance. The bushy tail has alternating black and white rings. Five long front toes work like human fingers for catching food and putting it into the mouth. The sensitive skin on the toes helps raccoons distinguish the texture of their food. In the suburbs and cities, raccoons use these toes to pry open trash containers. Raccoons are plantigrade, walking on the soles and heels of their feet. Body length is 18 to 25 inches (50 to 65 centimeters), and the tail measures another 8 to 12 inches (20 to 30 centimeters). They weigh 10 to 35 pounds (4 to 16 kilograms).

In cold climates, northern raccoons sleep in their dens for days or even months, living off fat reserves from summer and autumn feedings. They do not truly hibernate, because they get up during warm spells. (Leonard Lee Rue, III/Bruce Coleman Inc. Reproduced by permission.)

Geographic range: Northern raccoons are found in the United States, Mexico, Canada, Panama, the Netherlands, Russia, and Germany.

Habitat: Raccoons prefer forested areas, especially those near streams and rivers where they can forage for food. Forests provide nuts, berries, and tree hollows for dens. Highly adaptable, raccoons are equally at home in farmlands, cities, and the suburbs, inhabiting barns and attics.

Diet: Northern raccoons are opportunistic feeders, eating any food that is available. They enjoy fruits, berries, cereal grains, nuts, fish, crayfish, frogs, insects, and bird eggs. They dine on corn in rural areas and have adapted to eating garbage in suburban and urban areas.

Behavior and reproduction: Northern raccoons are solitary, except when mating, raising young, or gathering at human environments, such as garbage pits. They are nocturnal, sometimes spending the day resting on branches high up in trees. Expert climbers, they can descend a tree headfirst. They are also good swimmers. Although they typically walk leisurely, they can run as fast as 15 miles per hour (24 kilometers per hour).

Raccoons mate in late winter, with males having several partners. In the spring, the female gives birth to a litter of one to seven cubs in a tree hollow or abandoned animal burrow (a hole or a tunnel). The mother sometimes carries a newborn by the nape of the neck, the way cats do with kittens. The male does not participate in parenting. In cold climates, raccoons sleep in their dens for days or even months, living off fat reserves from summer and autumn feedings. However, they do not truly hibernate, getting up during warm spells.

Northern raccoons and people: Raccoons are hunted for their meat. Their fur is made into caps and coats. They are considered pests for raiding cornfields, chicken coops, and garbage bins. They carry the rabies virus, which can be passed on to humans through bites.

Conservation status: The northern raccoon is not a threatened species. ■

Red panda (*Ailurus fulgens*)

RED PANDA
Ailurus fulgens

Physical characteristics: The red panda has a body length of 20 to 24 inches (50 to 60 centimeters) and a tail length of 12 to 20 inches (30 to 50 centimeters). Its light weight of 6.5 to 11 pounds (3 to 5 kilograms) allows for climbing higher, thinner tree branches, with the long, bushy tail helping keep its balance. The tail has alternating reddish brown and tan rings. Reddish brown waterproof guard hairs protect a dense woolly underfur. Brownish black fur covers the back of the ears, belly, throat, and legs. Large pointed ears fringed with white sit atop a round head. White fur covers the cheeks and the areas over the small eyes and around the black nose. Large reddish brown tear marks run from the eyes to the corners of the mouth.

Each front paw has an extended wrist bone, used for grasping bamboo, its main food. Powerful jaw muscles and broad teeth are adapted for chewing the tough bamboo. Although flat-footed, the panda is considered semiplantigrade because the heels of its back feet do not touch the ground. Thick white fur keeps the soles warm in cold weather. The sharp claws can be pulled back like a cat's to keep from getting dull when walking on hard surfaces.

The red panda has to eat lots of leaves to get the nutrition it needs from them—it spends thirteen hours eating up to 2 to 3 pounds (1 to 1.4 kilograms) per day. (© Tim Davis/Photo Researchers, Inc. Reproduced by permission.)

Geographic range: The red panda occurs in Assam, Bhutan, China, India, Myanmar, Nepal, Sikkim, and Tibet.

Diet: The red panda is a folivore, eating almost exclusively the leaves of bamboo. On rare occasions, it eats fruits, berries, acorns, other grasses, as well as bamboo rats, insects, young birds, and bird eggs. It spends up to thirteen hours consuming 2 to 3 pounds (1 to 1.4 kilograms) of leaves. The panda has a carnivore's digestive system that is not adapted for processing plant fiber. Since it gets very little nutrients from the small amount of digested food, it has to eat plenty of leaves.

Behavior and reproduction: Red pandas sleep and rest in tree branches. They are active at night, daybreak, and dusk, mostly foraging for bamboo. Although loners, they communicate through vocalizations and body language. They scent mark territorial boundaries with anal secretions, urine, and feces. Sweat glands between the paw pads secrete fluid that helps pandas find their way around their home range. While territorial, red pandas are not aggressive. They warn each other off by bobbing their heads, raising the forepaws, and hissing.

Pandas pair off to mate, separating soon after. Due to delayed implantation during which the fertilized egg does not attach to the uterus for up to three months, newborns weigh just about 4.4 ounces (about 120 grams). The litter may consist of one to four cubs, but typically just two. To produce enough milk, the mother increases her bamboo intake threefold. The cubs stay with her for about a year or until she is ready to breed again.

Red pandas and people: Red pandas are popular zoo animals. Some Asian cultures make caps from the fur, believed to bring good fortune, especially to newlyweds.

Conservation status: The IUCN lists the red panda as Endangered due to habitat loss and fragmentation resulting from clearing forests for agriculture, timber, and fuel. Poachers (illegal hunters) harvest fur for trade. ■

FOR MORE INFORMATION

Books:

Glatston, Angela R. *Status Survey and Conservation Action Plan for Procyonids and Ailurids: The Red Panda, Olingos, Coatis, Raccoons, and their Relatives.* Gland, Switzerland: IUCN, 1994.

Kite, Patricia. *Raccoons.* Minneapolis: Lerner Publications Company, 2004.

MacClintock, Dorcas. *Red Pandas: A Natural History.* New York: Charles Scribner's Sons, 1988.

Nowak, Ronald M. "Raccoons." *Walker's Mammals of the World Online.* Baltimore: Johns Hopkins University Press, 1997. http://www.press.jhu.edu/books/walkers_mammals_of_the_world/carnivora/carnivora.procyonidae.procyon.html (accessed on July 6, 2004).

Zeveloff, Samuel I. *Raccoons: A Natural History.* Washington, D.C.: Smithsonian Institution Press, 2002.

Periodicals:

Dorn, Jonathan. "Who Was That Masked Critter?" *Backpacker* (December 1995): 24–26.

Gilbert, Bil. "Ringtails Like To Be Appreciated: Although They Are by Nature Loners, These Clever 'Cats' Don't Mind a Little Human Companionship." *Smithsonian* (August 2000): 64–70.

Lotze, Joerg-Henner, and Sydney Anderson. "*Procyon lotor.*" *Mammalian Species* 119 (June 8, 1979): 1–8.

Roberts, Miles. "Red Panda: The Fire Cat." *ZooGoer* 21, no. 2 (1992). Online at http://nationalzoo.si.edu/publications/zoogoer/1992/2/redpandasfirecat.cfm (accessed on July 6, 2004).

Roberts, Miles S., and John L. Gittelman. "*Ailurus fulgens.*" *Mammalian Species* 222 (November 14, 1984): 1–8.

Web sites:

Heath, Terrell, and Josh Platnick. "*Ailurus fulgens* (Red Panda)." Animal Diversity web. http://animaldiversity.ummz.umich.edu/site/accounts/information/Ailurus_fulgens.html (accessed on July 6, 2004).

"Procyonids: Raccoons, Ringtails & Coatis." Arizona-Sonora Desert Museum. http://www.desertmuseum.org/books/nhsd_procyonids.html (accessed on July 6, 2004).

WEASELS, BADGERS, SKUNKS, AND OTTERS
Mustelidae

Class: Mammalia
Order: Carnivora
Family: Mustelidae
Number of species: 65 species

phylum
class
subclass
order
monotypic order
suborder
▲ family

PHYSICAL CHARACTERISTICS

Mustelids, members of the family Mustelidae, may either have a slim, elongated body and long tail like weasels, mink, martens, and otters, or a stocky body and short tail like badgers and wolverines. Some have webbed feet for swimming. Their fur may be uniform in color, striped, or spotted. They may be white, silver, brown, or black in color. The smallest mustelid, the least weasel, is also the smallest carnivore, weighing about 1.76 ounces (50 grams).

GEOGRAPHIC RANGE

Mustelids are found on all continents except Antarctica. They live in such countries as the United States, Canada, Mexico, Japan, Mongolia, Great Britain, Ireland, Finland, Algeria, and Morocco.

HABITAT

Mustelids inhabit a wide range of habitats. Sea otters live exclusively in the ocean, while river otters forage for food in water but den (make a den, or place to live) on land. Some live in the desert like the honey badgers, and others in tundra marshes, like ermines. Some take over their prey's dens, such as black-footed ferrets. Others, including skunks and badgers live near humans under abandoned buildings, in golf courses, and in parks.

DIET

Mustelids are either true carnivores, such as weasels, martens, and otters, feeding mainly on meat, or omnivores, like skunks, badgers, and tayras, consuming both animals and plants. Their diet consists of rodents, rabbits, reptiles, birds, insects, fruits, roots, and seeds.

BEHAVIOR AND REPRODUCTION

Mustelids are mostly nocturnal, active at night. Most are solitary, except for otters and European badgers, which form social groups. Some are excellent swimmers and skillful climbers. Musk secreted by anal glands is used to scent mark territory, as a defense mechanism in skunks, or for communication.

Only the giant otter mates with just one partner. Some species experience delayed implantation, during which the fertilized egg waits several months before attaching to the uterus to continue development. Females have a litter of one to twelve offspring, depending on the species. Males do not participate in parenting.

MUSTELIDS AND PEOPLE

Mustelids are hunted by humans for their fur. Ferrets are kept as pets, while otters are kept in zoo exhibits. Some are considered pests for spraying musk and for digging up lawns and golf courses. Others carry diseases.

CONSERVATION STATUS

The United States classifies the black-footed ferret as Endangered due to habitat loss to agriculture and the declining population of prairie dogs, its main prey. The IUCN lists the black-footed ferret as Extinct in the Wild, and four otters, two weasels, and one mink as Endangered, facing a very high risk of extinction in the wild.

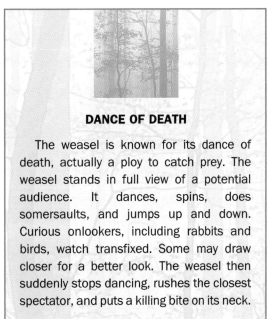

DANCE OF DEATH

The weasel is known for its dance of death, actually a ploy to catch prey. The weasel stands in full view of a potential audience. It dances, spins, does somersaults, and jumps up and down. Curious onlookers, including rabbits and birds, watch transfixed. Some may draw closer for a better look. The weasel then suddenly stops dancing, rushes the closest spectator, and puts a killing bite on its neck.

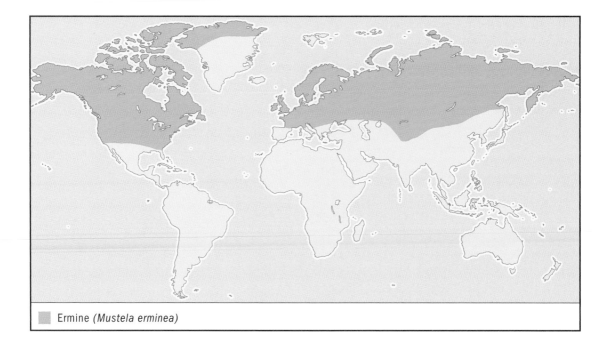

Ermine (Mustela erminea)

SPECIES
ACCOUNTS

ERMINE
Mustela erminea

Physical characteristics: Ermines have slender bodies, useful for pursuing prey through narrow passages. They have a triangular head, rounded ears, and a long neck. Long, sensitive whiskers help track prey. The fur changes with the season and acts as a camouflage (KAM-uh-flaj), white in winter to blend in with the snow and brown with yellowish undersides and feet in summer. Their tails measure 2 to 4 inches (3 to 10 centimeters) and have black tips all year-round, which helps distract attention from the predator's body. The body is 6 to 10 inches (15 to 25 centimeters) long. Ermines weigh just 4.4 to 12.3 ounces (125 to 350 grams).

Geographic range: Ermines live in the United States and Canada, Asia (including Japan, India, Mongolia, and Siberia), Europe (including Scandinavia and Ireland), Algeria, and Greenland.

Habitat: Ermines prefer forests, grasslands, and marshy plains that provide cover and prey. They live in tree roots, hollow logs, and

burrows, holes or tunnels, inherited from their prey, usually lining their nest with fur from their prey.

Diet: Ermines are carnivorous, eating rodents, rabbits, ground squirrels, birds, and insects. They eat as much as half their body weight in food and store extra food for later use.

Behavior and reproduction: Ermines are loners, except for breeding pairs and mother-offspring groups. They use musk, an anal secretion, to mark territory and as a signal for mating. Ermines also communicate through squeaks, trills, and screeches. They are active throughout the day and night. Expert hunters, they prey on animals several times their size, killing them with a bite at the back of the neck.

Ermines mate in late spring to early summer, but the fertilized egg undergoes delayed implantation, waiting nine to ten months before attaching to the uterus to resume development. Females give birth to one or two litters of four to eight offspring the following spring and raise the young alone. Females become sexually mature, capable of

An ermine turns from its brown fur color for summer to its white color for winter. The fur changes with the season and acts as a camouflage, helping the animal blend in with its surroundings. (Erwin and Peggy Bauer/Bruce Coleman Inc. Reproduced by permission.)

reproducing, at two months of age, while males attain sexual maturity at one year. It is not unusual for adult males to mate with very young females, sometimes before they are weaned from their mother's milk. This ensures new generations even if males might not be around for mating.

Ermines and people: Some people value ermines for killing rats and mice. Americans used the black-tipped tails as ornaments, while European royalties made ceremonial robes out of the whole fur.

Conservation status: Ermines are not a threatened species.   ∎

Striped skunk (Mephitis mephitis)

STRIPED SKUNK
Mephitis mephitis

Physical characteristics: Striped skunks have silky black fur. A white stripe starts on top of the head, and separates into two stripes down the sides of the back. Anal glands produce strong-smelling musk that protects against intruders. Sharp forefeet claws are designed for digging. The body is 13 to 18 inches (33 to 45 centimeters) long, and the tail measures 7 to 10 inches (18 to 25 centimeters). They weigh about 4 to 18 pounds (2 to 8 kilograms).

Geographic range: Striped skunks live in the United States, Canada, and Mexico.

Habitat: Striped skunks prefer a mixture of farmland, forest, and grassland, where they den in barns, under wood piles and in underground burrows. They adapt to desert conditions, sleeping in cool

A young striped skunk forages for insects. Rodents and insects make up most of a skunk's diet. (Erwin and Peggy Bauer/Bruce Coleman Inc. Reproduced by permission.)

dens during the day and foraging at night when their prey are active. They also thrive in the tundra, especially in marshes during the summer thaw. Skunks also live in suburban areas.

Diet: Striped skunks are opportunistic feeders, eating whatever food is available. Their main diet consists of small rodents and insects. They also consume reptiles, frogs, worms, birds, bird eggs, fruits, and seeds.

Behavior and reproduction: Striped skunks are active at night. They dig underground dens, use a hollowed tree stump, or share a home with rabbits and raccoons. During severe winters, they become inactive for several months, living off stored fat in their body. They do not truly hibernate, moving about when the weather warms up. Males are typically solitary but several females may den together. Mating occurs in February and March, with the males having several partners. Litters of four to ten young are born in May and are raised by the females. The young stay with the mother for up to two years.

When threatened, striped skunks give warning by stamping their front feet and growling. If the intruder does not leave, skunks raise their tails and spray a foul-smelling musk. The spray can travel up to 10 feet (3 meters), causing nausea and burning the eyes and nose.

Striped skunks and people: Skunk musk, with its odor removed, is an important perfume ingredient that enables perfume to evaporate slowly and emit fragrance longer. Striped skunks kill rodents and insects that destroy crops but they sometimes assault chickens and damage beehives. In North America, they are carriers of rabies, an often deadly disease affecting the central nervous system and transmitted through the skunk's saliva.

Conservation status: Striped skunks are not threatened. ■

European otter (Lutra lutra)

EUROPEAN OTTER
Lutra lutra

Physical characteristics: European otters are river otters with an elongated body and a broad, flat head. When diving, otters close the valves in their ears and nose to keep water out. The fully webbed feet work like paddles, while the flattened, muscled tail acts as a rudder for steering underwater. Sensitive whiskers help them find food, especially in muddy waters. The dark brown fur has two layers: a dense, wooly underfur and coarse, waterproof guard hairs. European otters weigh about 15 to 33 pounds (7 to 15 kilograms). Their body length is 25 to 33 inches (65 to 85 centimeters), and the tail length is 15 to 20 inches (36 to 52 centimeters).

Geographic range: European otters are found in Europe including Great Britain, France, Portugal, Spain, Ireland, Norway, Greece, Scotland, Albania, and Finland, Asia including Japan, Taiwan, Java, Sri Lanka, and Sumatra, and North Africa.

Habitat: European otters are found in freshwater habitats including rivers, streams, lakes, and ponds. They live along seashores where

freshwater pools are formed from abundant rainfall. They den on land, inhabiting swamps along rivers and lakes, and on dry land among tree roots and abandoned animal burrows.

Diet: European otters consume fish, frogs, crabs, small rodents, and aquatic birds. They eat small prey in the water, but haul out larger prey to shore. They eat the equivalent of 20 percent of their body weight every day.

Behavior and reproduction: Although European otters forage for food in water, they den and breed on land, and are active at night. Otters seek freshwater for drinking and for washing sea salt from their guard hairs to keep them waterproof. They scent mark territories with anal secretions and deposit feces on logs and rocks to keep out trespassers. They are playful animals, often seen sliding down mud banks and icy slides. They communicate through chirps, chuckles, and whistles.

Breeding starts in February in water or on land. Males have two or more mating partners. The mother gives birth to two to four kits in April or June. The father leaves after the babies are born, while the young stay with the mother for about a year.

European otters and people: European otters are legally protected in some countries. Commercial fishermen consider them pests for raiding fisheries.

Conservation status: The IUCN lists the European otter as Vulnerable, facing a high risk of extinction in the wild, due to habitat destruction from dam construction, drainage of wetlands, and conversion of rivers into canals, as well as water pollution from agriculture and industries. Illegal hunting continues in many areas. Accidental trapping in fishermen's nets is also a common occurrence. ∎

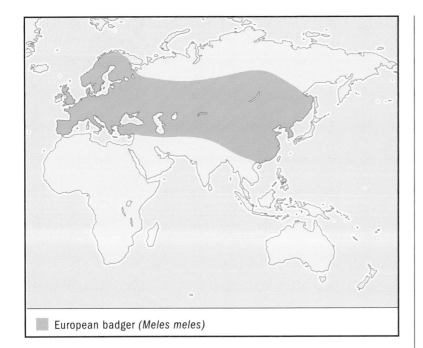

European badger *(Meles meles)*

EUROPEAN BADGER
Meles meles

Physical characteristics: European badgers have broad bodies, short legs, and short tails. They have gray backs, black undersides and legs. The white face has two parallel black stripes that start at the snout, cover the eyes, and extend to the ears. Their loose coat allows the badger to wriggle out of a predator's grasp or to quickly turn around and bite back. Long, strong front claws are designed for digging dirt and wasp nests, beehives, and insect larvae in grass roots. A see-through layer of skin protects the eyes from flying dirt and provides moisture. The back feet work like shovels for pushing out dirt. The badger weighs 22 to 44 pounds (10 to 20 kilograms), with a body length of 24 to 33 inches (60 to 85 centimeters) and a tail length of 6 to 8 inches (15 to 20 centimeters).

Geographic range: European badgers occur in all European countries and a number of Asian countries, including China, Japan, and Iran.

Habitat: European badgers prefer dense forests, but also inhabit open fields, hedgerows, and parks.

European badgers are nocturnal and live together in large underground connected tunnels called "setts." (Hans Reinhard/Bruce Coleman Inc. Reproduced by permission.)

Diet: Earthworms make up about 50 percent of the European badger's diet. They also feed on small rodents, hedgehogs, snails, insects and their larvae, as well as fruits, seeds, mushrooms, and roots.

Behavior and reproduction: European badgers live together in social groups called clans, consisting of twelve to fourteen adults and their cubs. A dominant male and female rule the clan. Badgers are territorial, marking the boundaries of their home range with feces and an anal secretion called musk. They also mark one another with musk for easy identification. Badgers forage for food at night. In winter, they sleep for days but do not truly hibernate.

Badgers mate during most of the year but implantation of the fertilized egg in the uterus can be delayed by about ten months, resulting in almost all cubs being born in February or March, when food is abundant. A litter averages two to three cubs, but may have as many as five. The young stay with their mother until fall.

European badgers and people: European badgers have damaged gardens, lawns, and golf courses. Scientific experiments in Great Britain found that badger are carriers of bovine tuberculosis (bTB), and can transmit the disease to cattle. Government-sponsored killing of badgers in areas where cattle had developed bTB ended because it did not reduce cattle infection. The government continues to monitor the situation.

Conservation status: European badgers are not considered a threatened species. ■

FOR MORE INFORMATION

Books:

Darbyshire, John, and Laurie Campbell. *Badgers*. Moray, U.K.: Colin Baxter Photography, 1998.

Foster-Turley, Pat, Sheila Macdonald, Chris Mason, and the IUCN/SSC Otter Specialist Group, eds. *Otters: An Action Plan for their Conservation*. Gland, Switzerland: IUCN, 1990.

Ivy, Bill. *Weasels*. Danbury, CT: Grolier Educational Corporation, 1986.

Love, John A. *Sea Otters*. Golden, CO: Fulcrum Publishing, 1992.

Nowak, Ronald M. "Old World Badger." *Walker's Mammals of the World Online 5.1.* Baltimore: Johns Hopkins University Press, 1997. http://www.press.jhu.edu/books/walkers_mammals_of_the_world/ carnivora/carnivora.mustelidae.meles.html (accessed July 7, 2004).

Paine, Stefani. *The World of the Sea Otter.* San Francisco, CA: Sierra Club Books, 1993.

Periodicals:

Bauman, Richard. "Getting Skunked: Understanding the Antics Behind the Smell." *Backpacker* (May 1993): 30–31.

Conniff, Richard. "You Can Call Him 'Cute' or You Can Call Him Hungry." *Smithsonian* (February 1997): 81–91.

King, Carolyn M. "*Mustela erminea.*" *Mammalian Species* 195 (April 8, 1983): 1–8.

Line, Les. "The Benefits of Badgers." *National Wildlife* (December-January 1995): 18–23.

Wade-Smith, Julia, and B. J. Verts. "*Mephitis mephitis.*" *Mammalian Species* 173 (May 25, 1982): 1–7.

Weidensaul, Scott. "The Rarest of the Rare." *Smithsonian* (November 2000): 118–128.

Web sites:

"Black-footed ferret." U.S. Fish & Wildlife Service. http://endangered.fws.gov/i/A07.html (accessed on July 7, 2004).

National Federation of Badger Groups. http://www.badger.org.uk/tb/ (accessed on July 7, 2004).

Division of Fish, Wildlife and Marine Resources. "Furbearer Profiles: The Striped Skunk." New York State Department of Environmental Conservation. http://www.dec.state.ny.us/website/dfwmr/wildlife/wildgame/ skunkinny.htm (accessed on July 7, 2004).

Badgerland Home Page. http://www.badgerland.co.uk/main.html (accessed on July 7, 2004).

"Mustelids." Arizona-Sonora Desert Museum. http://www.desertmuseum .org/books/nhsd_mustelids.html (accessed on July 7, 2004).

Class: Mammalia

Order: Carnivora

Family: Viverridae

Number of species: 34 species

family
CHAPTER

phylum

class

subclass

order

monotypic order

suborder

▲ family

PHYSICAL CHARACTERISTICS

Viverrids (civets, genets, and linsangs) have long, slender bodies and short legs. Some have a uniform coloration, while others are marked with spots, bars, or both. The fur is short. The tail, sometimes longer than the body, is bushy and may be ringed with alternating dark and light colors. The snout is pointed, and the ears are erect. Most have five toes on each paw. Viverrids are the only carnivores with perineal (per-uh-NEE-uhl) glands (perfume glands between the anus and the genital organs) that produce a strong-smelling substance used for defense, territory marking, and sexual communication. These glands are most developed in civets and genets.

GEOGRAPHIC RANGE

Viverrids are found in western Europe (including France, Portugal, and Spain), Southeast Asia (including Thailand, Malaysia, and Indonesia), and most of Africa.

HABITAT

Viverrids occupy tropical deciduous forests that provide canopies (uppermost layer of a forest consisting of spreading branches). They also inhabit tall grasses and thick brush for cover. Some prefer wetlands, while others live near rivers and streams.

DIET

Most viverrids eat rodents, insects, reptiles, frogs, birds, crabs, carrion (dead and decaying flesh), eggs, fruits, and nuts.

Palm civets are predominantly frugivores, eating pulpy fruits and berries.

BEHAVIOR AND REPRODUCTION

Viverrids are generally solitary, although some may live in pairs or small groups. The palm civet and the African linsang are almost exclusively arboreal (tree-dwelling). The otter civet and the aquatic genet live near rivers and streams.

Most viverrids scent mark territories and tree branches with perineal secretions. They also deposit feces on rocks, topping them with perineal secretions to advertise ownership. Some species produce sounds, including hisses, screams, and coughs. Some breed throughout the year. Others breed during certain seasons. Some may give birth two or three times a year. The average litter size is two to three kittens; up to six may be born. Kittens are born with a full coat, although the markings may not be clear. Males do not share in parenting.

VIVERRIDS AND PEOPLE

Viverrid meat is consumed by some people. Some species are kept as pets to control rodents. Humans sometimes kill those that attack poultry and lambs. Oil from the civet is valued by perfume makers for enhancing the quality of fragrances.

In 2002, an outbreak of severe acute respiratory syndrome (SARS) in southern China was linked to the consumption of masked palm civet. SARS is an infectious, potentially deadly disease. When the World Health Organization announced the end of the SARS outbreak in July 2003, more than 8,000 cases had been reported in 27 countries, with 774 deaths. In January 2004, when SARS resurfaced in China, authorities ordered the killing of all palm civets raised on farms. Other animals, including the raccoon dog and the Chinese ferret badger, also carry the SARS virus. These are not eaten by humans and have not been destroyed.

CONSERVATION STATUS

The IUCN lists eight species as threatened. The Malabar civet is classified as Critically Endangered, facing an extremely high risk of extinction, due to habitat loss, predation, and hunting by humans. The otter civet and the crested genet are listed as Endangered, facing a very high risk of extinction, because of habitat loss/degradation, predation, and hunting by humans.

Five species are listed as Vulnerable, facing a high risk of extinction, mostly because of habitat loss/destruction and hunting by humans. These are Owston's palm civet, Hose's palm civet, the Malagasy civet, the Sulawesi palm civet, and Jerdon's palm civet.

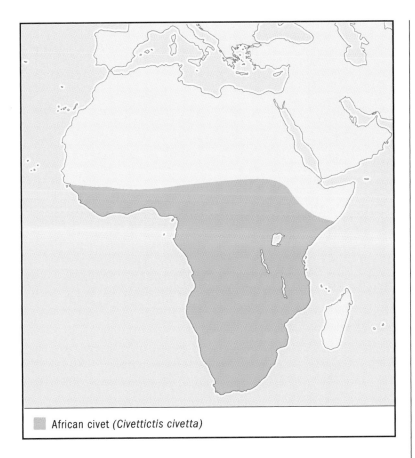

African civet (*Civettictis civetta*)

AFRICAN CIVET
Civettictis civetta

Physical characteristics: The African civet's fur ranges from silvery gray to creamy yellow with black-brown markings arranged in rows. A black mane of hair from the neck to the tail is erected when the civet gets scared or excited, making the animal seem larger. A black mask covers the eyes, with grayish fur above the eyes all the way to the small, round ears. The snout is black, with white on each side. A white stripe bordered by black stripes runs from the neck down to the front of the shoulders. This distinctive feature may serve to direct harmless, playful bites during mock-fighting or mating. The tail is partly ringed with alternating black and lighter colors, with solid black on the bottom half. Black legs and feet have long, curved claws. The perineal glands produce an oily substance called civet that

African civets are active at night, feeding mainly on fruits, but also eating some rodents, insects, reptiles, and other meat. (Cyril C. Laubscher. Bruce Coleman, Inc. Reproduced by permission.)

is used in the perfume industry. The civet uses this secretion for scent marking its territory. The body length is 27 to 33 inches (67 to 84 centimeters), and the tail is another 13 to 19 inches (34 to 47 centimeters). The largest of the viverrids, the African civet weighs about 22 to 38 pounds (10 to 17 kilograms).

Geographic range: African civets occur in countries south of the Sahara Desert, including Senegal, Somalia, the Democratic Republic of the Congo, Zimbabwe, Mozambique, and the island of Zanzibar.

Habitat: African civets prefer woodlands and areas of tall grasses and dense shrubs for resting and cover. Mothers and young nest in tangled roots and burrows (holes) abandoned by other animals.

Diet: African civets are omnivores, feeding on plants and animals. They eat mainly fruits, supplementing them with rodents, insects, reptiles, frogs, birds, crabs, and carrion. They can eat up to 4 pounds (2 kilograms) of food per feeding, but can fast (go without food) for up to two weeks. They sometimes take poultry and lambs in human environments.

Behavior and reproduction: African civets are solitary, except when mating and raising young. They are nocturnal (active at night), sleeping by day in tangled growths of vegetation or in tall grasses. They defend territories, marking boundaries with perineal secretion. Females use this secretion to advertise readiness to mate. Civets also deposit feces in piles, topped with the secretion, for identification and to claim ownership of a territory. Civets communicate through different sounds, including screams, growls, and coughs.

Mating occurs throughout the year. Females give birth two to three times a year, usually to two to three young. Young civets are quite developed when born, having a full coat with faint markings and able to crawl right away. The mother introduces solid food to her young after about a month and a half. Before this event, the young perform a unique behavior called mouth suckling, in which they drink the mother's saliva by licking her mouth. However, they continue nursing up to fourteen to sixteen weeks of age.

African civets and people: For centuries, the perfume industry has used the perineal secretion from African civets, called civet or civet oil, to make fragrances last longer. Although artificial civet oil has been available since the 1940s, some perfumers prefer the real thing. In Ethiopia, civet continues to be extracted from caged animals. African civets are sometimes considered pests for preying on poultry and lambs.

Conservation status: The African civet is not a threatened species. ∎

Common genet *(Genetta genetta)*

COMMON GENET
Genetta genetta

Physical characteristics: The common genet has a slender, flexible body that enables it to go through narrow openings to pursue rodents, their main prey. A yellowish or grayish coat is covered with black or brown markings arranged in rows. When threatened or scared, the hair covering the back is erected to give the appearance of a larger size. The long tail has alternating dark and light rings. The snout is pointed, and the ears are rounded. White coloration covers the areas around the eyes and mouth. The sharp claws, used for climbing trees and catching prey, are sharpened on tree barks and kept in a protective sheath when not in use. Secretions from the perineal glands are used to mark territory and as a means of communication. The body length is 17 to 22 inches (43 to 55 centimeters). The tail measures 13 to 16 inches (33 to 51 centimeters). Weight is about 3 to 6 pounds (1.5 to 2.5 kilograms).

Geographic range: The common genet is found in France, Portugal, Spain, Arabia, northern Africa (including Algeria, Tunisia, Egypt), and all African countries south of the Sahara Desert.

Habitat: Common genets inhabit forested areas where they have trees for climbing and tree hollows for sleeping and resting. Grasslands provide cover for stalking and ambushing prey. They also live near humans, such as in barns and parks.

Diet: Common genets are omnivores, eating rodents, frogs, reptiles, insects, and fruits. They prey on nesting birds and occasionally take poultry.

Behavior and reproduction: The common genets are equally at home on the ground and in tree branches. They are active at night, sleeping during the day in a tree hollow or a burrow abandoned by another animal. They are solitary, communicating with one another using perineal secretions to mark ground surfaces and tree branches. They make catlike sounds, such as meows and purrs. They also growl and hiss. Genets pair off briefly to mate, mostly in February and March. In summer, the mother gives birth to a litter of one to four kittens, but normally two to three, nursing them for about two months.

Common genets and people: Genets are sometimes kept as pets to control rodents. They occasionally prey on poultry and game birds.

Conservation status: The common genet is not a threatened species.   ■

FOR MORE INFORMATION

Books:

Attenborough, David. *The Life of Mammals.* Princeton, NJ: Princeton University Press, 2002.

Estes, Richard D. *The Behavior Guide to African Mammals: Including Hoofed Mammals, Carnivores, Primates.* Berkeley, CA: The University of California Press, 1991.

Kruuk, Hans. *Hunter and Hunted: Relationships Between Carnivores and People.* Cambridge, U.K.: Cambridge University Press, 2002.

Nowak, Ronald M. "African Civet." *Walker's Mammals of the World Online 5.1.* Baltimore: Johns Hopkins University Press, 1997. http://www. press.jhu.edu/books/walkers_mammals_of_the_ world/ carnivora/carnivora.viverridae.civettictis.html (accessed on June 23, 2004).

Nowak, Ronald M. "Civets, Genets, Linsangs, Mongooses, and Fossas." *Walker's Mammals of the World Online. 5.1.* Baltimore: Johns Hopkins University Press, 1997. http://www.press.jhu.edu/books/ walkers_mammals_of_the_world/carnivora/carnivora.viverridae.html (accessed on June 23, 2004).

Nowak, Ronald M. "Genets." *Walker's Mammals of the World Online. 5.1.* Baltimore: Johns Hopkins University Press, 1997. http://www.press. jhu.edu/books/walkers_mammals_of_the_world/carnivora/carnivora. viverridae.genetta.html (accessed on June 23, 2004).

Schreiber, Arnd, Roland Wirth, Michael Riffel, and Harry Van Rompaey. *Weasels, Civets, Mongooses, and their Relatives: An Action Plan for the Conservation of Mustelids and Viverrids.* Gland, Switzerland: IUCN, 1989.

Periodicals:

Ray, Justina C. "*Civettictis civetta.*" *Mammalian Species* 488 (June 23, 1995): 1–7.

family
CHAPTER

PHYSICAL CHARACTERISTICS

Mongooses are a family, Herpestidae, of small to medium-sized, mainly carnivorous Old World mammals. Their overall appearance suggests a small, generalized mammalian carnivore. They have long bodies, short but powerful legs, and long, often bushy tails. In some ways, they converge with (resemble) the mustelids (mammal family Mustelidae: weasels, badgers, skunks, otters, wolverines) of the New World.

Family Herpestidae, including species in Madagascar, includes about thirty-five species and seventeen genera (JEN-uh-ruh), although not all taxonomists, or classifiers of animal types, agree as to the exact number of genera and species. The large island of Madagascar, off the southeast coast of Africa, has eight mongoose species arranged in four genera, probably all descended from a single founder species that rafted on floating vegetation from Africa. The Malagasy mongooses are classified in a subfamily of their own, the Galidiinae. All other mongoose species are classified within subfamily Herpestinae.

Adult head-and-body length throughout family Herpestidae runs 9 to 25.5 inches (23 to 65 centimeters), tail length 9 to 20 inches (23 to 51 centimeters), and weight just under 1 pound to 9 pounds (0.4 to 4.0 kilograms). The exception to these measurements is the fossa of Madagascar, the largest of the Herpestidae and the most un-mongoose-like of all mongoose species. A fossa can grow up to 31.5 inches (80 centimeters) head-and-body length, with a tail just as long, and an adult weight of 20 pounds (9.1 kilograms).

phylum

class

subclass

order

monotypic order

suborder

▲ **family**

**MONGOOSES AND HORNBILLS
GETTING ALONG**

The dwarf mongoose has a mutually beneficial relationship with two bird species, the red-billed hornbill and the eastern yellow-billed hornbill. In the scrub country of eastern Kenya, the mongoose and either of the hornbill species forage together, eating the same prey, the hornbills keeping their senses alert for the presence of threat animals, especially birds of prey. The companionship allows the mongooses to forage in peace, while the birds benefit from creatures flushed out by the mongooses. The hornbills sound off with warning calls when a predator approaches, even warning at the sight of predators of mongooses that are not enemies of hornbills.

Fur colors in herpestids are various shades of brown and gray, with lighter, sometimes white, fur on the underside. Some species carry stripes or stipplings on their darker fur. The fur can vary in texture as well, from soft to coarse, short to long. There are five clawed digits on each of the four paws, the claws of the forefeet long, sharp, and curved. Except for the fossa, the claws are not retractable, meaning they cannot pull them back into the paw. The small head and face taper to a pointed muzzle, sometimes with a straight bridge from crown to the end of the snout, or there may be a distinct, sloped forehead where the head and muzzle join. The ears are short and rounded.

Herpestids carry glands for scent-marking in their cheeks and near their anuses. Some species can shoot out a foul-smelling fluid from the anal glands.

GEOGRAPHIC RANGE

Mongooses live in mainland Africa, southern Europe, Madagascar, southern Asia including India, the Malay Peninsula as far as and including Sumatra, Borneo and Java; also the islands of Hainan and Taiwan.

HABITAT

Mongooses live in various types of forest, including humid tropical rainforest, also dry grasslands and near-desert. They shelter in self-made burrows in the ground or in termite mounds, or in natural shelters like hollow logs and spaces within rock piles.

DIET

Mongoose species have generalized, mainly carnivorous diets, helping themselves to insects, crabs, millipedes, earthworms, reptiles, amphibians, mammals, birds, birds' eggs, fruits, and roots. Before eating toads or caterpillars, a mongoose will roll them back and forth on the ground to wipe off skin poisons of toads and irritating hairs of caterpillars. Among mongoose species that eat bird eggs, a mongoose will break open an individual egg by holding it in its forepaws and pitching it backward between its hindlimbs and into a rock, or by standing up on its hind legs and dropping the egg. Several species eat fruit as supplements to a mainly meat diet. Some species swim in ponds and streams, searching for fish and other aquatic animals.

An individual mongoose baits a snake by skillfully avoiding and dodging the reptile's lunges until it tires and slows down in its actions, enabling the mongoose to dart in and seize the snake behind its head, killing it by biting, then eating the snake at leisure. Mongooses are not immune to the venom, so that a mongoose-on-snake tussle is always dangerous and can end in death for either party.

BEHAVIOR AND REPRODUCTION

Mongooses are energetic, aggressive, and playful. They may hunt and forage alone or in groups. Some species are nocturnal, active at night, others are diurnal, active during the day. Diurnal species often start their days by sunning, outstretched on rocks or the ground near their shelters, and exercising to limber themselves up for a day of foraging.

Mongooses live in colonies of up to fifty individuals. These may live in burrow networks or just build temporary shelters for themselves during migratory foraging.

Some mongoose species breed seasonally, others breed throughout the year, females giving birth two or three times annually. Gestation periods range from forty-two to eighty-four days. There are one to four young per litter. Captive Egyptian mongooses have lived for over twenty years.

MONGOOSES AND PEOPLE

Mongooses and humanity share intertwined histories. The animals have been the source of innumerable folk tales in their native lands, e.g., "Rikki-tikki-tavi," the famous short story by British writer Rudyard Kipling, based on native legends of India. Mongooses have been praised for destroying pests and condemned for preying on non-pests, especially domestic poultry.

From ancient times until the present, mongooses have been introduced by humanity to mainlands and islands over much of the world, in attempts to keep down problem populations of rats and snakes: Italy, Spain, Portugal, Yugoslavia, many of the Caribbean islands, and the islands of Hawaii and Fiji. Since mongooses are so highly adaptable, they soon outdo the original problem they were introduced to control by becoming pests themselves, preying on harmless and beneficial local bird and mammal species, and raiding poultry. A number of countries that have learned the lesson the hard way and now outlaw the possession or importation of mongooses.

CONSERVATION STATUS

The World Conservation Union (IUCN), includes on its Red List of Threatened Species, four mongoose species considered Vulnerable, facing a high risk of extinction, and five Endangered, facing a very high risk of extinction. Three Vulnerable and three Endangered species are in Madagascar. The main threats to mongoose species are habitat destruction, and, on Madagascar, habitat loss plus competition and predation by introduced predators like dogs and cats. Nevertheless, family Herpestidae, overall, is flourishing.

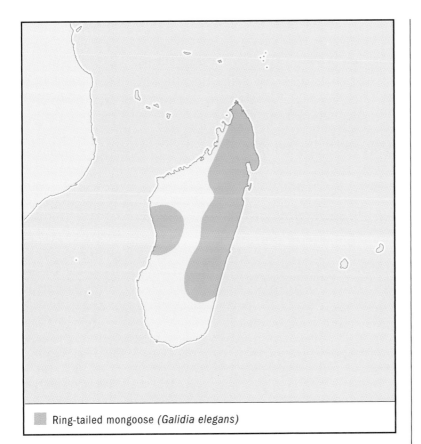

Ring-tailed mongoose (Galidia elegans)

RING-TAILED MONGOOSE
Galidia elegans

Physical characteristics: In appearance, the ring-tailed mongoose more or less follows the general mongoose body plan, while being a particularly beautiful and striking species, with red-brown to dark brown body fur and a long, bushy tail striped alternately with broad, red-brown and black rings. The underside is very dark to black. The head-and-body length of an adult Malagasy ring-tailed mongoose runs 12.5 to 14 inches (32 to 36 centimeters), tail length, 10.5 to 12.5 inches (27 to 32 centimeters), and body weight of 1.5 to 2.2 pounds (0.7 to 1 kilograms).

Geographic range: This mongoose lives in eastern and western Madagascar.

Ring-tailed mongooses feed on small mammals, birds, birds' eggs, frogs, fish, reptiles, insects, and fruits. (Photograph by Harald Schütz. Reproduced by permission.)

Habitat: The ring-tailed mongoose inhabits humid tropical rainforest along Madagascar's east and northwestern coasts, and drier, seasonal forest along much of the west coast.

Diet: Ring-tailed mongooses feed on small mammals, birds, birds' eggs, frogs, fish, reptiles, insects, and fruits. They also prey on two small primate species native to Madagascar, the greater dwarf lemur, and the brown mouse lemur.

Behavior and reproduction: Ring-tailed mongooses mate from April to November, and a single young is born from July to February. The gestation period runs seventy-nine to ninety-two days. The young is sexually mature at two years of age. A captive ring-tailed mongoose lived for over thirteen years.

Malagasy ring-tailed mongooses forage and hunt during daylight. They can swim and climb trees easily but do most foraging on the ground. These mongooses forage and hunt in groups of up to five, each group made up of a mated pair and offspring. As they wander, the mongooses mark trees and rocks of their territory with anal scent glands. They shelter in burrows during nights.

The ring-tailed mongoose and people: This animal seems to have little fear of humanity other than natural caution, and will investigate native villages and biological research camps, stealing whatever human garbage or food they can lay hands on. They may add domestic poultry to their diets, resulting in people hunting and harrassing them.

Conservation status: This mongoose is listed as Vulnerable by the IUCN. Some naturalists, after very recent surveys of the species in Madagascar, consider it of little or no conservation concern because of its high numbers and adaptability.   ■

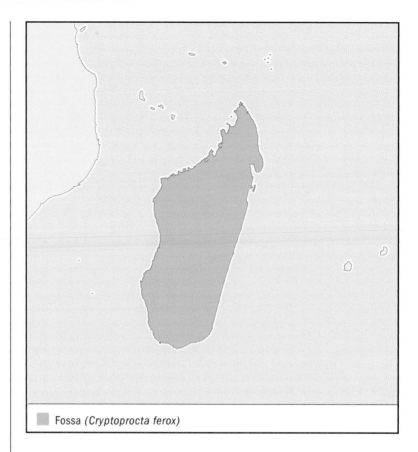

Fossa *(Cryptoprocta ferox)*

FOSSA
Cryptoprocta ferox

Physical characteristics: Its name derived from a native Malagasy word, and pronounced "foosh," this puzzling animal is as worthy of biodiversity poster status as the more famous lemurs of Madagascar.

The fossa is the largest of all mongoose species, with an adult head-and-body length of 24 to 31.5 inches (61 to 80 centimeters), a tail as long as the head and body, and an adult weight of eleven to twenty pounds (5 to 10 kilograms). A fossa looks like a combination of dog, cat, and mongoose, and has retractable claws, like a cat's, something not seen in other mongoose species. If approaching head-on, a fossa gives the impression of a scaled-down puma, but a side view shows the snout to be longer than that of the true cats, but shorter and wider than the norm among mongoose species. The gray-brown nostril pad

is furless and prominent, like a dog's. The overall appearance and behavior suggests a cat rather than a dog.

The body is long and sleek and the legs are short but powerful, as in a mongoose. The coat color is rich reddish-brown, the undersides lighter but stained with an orange secretion from skin glands. This secretion is more abundant in males than in females. There are five padded digits on each of the four feet. Though its movements are often considered plantigrade, meaning that the entire foot, from the toetips to the back of the heel, touch the ground when walking, fossas have also been seen to walk digitigrade, that is, only on the toetips. The large, prominent eyes are brown and lustrous, and have pupils that can retract to vertical slits, as in cats. The ears are large, prominent, and narrower than in typical mongoose species.

The fossa was originally classified as a direct descendant, little changed, of the ancestor species that gave rise to cats (Felidae) and dogs (Canidae). That classification arose from both to the appearance of the fossa and to the notion that Madagascar was a natural refuge for primitive mammal species driven to extinction elsewhere by more advanced species. At the same time, the fossa is the living creature closest in form to the dog-cat ancestor. Its classification is still uncertain. Genetic comparison studies strongly support the fossa and the other Malgasy mammal carnivores as being descendants, having changed forms over the ages through adaptive evolution, of a single colonizing species of mongoose. The founder species must have floated from Africa to Madagascar twenty to thirty million years ago. The fossa is the end result of adaptive evolution by which a mongoose, over countless generations, became something like a cat. At the same time, the fossa keeps a number of mongoose-like features. Scientists have found remains of a larger species related to the fossa, since named *Cryptoprocta spelea.*

Geographic range: Fossas live in all of the forested areas of Madagascar.

Habitat: Fossas live in the humid tropical rainforests of Madagascar's east coast and the drier forests along its western coast.

Diet: The fossa is carnivorous and able to deal with nearly all sorts of small to large prey animals on Madagascar, including the larger lemur species, which can be bigger than house cats. Fossas also prey upon snakes, tenrecs (native insectivorous mammals of Madagascar), and rodents, most often introduced rats. Fossas only rarely feed on insects and other invertebrates.

Behavior and reproduction: Fossas hunt at any time of night or day. They can swim and are adept at climbing and jumping among trees while chasing prey. The animals can turn their ankles so that their hindfeet face rearward, a unique adaptation that aids them in keeping a grip on treetrunks. The long tail acts as a balance while the fossa climbs or jumps between trees. Fossas hunt alone, or in family groups made up of a mother and her young.

There is a single annual mating season from October into December. Gestation lasts six to seven weeks. Litters number two to four young. Fossa young are very cute and endearing. They have big ears and eyes, their faces suggest a combination of domestic kitten, puppy, and lion cub, and they stare out at the world with the intent, slightly bewildered stare of young domestic kittens.

Mating is a complex affair, resembling that of cats. A female in heat stations herself in a tree, while several males, following her scent, gather around the tree, vocalizing and fighting among themselves. Then, one at a time, the males climb the tree and are accepted or rejected by the female. If she accepts a male, she will usually walk farther out on a branch but allow the male to mount her from behind, his forepaws resting on her neck, while he gently grips the female's nape in his jaws. A single mating can last for several hours, and the female will mate with several of the gathered males.

Only the mother raises the young, in a tree hollow or a hollowed-out termite nest. The young of both sexes reach sexual maturity at four years. A most interesting phenomenon among female fossa young is that they pass through a brief pseudo-masculine stage in their second year, during times of becoming less dependent on the mother and reaching sexual maturity. Their genitals come to resemble those of an adult male, they leave ano-genital scent markings on objects, as do adult males (adult females do not, except in mating season), and the female young secrete more of the fur-staining orange fluid than do adult females. Why this occurs is unanswered, and the young females lose the masculine characteristics as they approach sexual maturity.

Fossas have been known to live for twenty years in captivity.

Fossas and people: The fossa has not fared well with humans in Madagascar. Fossas raid chicken coops, leaving resentment behind, and an aura of superstitious fear surrounds them.

Conservation status: The fossa is listed as Endangered by the IUCN. Although widespread throughout Madagascar, the fossa's population density and total population are low, making it especially vulnerable to deforestation, which is ongoing and rampant in Madagascar. ■

FOR MORE INFORMATION

Books:

Estes, R. *The Behavior Guide to African Mammals.* Berkeley and Los Angeles: University of California Press, Ltd., 1991.

Garbutt, N. *Mammals of Madagascar.* New Haven, CT.: Yale University Press, 1991.

Goodman, Steven M., and Jonathan P. Benstead, eds. *The Natural History of Madagascar.* Chicago and London: University of Chicago Press, 2003.

Jolly, Alison. *A World Like Our Own: Man and Nature in Madagascar.* New Haven, CT: Yale University Press, 1980.

Periodicals:

Creel, S., Nancy Creel, David E. Wildt, and Steven L. Monfort. "Behavioural and Endocrine Mechanisms of Reproductive Suppression in Serengeti Dwarf Mongooses." *Animal Behaviour* no. 43 (1992): 231–245.

Creel, S. R., "Inclusive Fitness and Reproductive Strategies in Dwarf Mongooses." *Behavioral Ecology* no. 5 (1994): 339–348.

Dollar, Luke, "Assessing IUCN Classifications of Poorly-Known Species: Madagascar's Carnivores as a Case Study." *Small Carnivore Conservation, the Newsletter and Journal of the IUCN/SSC Mustelid, Viverrid and Procyonid Specialist Group* no. 22 (2000): 17–20.

Hawkins, C. E., J. F. Dallas, P. A. Fowler, R. Woodroffe, and P. A. Racey. "Transient Masculinization in the Fossa, *Cryptoprocta ferox* (Carnivora, Viverridae)." *Biology of Reproduction* 66, no. 3 (March 2002): 610–615.

Rasa, O. A. E., "Behavioural Parameters of Vigilance in the Dwarf Mongoose: Social Acquisition of a Sex-Biased Role." *Behaviour* no. 110 (1989): 125–143

Rood, J. P., "Dwarf Mongoose Helpers at the Den." *Zeitschrift fur Tierpsychologie* no. 48 (1978): 277–287

Rood, J. P., "Mating Relationships and Breeding Suppression in the Dwarf Mongoose." *Animal Behavior* no. 28 (1980): 143–150.

Yoder, Anne D., et al. "Single Origin of Malagasy Carnivora from an African Ancestor." *Nature* 421 (2003): 734–737.

Web sites:

"Carnivores of Madagascar." Earthwatch. http://www.earthwatch.org/expeditions/dollar/meetthescientists.html (accessed on July 7, 2004).

family
CHAPTER

PHYSICAL CHARACTERISTICS

The spotted hyena (hi-EE-nah) is the largest of three species that include the striped and brown hyenas. Hyenas weigh about 57 to 190 pounds (26 to 86 kilograms). The aardwolf (ARD-wolf), included in the Hyaenidae family, weighs about 20 to 30 pounds (9 to 14 kilograms). All hyaenids (members of the Hyaenidae family), except the spotted hyena, have long, shaggy coats. A mane of hair down the back can be erected to make the animals look larger. All have a bushy tail and a sloping back. Anal gland secretions are used for marking territories. Spotted hyena females have genitals resembling those of males.

GEOGRAPHIC RANGE

Hyenas and aardwolves are found in the Middle East (including Turkey, Israel, and Saudi Arabia), Pakistan, India, and in Africa south of the Sahara Desert (except the rainforests of The Democratic Republic of the Congo).

HABITAT

Hyenas and aardwolves occupy grasslands, bush country (wild, uncultivated land), and open woodlands. They dig burrows (holes) underground or live in burrows abandoned by other animals.

DIET

The striped and brown hyenas are mainly scavengers, feeding off the leftover kills of other animals. They also eat hares (relatives of rabbits), rodents, reptiles, vegetables, and fruits. Brown hyenas along the Namib Desert eat South African fur seal pups

phylum

class

subclass

order

monotypic order

suborder

▲ **family**

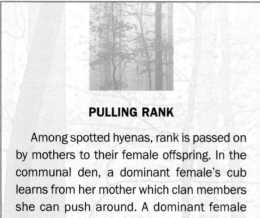

PULLING RANK

Among spotted hyenas, rank is passed on by mothers to their female offspring. In the communal den, a dominant female's cub learns from her mother which clan members she can push around. A dominant female will attack a subordinate female, which encourages her offspring to do the same. After repeated aggressive displays by her mother, the cub starts bullying the offspring of subordinate females. The dominant female participates in the bullying.

and other sea organisms. The spotted hyena mostly hunts its own prey, such as gazelles, antelopes, wildebeests, and zebras. Aardwolves feed almost exclusively on termites.

BEHAVIOR AND REPRODUCTION

Spotted and brown hyenas live in groups called clans, dominated by a female. Striped hyenas are solitary, but small family groups may share a den. Females of spotted and brown hyenas stay with the clan for life. Male spotted hyenas are driven from the clan upon puberty, while male brown hyenas may choose to stay with the clan or leave. Hyenas scent mark territories by depositing anal secretions on grass stalks. Aardwolves are solitary, although, like hyenas, they communicate through scent marking. Hyaenids are active at night or at dawn and dusk.

Spotted and striped hyenas breed year round, while brown hyenas are seasonal breeders. Litter size varies, with one to two cubs for the spotted hyena, up to four for the striped hyena, and as many as six for the brown hyena. Brown and striped hyenas wean their young at about one year, while the spotted hyena nurses for up to a year and a half. Aardwolves may be seasonal or nonseasonal breeders, giving birth to two to four cubs, who leave home by age one.

HYAENIDS AND PEOPLE

Some African cultures believe hyenas possess magical powers. Others consider hyenas as pests for preying on domestic livestock. The brown hyena is a popular exhibit animal in zoos. In Africa, garbage is left out for the spotted and striped hyenas to eat. Aardwolves are useful to humans for eating termites.

CONSERVATION STATUS

The World Conservation Union (IUCN) lists the brown and striped hyenas as not currently threatened, but may become threatened because of, among other things, accidental killing from the poison-spraying of pests. The spotted hyena also may become threatened because of killing by humans and habitat loss or degradation as a result of land clearing for agriculture and livestock. The aardwolf is not a threatened species.

Spotted hyena (*Crocuta crocuta*)

SPOTTED HYENA
Crocuta crocuta

Physical characteristics: Spotted hyenas range in color from sandy to brown, with black or dark brown spots. The short, bushy tail is black. The sloping back, caused by front legs that are longer than the hind legs, allows for long-distance pursuit of prey. The massive jaws can crush bones, teeth, hooves, and horns. The neck and back are covered with a short mane of hair that can be raised to make the hyena seem larger.

Females are larger than males. In southern Africa, females weigh up to 190 pounds (85 kilograms) and males up to 135 pounds (60 kilograms). Eastern African hyenas are lighter, with females weighing about 125 pounds (55 kilograms) and males about 110 pounds (49 kilograms). The female's genital organ resembles that of the male

Spotted hyenas hunt animals that are much larger than they are, such as antelopes, zebras, and young giraffes. (Norman O. Tomalin/Bruce Coleman Inc. Reproduced by permission.)

because of overproduction of testosterone, the male hormone responsible for the development of the penis. The female mates and gives birth through her pseudopenis (SUE-doh-pee-nis).

Geographic range: Spotted hyenas are found in Africa in countries such as Chad, Sudan, Angola, Zambia, and Zimbabwe.

Habitat: Spotted hyenas prefer grasslands inhabited by their herbivorous (plant-eating) prey, such as antelopes and wildebeests. They also occupy woodlands and semi-deserts.

Diet: Spotted hyenas mostly hunt rather than scavenge food. They prey on animals several times their size, including gazelles, antelopes, wildebeests, and zebras. They also eat the young of giraffes, hippotamuses, and rhinoceroses, as well as reptiles, domestic livestock, and human garbage. They tear pieces of flesh from prey, killing it in a few minutes. They eat very fast, consuming flesh, skin, teeth, bones, horns, and even hooves. A hyena can eat 33 pounds (15 kilograms) of meat per feeding, throwing up indigestible food as pellets.

Behavior and reproduction: Hyenas live in clans of as many as eighty members, ruled by a dominant female. Daughters inherit their mothers' status. Males are submissive to all females and to the dominant female's offspring. Young males are expelled from their homes between ages two to four. They join other clans, starting at the lowest rank. Sons of dominant females may be allowed to stay longer and are more likely to become dominant males in the clan they join. Female members occupy the same territory, defending it against intruders, sometimes to the death.

Spotted hyenas are either nocturnal (active at night) or crepuscular (active at dusk and dawn). They hunt alone, although they will join forces to catch large prey. They chase down their prey, running 25 to 31 miles (40 to 50 kilometers) per hour and covering a distance of up to 3 miles (5 kilometers). They target young, old, and sick animals.

The spotted hyena is also called the "laughing hyena" because of its high, cackling laugh. It laughs when it is being chased or attacked or to show submission. Hyenas whoop to call clan members to defend territory or to hunt. Greetings involve sniffing each other's genital areas. They scent-mark territories with anal secretions and feces.

Adults get together only to mate, which may be at any time of the year. A long pregnancy (up to four months) results in well-developed cubs, usually one or two, born with teeth and able to walk. Cubs are kept in a small den inaccessible to adults and predators. When female cubs come out to nurse, they compete for their mother's milk, sometimes resulting in the death of the sibling who cannot nurse. Within the den, cubs may kill littermates during fights for dominance. After two to four weeks, the mother takes her young to a communal den, where cubs of all ages are raised together. Mothers do not nurse each other's young. Cubs learn to recognize clan members and establish social rankings. They are weaned from their mothers' milk at about fourteen to eighteen months. Males do not share in parenting.

Spotted hyenas and people: Some African cultures believe hyenas possess magical powers. Humans kill hyenas for preying on domestic livestock.

Conservation status: The IUCN lists the spotted hyena as Lower Risk/Conservation Dependent (could become threatened) due to killing by humans and habitat loss or degradation as a result of land clearing for agriculture and livestock.   ■

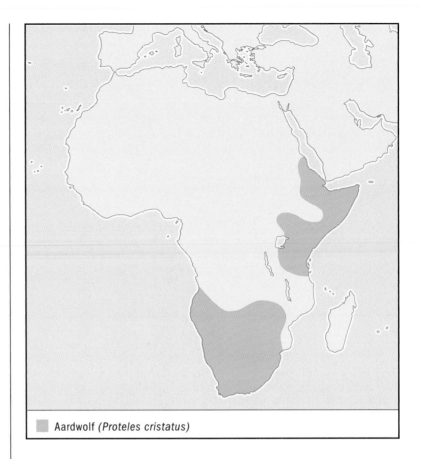

Aardwolf (*Proteles cristatus*)

AARDWOLF
Proteles cristatus

Physical characteristics: The aardwolf is yellowish white to reddish brown, with several black stripes along the body and legs. A dark mane running from the back of the head down to the tail can be erected to make the aardwolf seem bigger. A sloping back results from hind legs that are longer than the forelegs. The teeth are very small and widely spaced. The spatula-shaped tongue and sticky saliva are adapted for licking up termites. Sharp canine teeth are designed for fighting enemies. Both sexes are about the same size, about 20 pounds (9 kilograms) in southern Africa and up to 30 pounds (14 kilograms) in East Africa.

Geographic range: Aardwolves are found in Africa, including South Africa, Botswana, Zambia, Kenya, and Somalia.

Habitat: Aardwolves prefer grassland, open country, and rocky areas, where they live in burrows they have dug up or taken from aardvarks or springhares.

Diet: Aardwolves feed primarily on two varieties of termites that forage on the ground surface. They can eat about 200,000 termites a night. They also eat other insects, small birds, eggs, mice, and carrion (dead or decaying animal flesh).

Behavior and reproduction: Aardwolves are solitary, feeding at night when their favorite termites emerge. When these termites become inactive in winter, aardwolves switch to another termite species that are active in the late afternoon. When scared or threatened, aardwolves roar and growl. They scent mark territories by depositing anal secretions on grasses. Aardwolves within the same territory erect their back hair until they recognize each other. Mothers and young sniff each other's noses to establish identity. Aardwolves generally mate with just one partner, although a dominant male may mate with the partner of a subordinate male. The litter consists of two to four cubs. Males babysit the young, guarding the den against predators when the mothers feed. The young leave home by one year of age.

Aardwolves and people: Aardwolves may be hunted as a food source. They sometimes are poisoned when pesticides are sprayed to control locusts in some areas.

Conservation status: Aardwolves are not a threatened species. ∎

Aardwolves can eat 200,000 termites during one night of feeding. (© Terry Whittaker/ Corbis. Reproduced by permission.)

FOR MORE INFORMATION

Books:

Angier, Natalie. "Hyenas' Hormone Flow Puts Females in Charge." In *The Science Times Book of Mammals.* New York: The Lyons Press, 1999.

Estes, Richard D. *The Behavior Guide to African Mammals: Including Hoofed Mammals, Carnivores, Primates.* Berkeley, CA: The University of California Press, 1991.

Ewer, R. F. *The Carnivores.* Ithaca, NY: Comstock Publishing Associates, 1998.

Mills, Gus, Heribert Hofer, and IUCN/SSC Hyaena Specialist Group. *Status Survey and Conservation Action Plan: Hyaenas.* Gland, Switzerland, and Cambridge, U.K.: IUCN, 1998.

Morgan, Sally. *Hyenas.* Austin, TX: Raintree Steck-Vaughn Publishers, 2003.

Nowak, Ronald M. "Striped and Brown Hyenas." *Walker's Mammals of the World Online 5.1.* Baltimore: Johns Hopkins University Press, 1997. http://www.press.jhu.edu/books/walkers_mammals_of_the_world/carnivora/carnivora.hyaenidae.hyaena.html (accessed on June 21, 2004).

Periodicals:

Holekamp, Kay E, and Laura Smale. "Behavioral Development in the Spotted Hyena." *BioScience* (December 1998): 997–1005.

Koehler, C. E., and P. R. K. Richardson. "*Proteles cristatus.*" *Mammalian Species* 363 (October 23, 1990): 1–6.

Pickrell, John. "Rebranding the Hyena." *Science News* (April 27, 2002): 267–269.

Rieger, Ingo. "*Hyaena hyaena.*" *Mammalian Species* 150 (May 8, 1981): 1–5.

Web sites:

"Spotted Hyena." Woodland Park Zoo Animal Fact Sheets. http://www.zoo.org/educate/fact_sheets/savana/hyena.htm (accessed on June 21, 2004).

Class: Mammalia
Order: Carnivora
Family: Felidae
Number of species: 36 species

family
CHAPTER

PHYSICAL CHARACTERISTICS

Cats range in color from pale gray to brown, many with rosettes, spots, and stripes that help them blend in with their natural surroundings. The head is rounded, with a short snout. Ears are rounded or pointed. Sensitive whiskers are useful for night movements and for inflicting the fatal bite on a prey's body. Tiny, rough projections on the tongue are used to scrape meat off bones. Feet are padded for quiet stalking of prey. Claws in most species are retractable, or can be pulled back into a sheath of skin, to keep the nails sharp for climbing trees and clasping prey. The cat's ability to land on its feet from a fall is due to a flexible spine that can turn the body around.

GEOGRAPHIC RANGE

Cats naturally occur in most areas of the world, except Australia, the polar regions, and some oceanic islands.

HABITAT

Cats inhabit all types of habitats with the exception of tundra and polar ice. Most species occupy more than one type of habitat.

DIET

Large cats prey on ungulates (hoofed animals) such as deer, zebras, and wildebeests, but also eat other meat. Small cats eat rabbits, hares, rodents, snakes, frogs, fish, and birds. Many consume carrion (dead and decaying flesh).

phylum
class
subclass
order
monotypic order
suborder
▲ **family**

IS IT REALLY TEAMWORK?

Contrary to popular opinion, lions who hunt together do not necessarily team up to catch a prey animal. If members of the pride see that a lone member might be able to overcome the prey, they simply watch and wait to share the food. Only when the members realize that a large prey cannot be caught unassisted would they risk injury and jump in to help.

BEHAVIOR AND REPRODUCTION

Most cats are solitary, except when mating and raising young. Only lions form social groups. Cats defend territories but avoid physical confrontations through different means of communication. They scrape tree trunks and scent-mark with urine and feces. They use sounds, including roars, meows, purrs, hisses, and growls. They also use body language. Most hunt at night, but may show increased activity at dawn and dusk. Many are excellent climbers, and some are good swimmers. Males and females have several mating partners, producing an average of two to four kittens per litter. The young stay with their mother for up to eighteen months, longer for big cats.

CATS AND PEOPLE

The African wild cat is considered the ancestor of domestic cats. Experts believe ancient Egyptians tamed the cat to catch rodents. Cats are prized for their fur and as trophies. Some are popular exhibit animals in zoos. Large cats prey on humans and livestock.

CONSERVATION STATUS

The United States classifies the Florida panther and the eastern puma as Endangered. The World Conservation Union (IUCN) lists the Iberian lynx as Critically Endangered, facing an extremely high risk of extinction in the wild; four species as Endangered, facing a very high risk of extinction; twelve species as Vulnerable, facing a high risk of extinction; and eight species as Near Threatened, not currently threatened, but could become so.

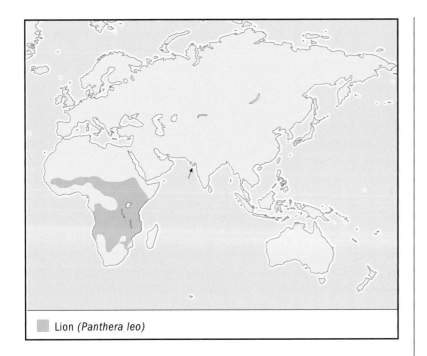

Lion *(Panthera leo)*

LION
Panthera leo

Physical characteristics: Lions have a short orange-brown coat tinged with gold. Males have manes, used for gender recognition at distances and protection during fights. A dark clump of fur covers the tail tip. Enormous shoulders and muscular legs are used to tackle large prey. Powerful jaws grasp prey and cut through tough skin. Lions measure 62 to 100 inches (160 to 250 centimeters), and another 24 to 40 inches (60 to 100 centimeters) for the tail. They weigh 270 to 570 pounds (120 to 260 kilograms).

Geographic range: Lions occur in countries south of the Saharan Desert, including Angola, Botswana, Ethiopia, Kenya, and Tanzania. The Asiatic lion lives in western India.

Habitat: Lions prefer a mixture of thick bush, scrub, and grass that afford cover for stalking and ambushing prey. They also live in open woodlands and deserts.

Female lions may give birth to one to six cubs at a time. Mothers help to nurse and raise each other's cubs. (Joe McDonald/Bruce Coleman Inc. Reproduced by permission.)

Diet: Lions prey on buffalo, zebra, and wildebeest. They also eat rodents, lizards, birds, and grass. An adult male eats as much as 110 pounds (50 kilograms) per feeding, but may fast (go without food) for several days.

Behavior and reproduction: Lions live in groups called prides, consisting of two to eighteen related females, their cubs, and one to seven unrelated males. Every two or three years, adult male groups called coalitions try to take over prides to mate with the females. If the newcomers win, they attempt to kill the resident cubs in order to produce their own. Mothers band together to defend their young.

Mothers who lose their young become receptive to mating, pairing off with several partners, and giving birth to one to six cubs. Mothers share nursing and cub rearing. Between ages two to four, young males are driven from the pride by dominant males or the new coalition. Females stay with the pride for life, doing most of the hunting at night. Males advertise territorial boundaries through urine markings and group roars.

Lions and people: Many African cultures believe the lion's body parts have magical and healing powers. Lions may be killed as threats to humans and livestock.

Conservation status: The lion is listed as Vulnerable and the Asiatic lion as Critically Endangered due to habitat and prey base (the animals lions hunt for food) loss, as well as killings by humans. ■

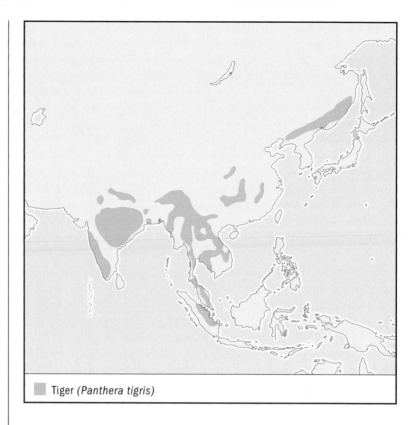

Tiger (*Panthera tigris*)

TIGER
Panthera tigris

Physical characteristics: The largest of cats, tigers range in color from pale yellow to reddish ochre (brownish yellow). Each tiger has a black stripe pattern that is uniquely its own. In the wild, tigers blend in with the natural background, especially against tall grasses, which break up their body shape. Males have a ruff of hair around the face. Ears are black with a white circle in the middle. The body length is 75 to 150 inches (190 to 310 centimeters). The tail measures 28 to 40 inches (70 to 100 centimeters). Tigers weigh 140 to 670 pounds (65 to 306 kilograms).

Geographic range: Tigers are found in Bangladesh, China, India, Myanmar, Sumatra, and Russia.

Habitat: Tigers inhabit coniferous and deciduous forests that provide prey and cover. They also inhabit jungle grasslands and mangrove swamps. They need water for drinking and swimming.

Diet: Tigers prey on deer, wild pigs, wild cattle, and occasionally young elephants and rhinoceroses, birds, reptiles, and fish. An adult eats up to 90 pounds (40 kilograms) per feeding. It hides surplus kill to eat later.

Behavior and reproduction: Tigers are solitary, hunting at night. Good swimmers, they will pursue an animal into the water. They roar to advertise ownership of a territory. They further communicate through scratches on trees and scent marks with urine, feces, and anal and cheek secretions.

A male and female pair off briefly, producing an average of two to three cubs. The mother rears the young for about two years. Young females stay close to their mother's home range, but young males may travel far to secure their own territories. When a male takes over another's territory, he kills the cubs because a tigress will not mate while caring for her young.

Tigers and people: Tigers represent either good or bad spirits in some religions. They are illegally hunted for their fur. Body parts are used by some Asian cultures for medicine. They are killed for attacking humans and livestock.

Conservation status: The tiger is listed as Endangered due to habitat loss, illegal hunting for fur and traditional medicine, and declining prey. ■

Puma (*Puma concolor*)

PUMA
Puma concolor

Physical characteristics: The puma, also known as cougar, panther, or mountain lion, has coloration ranging from silvery gray to reddish brown. Having the longest hind legs of all cats, the puma can jump 18 feet (5.5 meters) up a tree. Pumas measure 41 to 77 inches (105 to 196 centimeters), with another 26 to 31 inches

A puma can take down a large animal by breaking the animal's neck with its powerful jaws. (© Charles Krebs/Corbis. Reproduced by permission.)

(67 to 78 centimeters) for the tail. They weigh about 75 to 264 pounds (34 to 120 kilograms).

Geographic range: Pumas are found in the United States, Canada, Mexico, South America (including Argentina, Bolivia, and Venezuela), and Central America (including Costa Rica, Guatemala, and Panama).

Habitat: Pumas prefer forested areas with cover for hunting and resting. They are adaptable, also occupying mountain areas, swampland, and grassland. They thrive in the desert, getting moisture from the flesh of prey.

Diet: Pumas feed on deer and other large ungulates, large rodents, rabbits, raccoons, and even bats, grasshoppers, and occasionally domestic livestock. A puma eats 20 to 30 pounds (9.1 to 13.6 kilograms) of meat per feeding, burying extra kill and returning later to feed.

Behavior and reproduction: Pumas are solitary animals, mostly hunting at night. They mark territorial boundaries with urine, feces, and scrapes on tree trunks. Scent marks are also used for mating signals. Pumas cannot roar but communicate through squeaks, purrs, growls, and hisses. Both sexes have several partners, mating throughout the year. Females give birth every other year to one to six kittens, making the young leave her territory after about two years.

Pumas and people: Human expansion into puma habitat has resulted in close encounters with the animals. Pumas in the suburbs and cities are likely to be killed.

Conservation status: The United States classifies the Florida panther and the eastern puma as Endangered due to habitat loss to forest clearance, prey reduction, and human expansion. The IUCN lists the puma as Near Threatened. ∎

Snow leopard (*Uncia uncia*)

SNOW LEOPARD
Uncia uncia

Physical characteristics: Snow leopards are light gray with black-brown rosettes and spots and sides tinged with yellow. This leopard measures 39 to 51 inches (99 to 130 centimeters). The furry tail, nearly as long as the body, acts as a warm wrap during sleep or rest and provides balance during leaps. An enlarged nasal cavity warms cold air entering the body. Long hind legs are adapted for jumping up to 45 feet (14 meters), while wide, furred paws are designed for walking on snow. Snow leopards weigh 77 to 120 pounds (35 to 55 kilograms).

Geographic range: Snow leopards occur in Afghanistan, Bhutan, China, India, Kazakhstan, Kyrgyzstan, Mongolia, Nepal, Pakistan, Russia, Tajikistan, and Uzbekistan.

Snow leopards live in high mountain regions, preferring areas near cliffs and ridges. (Cincinnati Zoo. Reproduced by permission.)

Habitat: Snow leopards live in high mountain regions, preferring steep, broken areas near cliffs and ridges. They also inhabit arid or semi-arid shrubland.

Diet: Snow leopards feed mainly on blue sheep and ibex, a wild goat. They also eat small animals, including marmots, hares, and game birds. They may take livestock, including young yaks, sheep, goats, and horses. They occasionally eat plants.

Behavior and reproduction: Snow leopards are generally active at dawn and dusk. They are solitary but communicate by scent marking with urine, feces, and scratches on the ground and tree trunks. They cannot roar but make sounds, including screams, hisses, and mews. Leopards pair off only to mate, averaging two to three cubs. The cubs stay with their mother for about two years.

Snow leopards and people: Snow leopards' bones and body parts have replaced tiger parts in traditional Asian medicine. Illegal hunting for fur continues in some Asian countries. Snow leopards are also killed for preying on domestic livestock.

Conservation status: The IUCN lists the snow leopard as Endangered due to several factors: loss of prey, killing by herders, poaching, and habitat loss and fragmentation due to human activities, especially the raising of livestock. ■

Bobcat (*Lynx rufus*)

BOBCAT
Lynx rufus

Physical characteristics: Bobcats have a light gray to reddish brown coat covered with black spots and bars. The tip of the "bobbed," or short, tail is black on the upper side. The face is framed in bushy hair. Black ears with a white center have long hairs inside that are very sensitive to sound. A shoulder height of 18 to 23 inches (46 to 58 centimeters), thick fur, and large ears give the appearance of a larger size. Bobcats measure 24 to 42 inches (62 to 106 centimeters) in length, and the tail is another 5 to 8 inches (13 to 20 centimeters). It weighs 13 to 37 pounds (6 to 17 kilograms).

Geographic range: Bobcats are found in the United States, Canada, and Mexico.

Habitat: Bobcats inhabit coniferous forests, mixed coniferous and deciduous forests, swamps, and desert scrub. They prefer thick

understory (short vegetation under taller trees) for the cover provided by the dappled shade of tall trees.

Diet: Bobcats mainly eat rabbits and hares. They also feed on rodents, large birds, snakes, fruits, and carrion. They prey on deer, which are taken when resting.

Behavior and reproduction: Bobcats are active at all hours, but most active at dawn and dusk. They are good climbers and may rest in trees. They are also excellent swimmers. Bobcats scent mark territorial boundaries with urine and feces. They are solitary, except when mating and raising young. Males have several partners. An average litter consists of two to three kittens, which stay with their mother for nine to ten months. Young females stay close to their mothers' home ranges, while young males may travel far to establish their own territories.

Bobcats and people: In the 1960s and 1970s, bobcat furs were in high demand due to restrictions in the trade of other cat furs. Demand for the furs continues, and research regarding the harvest of bobcat fur continues as well.

Bobcats eat mainly hares and rabbits, but also prey on deer, which they can take when the deer are resting. (Erwin and Peggy Bauer/Bruce Coleman Inc. Reproduced by permission.)

Conservation status: The bobcat is not a threatened species. ■

FOR MORE INFORMATION

Books:

Aaseng, Nathan. *The Cougar.* San Diego, CA: Lucent Books, Inc., 2001.

Alderton, David. *Wild Cats of the World.* New York: Facts on File, Inc., 1993.

Lumpkin, Susan. *Small Cats.* New York: Facts on File, Inc., 1993.

Malaspina, Ann. *The Jaguar.* San Diego, CA: Lucent Books, Inc., 2001.

Schlaepfer, Gloria G. *Cheetahs.* New York: Benchmark Books, 2002.

Seidensticker, John. *Tigers.* Stillwater, MN: Voyageur Press, Inc., 1996.

Periodicals:

Newman, Cathy. "Nature's Masterwork: Cats." *National Geographic* (June 1997): 54–76.

Packer, Craig, and Anne E. Pusey. "Divided We Fall: Cooperation among Lions." *Scientific American* (May 1997): 52–59.

Web sites:

"All About Tigers." The Tiger Information Center. http://www.5tigers.org/Directory/allabouttigers.htm (accessed on June 23, 2004).

"Cheetahs in a Hot Spot." Public Broadcasting Service (PBS) Nature. http://www.pbs.org/wnet/nature/cheetahs/index.html (accessed on June 23, 2004).

"Great Cats." Smithsonian National Zoological Park. http://nationalzoo.si.edu/Animals/GreatCats/catfacts.cfm (accessed on June 23, 2004).

"Species Accounts." IUCN Species Survival Commission: Cat Specialist Group. http://lynx.uio.no/catfolk/sp-accts.htm (accessed on June 23, 2004).

EARED SEALS, FUR SEALS, AND SEA LIONS
Otariidae

Class: Mammalia
Order: Carnivora
Family: Otariidae
Number of species: 15 species

PHYSICAL CHARACTERISTICS

Otariids, eared seals, have streamlined, smooth, bodies that allow them to move easily through water. A layer of blubber, or fat, provides insulation. The dog-like head has small external flaps for ears. Long whiskers are sensors for finding food and alerting against predators. Flippers can be turned forward for walking on land. In water, the front flippers function as oars, while the back flippers steer and provide balance. Males are two to four times larger than females.

GEOGRAPHIC RANGE

Otariids haul out on land near the waters they inhabit, including the United States, Canada, Mexico, Argentina, Chile, Ecuador, Peru, Japan, Australia, and New Zealand.

HABITAT

When breeding or molting, shedding fur, otariids gather on rocky coastlines, sandy and gravel beaches, and caves. They also breed in mainland areas in Africa, Argentina, and Peru.

DIET

Otariids feed on krill, a small shrimp-like animal, fish, crustaceans like shrimps, crabs, and lobsters, mollusks such as clams, mussels, squid, and octopuses, and penguins. A small fur seal weighing 110 pounds (50 kilograms) consumes about 4 to 5 pounds (1.8 to 2.3 kilograms) of food per feeding.

ADJUSTABLE EYES

An eared seal's eyes are adapted for seeing in hazy seawater and bright sunlight. Underwater, the pupil, or opening at the front of the eye, expands to let in as much light as possible. In addition, a mirror-like layer behind the eyes reflects light back to the retina, increasing the amount of light entering the eyes. Out of the water, the pupil adjusts to the bright sunlight by narrowing into a tiny pinhole.

BEHAVIOR AND REPRODUCTION

Otariids are active both day and night. Expert divers, they swim to the deepest parts of the ocean floor to forage, find food. They breed annually, except for the Australian sea lion that breeds every seventeen-and-a-half months. Some species migrate far to rookeries, breeding colonies. Females give birth to one pup a year.

OTARIIDS AND PEOPLE

In the nineteenth century, fur seals were hunted for their fur, meat, and blubber. Today fishermen consider seals as competitors for fish. Seals' body parts may be used as aphrodisiacs, believed to increase sexual desire, or ornaments. Seals may be threatened by pollution caused by humans.

CONSERVATION STATUS

The World Conservation Union (IUCN) and the United States classify the Steller sea lion as Endangered, facing an extremely high risk of extinction in the wild. They are at risk due to extensive commercial fishing of pollock, its major prey fish, human pollution, accidental tangling in commercial fishing gear, and hunting by humans.

The IUCN lists many otariids as Vulnerable, facing a high risk of extinction in the wild. The Galápagos fur seal is vulnerable due to parasites and predators. The Juan Fernández fur seal is threatened by a limited population as a result of inbreeding. Guadalupe fur seals are vulnerable because of excessive harvesting. Northern fur seals are endangered by habitat loss or degradation due to human activities. Hooker's sea lions are at risk due to accidental entanglement in fishing gear and human hunting. Finally the Galápagos sea lion is vulnerable as a result of El Niño events, illegal hunting, and tangling in fishing gear.

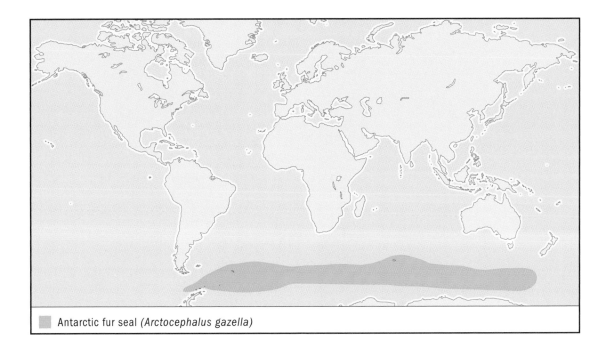

Antarctic fur seal (*Arctocephalus gazella*)

ANTARCTIC FUR SEAL
Arctocephalus gazella

Physical characteristics: Antarctic fur seals have a thick water-proof underfur and an overcoat of long guard hairs. Bulls, adult males, are dark brown or charcoal-gray. A long mane of hair protects bulls when fighting over breeding territories. Bulls measure about 6 feet 7 inches (2 meters) long and weigh up to 440 pounds (200 kilograms). Adult females, cows, are smaller in size, about 4 feet 5 inches (1.4 meters) long and weigh up to 110 pounds (50 kilograms). They are gray, with cream-colored throat and chest.

Geographic range: Antarctic fur seals live in the Southern Ocean surrounding Antarctica. They breed on the islands south of, or close to, the Antarctic polar front. About 95 percent breed on South Georgia in the South Atlantic Ocean.

Habitat: Antarctic fur seals live in the open seas and congregate on land to breed, molt, and rest.

Antarctic fur seal pups stay on land for about four months. Growing seals stay at sea for several years, returning only when they're ready to mate. (© Paul A. Souders/Corbis. Reproduced by permission.)

Diet: Antarctic fur seals are the only otariids that feed mainly on krill. They sometimes consume fish, squid, and birds.

Behavior and reproduction: Antarctic fur seals are solitary, alone, at sea, usually foraging at night. Adult and subadult males congregate on land to molt. Cows may assemble in herds but do not socialize. Growing seals stay at sea for several years, only returning to their birthplaces to mate for the first time.

In late October, bulls arrive at rookeries to claim territories. They quarrel, sometimes biting one another. Males fast, go without food, for as long as two months while protecting their territory. In November, cows arrive, choose a bull's territory, and give birth to a single pup conceived the previous year. A bull has an average of eleven to sixteen cows in his territory. At birth, the pup vocalizes with its mother. After nursing for a week to ten days, the cow mates with the territorial bull. The female then feeds at sea for up to six days. A returning mother calls out to her pup who answers back. After smelling the pup to make sure it is hers, and then nurses for three or more days. The periodic foraging and nursing lasts about four months. In April, all seals leave for the sea, each going its own way.

Antarctic fur seals and people: Once hunted almost to extinction for their fur, meat, and blubber, these seals are currently protected by international agreements and by the islands where they breed.

Conservation status: The Antarctic fur seal is not a threatened species. ■

California sea lion *(Zalophus californianus)*

CALIFORNIA SEA LION
Zalophus californianus

Physical characteristics: California sea lions have a torpedo-like body, with flippers for swimming and moving on land. Males have brown or black fur, a bulky upper body, and a thick mane over the shoulders. A crest, or a distinctive bump on the forehead, is topped with blonde or light brown hair. They weigh as much as 772 pounds (350 kilograms). Females are much lighter, weighing up to 220 pounds (100 kilograms), and are tan in color.

Geographic range: California sea lions live in the Pacific Ocean along central Mexico to southern California. In between breeding seasons, males migrate, travel, to feeding sites off Oregon, Washington, and British Columbia, Canada.

Habitat: California sea lions breed on sandy, gravel, or rocky beaches.

Diet: California sea lions are opportunistic feeders, eating whatever is available. They feed mainly on squid and octopuses, but also consume fish, including anchovies, salmon, rockfish, and small sharks. They eat at all hours of the day. They typically swallow small prey whole in water but take bigger prey to land to shake them into small pieces. Males prey on northern fur seal pups and small true seals.

Behavior and reproduction: California sea lions are active the whole day. They are the fastest marine carnivore and can swim up to 25 miles (40 kilometers) per hour. They often swim in groups, covering large distances by porpoising, leaping over water. They also rest together on the water surface in a horizontal position called rafting.

Breeding season lasts from May through July. Bulls wait for the pregnant cows to come ashore before establishing territories. After giving birth to one pup, mothers nurse their young, then forage at sea, sometimes taking the newborn with them. Three or four weeks later, mating occurs in the water. Mothers recognize their pup by sound and smell. A pup may nurse for a whole year at the rookery. The males leave for the ocean soon after breeding.

California sea lions and people: California sea lions are most familiar as talented performers in marine parks and circuses. Some fishermen consider them pests because they steal fish from nets. Sea lions have been trained by the U.S. Navy to detect suspicious swimmers and divers near military ships and ports because they have excellent underwater directional hearing and low-light vision and are able to make repeated deep dives. A sea lion can approach an intruder without being heard. Using its flippers, it will clamp a handcuffs-like device carried in its mouth onto the person's leg, allowing sailors to apprehend the suspect. The U.S. Navy has normally relied on sea lions to recover practice mines undersea.

Conservation status: The California sea lion is not a threatened species. ■

Galápagos sea lion (*Zalophus wollebaeki*)

GALÁPAGOS SEA LION
Zalophus wollebaeki

Physical characteristics: Male Galápagos sea lions are dark brown to black, weigh up to 550 pounds (250 kilograms), and have a bump on the forehead. Females are lighter, weighing as much as 176 pounds (80 kilograms) and are tan or blonde in color.

Geographic range: Galápagos sea lions inhabit the Galápagos Islands, a group of islands considered a province of Ecuador.

Habitat: Galápagos sea lions favor gently sloping sandy and rocky beaches for breeding.

Diet: Galápagos sea lions feed on squid and fish, including sardines, anchovies, mackerel, and rockfish in the upwelling waters, nutrient-rich waters rising from the ocean depths, along the coasts. During El Niño events, when fish populations either die or migrate, sea lions dive down deeper into the ocean to feed on lantern fish.

Behavior and reproduction: Galápagos sea lions stay on the islands year round. During the day, they forage in waters close to the islands. The breeding season is long, lasting from May to January. The cow nurses her pup for about a week, then feeds at sea, returning periodically to nurse. Three weeks after giving birth, cows are ready to mate. A bull may have as many as thirty cows in his territory. Some cows ignore boundaries, seeking males in other territories. Mating occurs in shallow water or on land. Bulls may help guard pups from sharks by a warning call or by moving them away from the water. Pups nurse for up to a year or until a sibling is born. Some cows nurse both the yearling and the newborn for another year.

Galápagos sea lions and people: Galápagos sea lions are popular tourist attractions on the islands. They are illegally hunted for their teeth for adornment, and the male genitals are believed to be aphrodisiacs, items that intensify or arouse sexual desires, in some Asian cultures.

Conservation status: The IUCN lists the Galápagos sea lion as Vulnerable due to El Niño events, tangling in fishing gear, and illegal hunting for body parts. ■

FOR MORE INFORMATION

Books:

Bonner, Nigel. *Seals and Sea Lions of the World.* New York: Facts on File, Inc., 1994.

DuTemple, Leslie A. *Seals and Sea Lions.* San Diego, CA: Lucent Books, Inc., 1999.

Grace, Eric S. *Sierra Club Wildlife Library: Seals.* Boston: Little, Brown and Company, 1991.

Jackson, Michael H. *Galápagos: A Natural History Guide.* Calgary, Canada: The University of Calgary Press, 1985.

Miller, David. *Seals & Sea Lions.* Stillwater, MN: Voyageur Press, 1998.

Nowak, Ronald M. "California Sea Lion." *Walker's Mammals of the World Online. 5.1* Baltimore: Johns Hopkins University Press, 1997. http://www.press.jhu.edu/books/walkers_mammals_of_the_world/pinnipedia/pinnipedia.otariidae.zalophus.html (accessed on July 7, 2004).

Patent, Dorothy Hinshaw. *Seals, Sea Lions and Walruses.* New York: Holiday House, 1990.

Reeves, Randall R., Brent S. Stewart, Phillip J. Clapham, and James A. Powell. *Guide to Marine Mammals of the World.* New York: Alfred A. Knopf, 2002.

Periodicals:

Holmes, Bob. "Exploring the Sensory Lives of Sea Lions." *Ranger Rick* (June 2000): 2.

Momatiuk, Yva, and John Eastcott. "The Art of Bullying (Behavior of Northern Fur Seals)." *National Wildlife* (August–September 1999): 50–56.

Nelson, Roxanne. "The Blubber Bunch at Pier 39." *Ranger Rick* (November 1996): 14–16.

Web sites:

Bruemmer, Fred. "Comeback on a Castaway's Island." National Wildlife Federation.   http://www.nwf.org/internationalwildlife/2001/seal.html (accessed on July 7, 2004).

"Golden Seals of the Skeleton Coast: Life amid the Wrecks." Public Broadcasting Service (PBS) Nature. http://www.pbs.org/wnet/nature/ goldenseals/index.html (accessed on July 7, 2004).

Murphy, Verity. "Let Slip the Sea Lions of War." BBC News Online. http://news.bbc.co.uk/1/hi/world/middle_east/2839155.stm (accessed on July 7, 2004).

"Pinniped Species Information Page." Seal Conservation Society. http://www.pinnipeds.org/species/species.htm (accessed on July 7, 2004).

"Steller Sea Lion Biology." North Pacific Universities Marine Mammal Research Consortium. http://www.marinemammal.org/steller_sea_lion/ fastfacts.html (accessed on July 7, 2004).

WALRUS

Odobenidae

Class: Mammalia

Order: Carnivora

Family: Odobenidae

One species: Walrus (*Odobenus rosmarus*)

family

CHAPTER

PHYSICAL CHARACTERISTICS

The walrus is the second largest pinniped, after the elephant seal. Walruses are 44 to 126 inches (112 to 320 centimeters) long and weigh 139 to 2,662 pounds (63 to 1,210 kilograms). Their streamlined, smooth, body allows for easy movement through water. They are sparsely covered with short, cinnamon brown hair, which is darker in young walruses. In older males, the hair is almost absent, giving a naked appearance. The wrinkled skin measures 0.75 to 2 inches (2 to 5 centimeters) thick. Adult males have large, coarse bumps on the neck and shoulders. Underneath the skin is a layer of blubber, or fat, about 0.4 to 6 inches (1 to 15 centimeters) thick, which protects against the cold and serves as storage for food energy.

Although its head is quite small compared to the rest of its body, the walrus has a powerful skull. If the seawater freezes while the walrus is underwater, it uses its skull like a sledgehammer to break through the ice overhead, up to 8 inches (20 centimeters) in thickness. The walrus has no external ears, just small openings covered by a fold of skin. About 600 to 700 stiff whiskers form a mustache and act as antennas for detecting prey. The thickened upper lip is used to feel around for food in the muddy sediments of the ocean floor. Two air pouches in the throat extend to the shoulders. They can be inflated to function as life preservers, enabling the walrus to sleep or rest in an upright position with its head above water. Males produce bell-like sounds with these inflated air pouches when courting females.

Walruses have webbed flippers. The back flippers act as paddles for swimming, while the front flippers do the steering. On land or ice, walruses use their flippers the same way eared seals use theirs. The back flippers are turned forward and, together with the front flippers, are used for moving around. However, unlike eared seals, walruses cannot lift their enormous body off the ground. They walk by pushing off the ground with the help of the belly and flippers. The thick blubber helps cushion its underparts while walking.

The walrus is known for its long, ivory tusks, which are enlarged upper canine, dagger-like, teeth. The teeth first extend out of the mouth when they are about one year old. The tusks serve many functions. They are used for hauling out (getting out of the water) onto the ice. This is where the first part of the walrus's scientific name came from. The Greek word *odobenus* means "tooth walker" or "one who walks on his teeth." The tusks are also used to threaten rivals for breeding territories and for actual fights. Dominant males typically have larger tusks and use them as power displays. Walruses sometimes use their tusks to support their head while sleeping or resting on ice. They sleep or rest vertically in water with the tusks hooked over the edge of an ice floe, a large sheet of floating ice. The tusks grow with age. In adult males, they can grow up to 3 feet (1 meter) long and weigh about 12 pounds (nearly 5.5 kilograms) each.

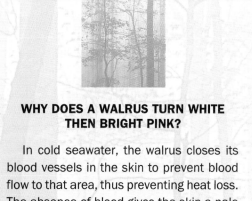

WHY DOES A WALRUS TURN WHITE THEN BRIGHT PINK?

In cold seawater, the walrus closes its blood vessels in the skin to prevent blood flow to that area, thus preventing heat loss. The absence of blood gives the skin a pale appearance. On land under the sun, the walrus's thick blubber makes it feel hot. To prevent overheating, blood vessels in the skin are opened to carry heat from inside the body and get rid of it through the skin, turning it pink.

GEOGRAPHIC RANGE

Walruses are found mainly in the coastal areas of the Arctic Ocean and adjoining seas. There are two populations of walruses. Pacific walruses are found in the Bering, Chukchi, and Laptev Seas. Atlantic walruses occupy the coastal regions of Greenland and northeastern Canada.

HABITAT

Walruses live mainly in the sea, occupying pack ice, large pieces of ice frozen together, that floats on the continental shelf, the shallow part of the ocean floor that starts at the shoreline. Males haul out on sandy, cobble, or boulder beaches.

DIET

Walruses eat primarily bivalve mollusks, clams and mussels. They also feed on marine worms, crabs, shrimp, octopus, squid, and sea cucumbers. They occasionally eat fish and seals, including spotted, ringed, and bearded seals. The walrus squirts the muddy sediments on the ocean floor with water from its mouth, exposing the mollusks. Then it sucks the meat out of the shell. An adult walrus consumes about 4 to 6 percent of its total body weight daily. It can eat 3,000 to 6,000 clams per meal.

BEHAVIOR AND REPRODUCTION

Walruses socialize in groups called herds, although males and females keep to their groups except when mating in the winter. They travel and forage together in small groups, and several hundred may haul out on ice floes. Thousands of walruses congregate on beaches to molt, shed, or rest. They typically lie close together, oftentimes draped over one another. However, they can annoy one another, at which point they hit their neighbors with their tusks. Sometimes fighting occurs. However, walruses are supportive of one another. They will help a neighbor who is being attacked by a polar bear or attempt to get a dead animal off an ice floe into the water to get it away from a hunter.

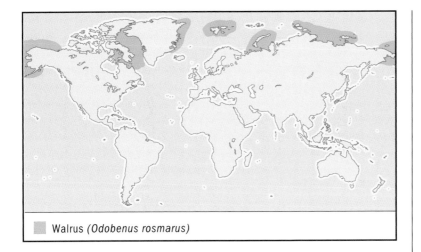

■ Walrus (*Odobenus rosmarus*)

Walruses follow the pack ice throughout the year. In spring, they migrate north toward the Arctic Ocean to feed. Males haul out onto beaches along the Alaskan and Russian coasts to molt and rest, while females migrate farther north. Females give birth on pack ice in the spring and summer. Unlike other pinnipeds, walruses do not mate right after giving birth.

In the fall, they follow expanding pack ice, this time heading south. In the winter, males follow herds of females and their young at sea. When the mother-offspring groups haul up on ice floes, the males remain in the water close by. The males go through a courtship display of producing bell-like sounds underwater, followed by whistles and teeth-clacking above the water. The males also fight for dominance, and only the winner will mate with the females of a certain herd. Mating occurs underwater, after which males rejoin their all-male group. This yearly migration north and south covers about 2,000 miles (3,000 kilometers), with walruses swimming or riding on moving ice.

Walruses spend about two-thirds of their lives in the water. They are slow swimmers, typically going up to 4.3 miles (7 kilometers) per hour, but can reach a speed of up to 22 miles (35 kilometers) per hour. They can stay underwater for 25 minutes, although they usually remain underwater for just 10 minutes because they forage on shallow ocean floors.

Pregnancy lasts fifteen months due to delayed implantation, during which the fertilized egg grows a little then waits four to five months before attaching to the uterus for further development. A single calf is born during the spring migration north. Nursing usually occurs in water, with the calf hanging upside down. The calf can swim at birth. Calves remain with their mothers for two years, although they forage for other food before being completely weaned from their mother's milk. Young females stay with female herds, while young males leave to join all-male herds. The long nursing period means that females do not give birth annually. Mothers are very protective of their young, fighting off intruders with their tusks. They carry their newborn on their back in the water. On land, they hold their calf close to their body with their front flippers when they perceive danger. Walruses have been known to guard one another's young and to adopt orphans.

WALRUSES AND PEOPLE

Native people of the Arctic have always associated the walrus with spiritual power. For thousands of years, they depended on walruses for subsistence, hunting them for food and fuel, as well as material for shelter, clothing, boats, sled, tools, and handicrafts. In the seventeenth century, Europeans first harvested walruses commercially, especially for their ivory tusks, eventually causing declining populations. Today, walruses are legally protected by the governments of the United States, Canada, and Russia. Only native people are allowed to hunt them.

CONSERVATION STATUS

Walruses are not a threatened species.

FOR MORE INFORMATION

Books:

Bonner, Nigel. "The Walrus." In *Seals and Sea Lions of the World.* New York: Facts on File, Inc., 1994.

Knudtson, Peter. *The World of the Walrus.* San Francisco: Sierra Club Books, 1998.

Nowak, Ronald M. "Walrus." *Walker's Mammals of the World Online 5.1.* Baltimore: Johns Hopkins University Press, 1997. http:// www.press. jhu.edu/books/walkers_mammals_of_the_world/pinnipedia/pinnipedia. odobenidae.odobenus.html (accessed on July 7, 2004).

Patent, Dorothy Hinshaw. *Seals, Sea Lions and Walruses.* New York: Holiday House, 1990.

Reeves, Randall R., Brent S. Stewart, Phillip J. Clapham, and James A. Powell. *Guide to Marine Mammals of the World.* New York: Alfred A. Knopf, 2002.

Periodicals:

Fay, Francis H. "*Odobenus rosmarus.*" *Mammalian Species* 238 (May 24, 1985): 1–7.

Lanken, Dane. "Grace Under Water." *Canadian Geographic* (March 2002): 48–53.

Rosing, Norbert. "Walrus: Giant of the Arctic Ice." *National Geographic* (September 2001): 62–78.

Schleichert, Elizabeth. "Giants of the North." *Ranger Rick* (November 1997): 4–11.

Web sites:

Alaska Science Center-Biological Science Office. "Pacific Walrus Research." U.S. Geological Survey. http://www.absc.usgs.gov/research/walrus/home.html (accessed on July 7, 2004).

Sea World Education Department. "Walrus." Sea World/Busch Gardens Animal Information Database. http://www.seaworld.org/infobooks/Walrus/home.html (accessed on July 7, 2004).

Vlessides, Michael. "In Search of the Tooth Walker." National Wildlife Federation. http://www.nwf.org/internationalwildlife/2000/walrusnd.html (accessed on July 7, 2004).

family

PHYSICAL CHARACTERISTICS

True seals have a tapered shape, with short hair covering their body. Underneath the thick skin are 5 to 6 inches (11 to 13 centimeters) of blubber, or fat, that conserves body heat and stores food energy. They are also called earless seals, because they do not have external ears. The ears are just tiny openings on each side of the rounded head. Unlike eared seals, true seals cannot rotate their back flippers for walking. For movement on land, they crawl on their undersides, with the rear end and front flippers pushing the body along. In water, the webbed back flippers act as paddles, while the front flippers are used for steering and balance.

GEOGRAPHIC RANGE

True seals inhabit all oceans, except the Indian Ocean. Some species live in inland lakes in Siberia, Russia, and Finland.

HABITAT

True seals forage, search for food, at sea, but haul out (get out of the water) to land to breed, molt, or shed fur, and rest. They prefer ice floes, large sheets of floating ice, or fast ice, ice attached to a land mass. They also inhabit sand, cobble, and boulder beaches, as well as caves and rocky outcrops.

DIET

True seals eat mostly fish. They also feed on krill, squid, octopuses, and other seals.

BEHAVIOR AND REPRODUCTION

True seals congregate on land or ice to breed and molt. The males and females of some species migrate, travel, separately from breeding to foraging areas. Others species do not migrate. Only the male elephant seals and gray seals gather groups of females during the breeding season. In some species, cows, females, nurse their young for just a few days, fattening up the pup, and then letting it fend for itself.

TRUE SEALS AND PEOPLE

Native people have always depended on seals for food, oil, and fur, taking only what they need for their local populations. Commercial sealers, on the other hand, have overhunted some species.

CONSERVATION STATUS

Three true seals are considered threatened species due mainly to habitat loss or degradation. The Caribbean and Hawaiian monk seals are listed as Endangered, facing a very high risk of extinction, by the U.S. Fish and Wildlife Service. The World Conservation Union (IUCN) lists the Mediterranean monk seal as Critically Endangered, facing an extremely high risk of extinction in the wild, the Hawaiian monk seal as Endangered, and the Caspian seal as Vulnerable, facing a high risk of extinction in the wild.

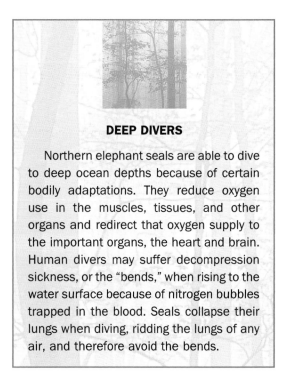

DEEP DIVERS

Northern elephant seals are able to dive to deep ocean depths because of certain bodily adaptations. They reduce oxygen use in the muscles, tissues, and other organs and redirect that oxygen supply to the important organs, the heart and brain. Human divers may suffer decompression sickness, or the "bends," when rising to the water surface because of nitrogen bubbles trapped in the blood. Seals collapse their lungs when diving, ridding the lungs of any air, and therefore avoid the bends.

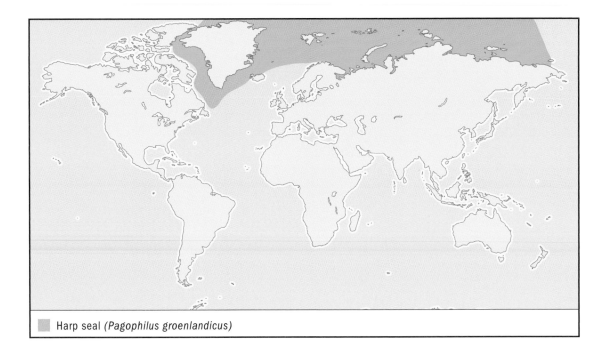

Harp seal (Pagophilus groenlandicus)

SPECIES ACCOUNTS

HARP SEAL
Pagophilus groenlandicus

Physical characteristics: Harp seals got their name from the harp pattern on their back. Adult males and females are light silvery gray with a black face. In males, the harp marking is black. In females, the marking may be broken into smaller patterns. Each seal measures about 5.6 feet (1.7 meters). Males weigh about 297 pounds (135 kilograms) and females about 240 pounds (109 kilograms). Harp seals have a thick layer of blubber that protects them from the cold and stores food energy. The front flippers have strong, sharp claws for hauling out of the water and moving across ice. The back flippers function as oars for swimming but cannot be turned forward for walking.

Geographic range: Harp seals live in the Arctic and the North Atlantic Oceans. They breed off the coast of northeastern Canada, off the east coast of Greenland, and in the White Sea off the northwestern coast of Russia.

Habitat: When not foraging or migrating, harp seals live on ice floes in the open sea. They breed and molt on offshore pack ice. They forage, search for food, under the ice or in open water.

Diet: Harp seals feed on a variety of fish, including capelin, cod, and herring. They also eat shrimp, crabs, and squid.

Behavior and reproduction: Harp seals feed and travel in large groups. They are playful, porpoising or making arcing leaps over water, like dolphins and sea lions. They are excellent divers, able to stay underwater for thirty minutes at a time. They vocalize underwater and on land.

Females gather on pack ice in late winter to give birth to single pups and nurse for about two weeks. Soon after, each cow mates in the water, then returns to sea, leaving her pup permanently. Within those two weeks, the pup grows from about 24 pounds (11 kilograms) to about 80 pounds (36 kilograms). After another two weeks, it sheds its white downy coat, replacing it with a shorter silvery gray coat. They learn to swim and find their own food. After mating, the adult

Harp seals nurse their pups for about two weeks, then leave the pups on their own. After another two weeks, the pup sheds its white downy coat, replacing it with a shorter silvery gray coat. (Tom Brakefield/Bruce Coleman Inc. Reproduced by permission.)

males leave to feed at sea, hauling up on shore to molt for about a month before continuing their northward journey.

Harp seals and people: In the 1970s and 1980s, pressure from conservationists caused the closing of American and European markets for seal products. The seal trade has continued, with new markets in Russia, China, Poland, and Ukraine bringing in millions of dollars for the fur alone. In addition, seal genitals are marketed to Asian markets as aphrodisiacs (aff-roh-DEE-zee-acks), substances that are supposed to increase sexual desire. In 2004, the Canadian government announced an additional quota of 100,000 seals available for hunting for an annual total of 350,000 seals.

Conservation status: Harp seals are not a threatened species.   ■

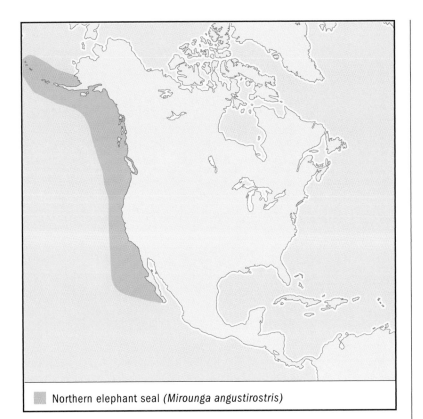

Northern elephant seal (*Mirounga angustirostris*)

NORTHERN ELEPHANT SEAL
Mirounga angustirostris

Physical characteristics: The northern elephant seal got its name from the male's nose, which resembles an elephant's trunk. Males weigh three or four times as much as females, averaging 3,750 pounds (1,704 kilograms) and measuring about 13.2 feet (4 meters). Females are about 1,122 pounds (510 kilograms) and 10.6 feet (3.2 meters) long. Males are dark brown. The thickened, pinkish throat and neck protect them against sharp teeth during fights at the rookeries, breeding grounds. The nose can be inflated to give a bigger appearance and to make loud noises for threat displays. Females are light to chocolate brown.

Geographic range: Northern elephant seals forage in the North Pacific Ocean and breed off the coast of northern California to Baja, Mexico.

The northern elephant seal's nose can be inflated to give a larger appearance and to make loud noises for threat displays. (Jen and Des Bartlett/Bruce Coleman Inc. Reproduced by permission.)

Habitat: Northern elephant seals forage at sea as far north as the Gulf of Alaska and the Aleutian Islands. They breed on sandy, cobble, and pebble beaches.

Diet: Northern elephant seals feed on deep-sea fish, such as Pacific whiting, ratfish, and shark, as well as squid, octopuses, crabs, and eels.

Behavior and reproduction: Northern elephant seals spend up to 90 percent of their time underwater, diving for twenty to thirty minutes, and then coming up for air for about three minutes. They have been recorded diving as deep as 1 mile (1.6 kilometers). Average diving depths range from 1,650 to 2,300 feet (about 500 to 700 meters). In winter, bulls haul out to establish breeding territories. Pregnant cows go ashore a month later, giving birth to single pups. After nursing for about a month, females mate with the territorial bull and with other subordinate males. She then goes back to the sea, leaving the pup to fend for itself. Both sexes fast, go without food, while on land, up to three months for the males. After foraging at sea, each migrates back to the breeding grounds to molt. Each year, seals shed both old skin and hair in what is called catastrophic molt. Northern elephant seals migrate a long distance twice a year, to breed and then to molt, traveling over 6,000 miles (10,000 kilometers) each way.

Northern elephant seals and people: Northern elephant seals were thought extinct by the late 1800s due to overharvesting for its blubber, primarily used in lamp oil. Since the early 1900s, when the seals appeared in Mexico and California, the U.S. government and Mexican government have taken steps to protect them.

Conservation status: Northern elephant seals are not a threatened species. ■

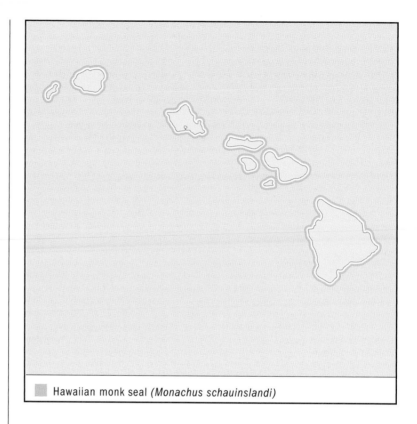

Hawaiian monk seal (*Monachus schauinslandi*)

HAWAIIAN MONK SEAL
Monachus schauinslandi

Physical characteristics: Adult Hawaiian monk seals have short, silvery gray coats, which turn lighter on their undersides. As a seal ages, its coat turns a deep brown with each molt. Females, at about 7.5 feet (2.3 meters) and 528 pounds (270 kilograms), are larger than males. Males measure about 6.9 feet (2.1 meters) long and weigh 385 pounds (175 kilograms).

Geographic range: Hawaiian monk seals are found in the United States.

Habitat: Hawaiian monk seals inhabit the Pacific Ocean waters surrounding the northwestern Hawaiian islands. They breed, rest, and molt on coral reef islands. A small number are found on the main

Hawaiian Islands. Cows choose breeding areas with a coral shelf that affords protection from the sun and sharks.

Diet: Hawaiian monk seals feed on deep-water fish and other fish found in the coral reefs. They also eat squid, octopuses, and lobsters.

Behavior and reproduction: Hawaiian monk seals are solitary, living alone, except during the breeding season. Females give birth to a single pup that they nurse for four to six weeks. A cow sometimes nurses another cow's pup. Females mate soon after they leave their pups, typically in the water. Bulls are believed to have several partners. In areas where males outnumber females, mobbing occurs, in which a group of adult males attempt to mate at once with an adult or an immature female, sometimes fatally injuring that individual.

These seals are active at night, sleeping during the heat of day. They do not migrate, but may spend many days foraging at sea before going ashore to sleep. They do not tolerant humans. When disturbed, they either do not go ashore to breed or give birth in a less preferred site. Pups usually do not survive under these conditions.

Hawaiian monk seals live in the Pacific Ocean waters surrounding the northwestern Hawaiian islands. They breed, rest, and molt on coral reef islands. (© Frans Lanting/Photo Researchers, Inc. Reproduced by permission.)

Hawaiian monk seals and people: Hawaiian monk seals have recently inhabited the main Hawaiian islands. Since they are listed as Endangered and, therefore, legally protected, their appearance on tourist beaches has prompted restrictions or closure that may turn people against them.

Conservation status: The U.S. Fish and Wildlife Service and IUCN lists the Hawaiian monk seal as Endangered due to habitat loss to human expansion, lack of young females for mating, male mobbing of females, reduced prey, and entanglement in ocean debris and commercial fishing gear. ■

FOR MORE INFORMATION

Books:

Bonner, Nigel. *Seals and Sea Lions of the World.* New York: Facts on File, Inc., 1994.

Cossi, Olga. *Harp Seals.* Minneapolis: Carolrhoda Books, Inc., 1991.

Grace, Eric S. *Sierra Club Wildlife Library: Seals.* Boston: Little, Brown and Company, 1991.

Le Boeuf, Burney J., and Richard M. Laws, eds. *Elephant Seals: Population Ecology, Behavior, and Physiology.* Berkeley, CA: University of California Press, 1994.

Patent, Dorothy Hinshaw. *Seals, Sea Lions and Walruses.* New York: Holiday House, 1990.

Reeves, Randall R., Brent S. Stewart, Phillip J. Clapham, and James A. Powell. *Guide to Marine Mammals of the World.* New York: Alfred A. Knopf, 2002.

Periodicals:

Bruemmer, Fred. "Five Days with Fat Hoods." *International Wildlife* (January/Febrary 1999). Online at http://www.nwf.org/internationalwildlife/1998/hoodseal.html (accessed on July 7, 2004).

Kovacs, Kit. "Bearded Seals: Going with the Floe." *National Geographic* (March 1997): 124–137.

Tennesen, Michael. "Testing the Depths of Life." *National Wildlife* (Feb/Mar 1999). Online at http://nwf.org/nationalwildlife/article. cfm?articleId=187&issueid=67 (accessed on July 7, 2004).

Williams, Terrie M. "Sunbathing Seals of Antarctica : The Puzzle Is How Do They Keep Cool? (Weddell Seals)." *Natural History* (October 2003): 50–56.

Web sites:

"The Hawaiian Monk Seal." Pacific Whale Foundation. http://www.pacificwhale.org/childrens/fsmonkseal.html (accessed on July 7, 2004).

"Hawaiian Monk Seal" Seal Conservation Society. http://www.pinnipeds.org/species/hawaimnk.htm (accessed on July 7, 2004.)

"Pagophilic Seals: Fast Facts." Pagophilus.org: Science and Conservation of Ice Loving Seals. http://www.pagophilus.org/index.html (accessed on July 7, 2004).

"Steller Sea Lion Biology." National Marine Mammal Laboratory. http://nmml.afsc.noaa.gov/AlaskaEcosystems/sslhome/StellerDescription.html (accessed on July 7, 2004).

Species List by Biome

CONIFEROUS FOREST
American black bear
American pika
American water shrew
Asian elephant
Bobcat
Brown-throated three-toed sloth
Chimpanzee
Common bentwing bat
Coypu
Desert cottontail
Eastern mole
Edible dormouse
Ermine
Gambian rat
Geoffroy's spider monkey
Giant panda
Gray squirrel
Gray wolf
Greater sac-winged bat
Hairy-footed jerboa
Human
Indian crested porcupine
Kirk's dikdik
Lar gibbon
Little brown bat
Malayan moonrat
Mandrill
Moose

Mountain beaver
Mountain hare
Nine-banded armadillo
North American beaver
North American porcupine
Northern pika
Pacarana
Pallas's long-tongued bat
Pallid bat
Pileated gibbon
Puma
Red deer
Red panda
Red-shanked douc langur
Reindeer
Rhesus macaque
Serow
Siamang
Siberian musk deer
Snow leopard
Snowshoe hare
South African porcupine
Southern tree hyrax
Star-nosed mole
Striped skunk
Tasmanian devil
Three-striped night monkey
Tiger
Valley pocket gopher
Venezuelan red howler monkey

Virginia opossum
Weeper capuchin
Western barbastelle
White-tailed deer
White-throated capuchin

DECIDUOUS FOREST
Aardvark
African civet
American bison
American black bear
American least shrew
American pika
American water shrew
Ashy chinchilla rat
Asian elephant
Aye-aye
Bobcat
Bornean orangutan
Bridled nail-tailed wallaby
Brush-tailed phascogale
Brush-tailed rock wallaby
Capybara
Central American agouti
Chimpanzee
Collared peccary
Common bentwing bat
Common brush-tailed possum
Common genet

Common ringtail
Common tenrec
Common wombat
Cotton-top tamarin
Coypu
Crowned lemur
Degu
Desert cottontail
Eastern chipmunk
Eastern gray kangaroo
Eastern mole
Eastern pygmy possum
Edible dormouse
Ermine
Eurasian wild pig
European badger
Forest elephant
Forest hog
Funnel-eared bat
Gambian rat
Geoffroy's spider monkey
Giant panda
Goeldi's monkey
Gray squirrel
Gray wolf
Greater dog-faced bat
Greater glider
Greater horseshoe bat
Greater sac-winged bat
Ground pangolin
Human
Indian crested porcupine
Indian muntjac
Indian rhinoceros
Koala
Lar gibbon
Lesser Malay mouse deer
Lesser New Zealand short-
  tailed bat
Lion
Little brown bat
Lord Derby's anomalure
Lowland tapir
Mara
Mountain beaver
Mountain hare

North American beaver
North American porcupine
Northern raccoon
Numbat
Paca
Pacarana
Pallas's long-tongued bat
Parnell's moustached bat
Pileated gibbon
Puma
Pygmy glider
Red deer
Red fox
Red kangaroo
Red panda
Red-tailed sportive lemur
Rhesus macaque
Ringtailed lemur
Rock cavy
Senegal bushbaby
Serow
Siamang
Silky anteater
South African porcupine
Southern flying squirrel
Spotted hyena
Star-nosed mole
Striped skunk
Sugar glider
Three-striped night monkey
Tiger
Valley pocket gopher
Venezuelan red howler
  monkey
Virginia opossum
Water buffalo
Weeper capuchin
Western barbastelle
Western European hedgehog
White rhinoceros
White-tailed deer
White-throated capuchin

DESERT
Australian jumping mouse
Bighorn sheep

Bobcat
Brazilian free-tailed bat
California leaf-nosed bat
Collared peccary
Damaraland mole-rat
Dassie rat
Desert cottontail
Dromedary camel
Egyptian slit-faced bat
Egyptian spiny mouse
Grant's desert golden mole
Gray wolf
Hairy-footed jerboa
Hardwicke's lesser mouse-
  tailed bat
Human
Kirk's dikdik
Lion
Mzab gundi
Naked mole-rat
North American porcupine
Pallid bat
Parnell's moustached bat
Pink fairy armadillo
Pronghorn
Puma
Red fox
Rhesus macaque
San Joaquin pocket mouse
Savanna elephant
Short-beaked echidna
Southern marsupial mole
Spotted hyena
Striped skunk
Trident leaf-nosed bat
Valley pocket gopher
Virginia opossum
White-footed sportive lemur

GRASSLAND
Aardvark
Aardwolf
African civet
Alpaca
Alpine marmot
American bison

American black bear
American least shrew
American pika
Ashy chinchilla rat
Asian elephant
Australian false vampire bat
Australian jumping mouse
Black wildebeest
Black-bellied hamster
Black-tailed prairie dog
Brazilian free-tailed bat
Bridled nail-tailed wallaby
California leaf-nosed bat
Capybara
Central American agouti
Chimpanzee
Common bentwing bat
Common genet
Common tenrec
Coypu
Degu
Dwarf epauletted fruit bat
Eastern barred bandicoot
Eastern chipmunk
Eastern gray kangaroo
Eastern mole
Egyptian rousette
Egyptian slit-faced bat
Egyptian spiny mouse
Ermine
Eurasian wild pig
Forest elephant
Gambian rat
Giant anteater
Giant kangaroo rat
Giraffe
Grant's desert golden mole
Gray wolf
Greater bilby
Greater dog-faced bat
Greater horseshoe bat
Grevy's zebra
Ground pangolin
Hardwicke's lesser mouse-
    tailed bat
Hispaniolan solenodon
Hispid cotton rat

Human
Indian crested porcupine
Indian muntjac
Indian rhinoceros
Kiang
Lesser New Zealand short-
    tailed bat
Lion
Llama
Long-tailed chinchilla
Lowland tapir
Maned wolf
Mara
Naked bat
Nine-banded armadillo
Northern pika
Numbat
Paca
Pallas's long-tongued bat
Pallid bat
Parnell's moustached bat
Pearson's tuco-tuco
Pink fairy armadillo
Pronghorn
Przewalski's horse
Puma
Red deer
Red fox
Red kangaroo
Rock cavy
Rock hyrax
San Joaquin pocket mouse
Savanna elephant
Senegal bushbaby
Short-beaked echidna
Smoky bat
Snow leopard
South African porcupine
Spix's disk-winged bat
Spotted hyena
Springhare
Star-nosed mole
Striped skunk
Tasmanian wolf
Thomson's gazelle
Tiger
Valley pocket gopher

Vampire bat
Virginia opossum
Water buffalo
Western European hedgehog
Western red colobus
White rhinoceros
Yellow-streaked tenrec

LAKE AND POND
American water shrew
Babirusa
Capybara
Central American agouti
Common hippopotamus
Coypu
Duck-billed platypus
European otter
Greater bulldog bat
Malayan tapir
Muskrat
North American beaver
North American porcupine
Prehensile-tailed porcupine
Tiger

OCEAN
Antarctic fur seal
Beluga
Blue whale
Burmeister's porpoise
California sea lion
Common bottlenosed dolphin
Dugong
Franciscana dolphin
Galápagos sea lion
Gray whale
Harbor porpoise
Harp seal
Hawaiian monk seal
Humpback whale
Killer whale
Narwhal
North Atlantic right whale
Northern bottlenosed whale
Northern elephant seal
Northern minke whale

Pygmy right whale
Pygmy sperm whale
Shepherd's beaked whale
Sperm whale
Spinner dolphin
Steller's sea cow
Walrus
West Indian manatee

RAINFOREST

Australian false vampire bat
Aye-aye
Babirusa
Bald uakari
Bennett's tree kangaroo
Bornean orangutan
Brazilian free-tailed bat
Brown-throated three-toed
  sloth
Brush-tailed rock wallaby
Central American agouti
Checkered sengi
Chevrotains
Chimpanzee
Collared peccary
Colombian woolly monkey
Common brush-tailed possum
Common ringtail
Common squirrel monkey
Common tenrec
Common tree shrew
Cotton-top tamarin
Coypu
Crowned lemur
Cuban hutia
Eastern pygmy possum
Eurasian wild pig
Forest elephant
Fossa
Funnel-eared bat
Geoffroy's spider monkey
Giant anteater
Goeldi's monkey
Greater sac-winged bat
Ground cuscus
Hispaniolan solenodon

Hoffman's two-toed sloth
Human
Indian crested porcupine
Indian flying fox
Indian muntjac
Indri
Kitti's hog-nosed bat
Lar gibbon
Lesser New Zealand short-
  tailed bat
Lord Derby's anomalure
Lowland tapir
Malayan colugo
Malayan tapir
Mandrill
Masked titi
Milne-Edwards's sifaka
Monito del monte
Mountain beaver
Musky rat-kangaroo
Naked bat
North American beaver
Northern bettong
Northern greater bushbaby
Okapi
Old World sucker-footed bat
Paca
Pacarana
Philippine tarsier
Pileated gibbon
Potto
Prehensile-tailed porcupine
Proboscis monkey
Pygmy hippopotamus
Pygmy marmoset
Pygmy slow loris
Queensland tube-nosed bat
Red mouse lemur
Red-shanked douc langur
Rhesus macaque
Ring-tailed mongoose
Rock hyrax
Rufous spiny bandicoot
Short-beaked echidna
Siamang
Siberian musk deer
Silky anteater

Silky shrew opossum
Smoky bat
Southern pudu
Spiny rat
Spix's disk-winged bat
Sugar glider
Sumatran rhinoceros
Three-striped night monkey
Valley pocket gopher
Vampire bat
Venezuelan red howler
  monkey
Virginia opossum
Water opossum
Weeper capuchin
Western gorilla
Western red colobus
Western tarsier
White bat
White-faced saki
White-tailed deer
White-throated capuchin
Yellow-streaked tenrec

RIVER AND STREAM

American water shrew
Aye-aye
Babirusa
Baiji
Black-bellied hamster
Boto
Capybara
Central American agouti
Common hippopotamus
Common squirrel monkey
Coypu
Duck-billed platypus
European otter
Ganges and Indus dolphin
Greater bulldog bat
Greater cane rat
Lowland tapir
Malayan tapir
Mountain beaver
Muskrat
North American beaver

North American porcupine
Northern raccoon
Old World sucker-footed bat
Paca
Prehensile-tailed porcupine
Pygmy hippopotamus
Smoky bat
Tiger
Virginia opossum
Water opossum
West Indian manatee
White-footed sportive lemur

SEASHORE
Antarctic fur seal
California sea lion
Cape horseshoe bat
European otter
Galápagos sea lion
Grant's desert golden mole
Greater bulldog bat
Harp seal
Hawaiian monk seal
Honey possum
Lesser New Zealand short-
   tailed bat

Marianas fruit bat
Northern elephant seal
Pearson's tuco-tuco
Walrus

TUNDRA
American black bear
Ermine
Gray wolf
Hairy-footed jerboa
Human
Long-tailed chinchilla
Moose
Mountain hare
North American porcupine
Northern pika
Norway lemming
Polar bear
Red fox
Reindeer
Snowshoe hare
Striped skunk

WETLAND
American black bear

Bobcat
Bornean orangutan
Brazilian free-tailed bat
Capybara
Common squirrel monkey
Coypu
European otter
Giant anteater
Greater bulldog bat
Greater cane rat
Greater dog-faced bat
Indian flying fox
Malayan moonrat
Marianas fruit bat
North American beaver
Northern raccoon
Old World sucker-footed bat
Pacarana
Parnell's moustached bat
Proboscis monkey
Puma
Rhesus macaque
Spix's disk-winged bat
Star-nosed mole
Tiger
Valley pocket gopher

Species List by Geographic Range

AFGHANISTAN
Common bentwing bat
Dromedary camel
Eurasian wild pig
Gray wolf
Greater horseshoe bat
Hardwicke's lesser mouse-
  tailed bat
Red deer
Red fox
Rhesus macaque
Snow leopard
Trident leaf-nosed bat

ALBANIA
Blue whale
Common bentwing bat
Common bottlenosed dolphin
Edible dormouse
Eurasian wild pig
European badger
European otter
Gray wolf
Greater horseshoe bat
Humpback whale
Northern minke whale
Pygmy sperm whale
Red deer
Red fox
Sperm whale

ALGERIA
Blue whale
Common bentwing bat
Common bottlenosed dolphin
Common genet
Dromedary camel
Eurasian wild pig
European otter
Greater horseshoe bat
Humpback whale
Killer whale
Mzab gundi
Northern bottlenosed whale
Northern minke whale
Pygmy sperm whale
Red deer
Red fox
Sperm whale
Trident leaf-nosed bat

ANDORRA
European badger
Red fox

ANGOLA
Aardvark
African civet
Blue whale
Common bentwing bat

Common bottlenosed dolphin
Common genet
Dassie rat
Egyptian slit-faced bat
Gambian rat
Giraffe
Ground pangolin
Humpback whale
Kirk's dikdik
Lion
Northern minke whale
Pygmy sperm whale
South African porcupine
Sperm whale
Spinner dolphin
Spotted hyena
Springhare
Western gorilla
White rhinoceros

ANTARCTICA
Antarctic fur seal
Blue whale
Northern minke whale

ARGENTINA
Blue whale
Brazilian free-tailed bat
Brown-throated three-toed sloth

Burmeister's porpoise
Capybara
Central American agouti
Collared peccary
Common bottlenosed dolphin
Coypu
Franciscana dolphin
Giant anteater
Greater bulldog bat
Humpback whale
Killer whale
Llama
Lowland tapir
Maned wolf
Mara
Monito del monte
Northern minke whale
Pallas's long-tongued bat
Pearson's tuco-tuco
Pink fairy armadillo
Prehensile-tailed porcupine
Puma
Pygmy right whale
Red deer
Shepherd's beaked whale
Southern pudu
Sperm whale
Three-toed tree sloths
Vampire bat
Water opossum

ARMENIA
Common bentwing bat
Edible dormouse
Eurasian wild pig
European badger
Gray wolf
Red deer
Red fox

AUSTRALIA
Australian false vampire bat
Australian jumping mouse
Bennett's tree kangaroo
Blue whale
Bridled nail-tailed wallaby

Brush-tailed phascogale
Brush-tailed rock wallaby
Common bentwing bat
Common bottlenosed dolphin
Common brush-tailed possum
Common ringtail
Common wombat
Duck-billed platypus
Dugong
Eastern barred bandicoot
Eastern gray kangaroo
Eastern pygmy possum
Greater bilby
Greater glider
Honey possum
Humpback whale
Killer whale
Koala
Musky rat-kangaroo
Northern bettong
Northern minke whale
Numbat
Pygmy glider
Pygmy right whale
Pygmy sperm whale
Queensland tube-nosed bat
Red fox
Red kangaroo
Rufous spiny bandicoot
Short-beaked echidna
Southern marsupial mole
Sperm whale
Spinner dolphin
Sugar glider
Tasmanian devil
Tasmanian wolf

AUSTRIA
Alpine marmot
Common bentwing bat
Edible dormouse
Ermine
Eurasian wild pig
European badger
Greater horseshoe bat
Mountain hare

Red deer
Red fox
Western European hedgehog

AZERBAIJAN
Common bentwing bat
Edible dormouse
Eurasian wild pig
European badger
Gray wolf
Red deer
Red fox

BANGLADESH
Asian elephant
Blue whale
Common bentwing bat
Common bottlenosed dolphin
Eurasian wild pig
Ganges and Indus dolphin
Gray wolf
Greater horseshoe bat
Humpback whale
Indian crested porcupine
Indian flying fox
Indian muntjac
Indian rhinoceros
Northern minke whale
Pygmy sperm whale
Red fox
Rhesus macaque
Serow
Sperm whale
Spinner dolphin
Tiger

BELARUS
Black-bellied hamster
Edible dormouse
Ermine
Eurasian wild pig
European badger
Gray wolf
Moose
Mountain hare

Red deer
Red fox

BELGIUM
Black-bellied hamster
Blue whale
Common bottlenosed dolphin
Edible dormouse
Ermine
Eurasian wild pig
European badger
Greater horseshoe bat
Harbor porpoise
Humpback whale
Killer whale
North Atlantic right whale
Northern minke whale
Pygmy sperm whale
Sperm whale
Western European hedgehog

BELIZE
Blue whale
Brazilian free-tailed bat
Central American agouti
Collared peccary
Common bottlenosed dolphin
Funnel-eared bat
Geoffroy's spider monkey
Giant anteater
Greater bulldog bat
Greater dog-faced bat
Greater sac-winged bat
Hispid cotton rat
Humpback whale
Nine-banded armadillo
Northern minke whale
Paca
Pallas's long-tongued bat
Parnell's moustached bat
Pygmy sperm whale
Silky anteater
Sperm whale
Spinner dolphin
Spix's disk-winged bat
Vampire bat

Virginia opossum
Water opossum
White-tailed deer

BENIN
Aardvark
African civet
Blue whale
Common bottlenosed dolphin
Common genet
Gambian rat
Humpback whale
Lord Derby's anomalure
Northern minke whale
Pygmy sperm whale
Rock hyrax
Senegal bushbaby
South African porcupine
Sperm whale
Spinner dolphin

BHUTAN
Asian elephant
Common bentwing bat
Gray wolf
Greater horseshoe bat
Indian crested porcupine
Red fox
Red panda
Rhesus macaque
Serow
Snow leopard
Water buffalo

BOLIVIA
Alpaca
Ashy chinchilla rat
Boto
Brazilian free-tailed bat
Brown-throated three-toed
  sloth
Capybara
Central American agouti
Collared peccary
Coypu
Giant anteater
Goeldi's monkey

Greater bulldog bat
Greater dog-faced bat
Greater sac-winged bat
Hoffman's two-toed sloth
Llama
Lowland tapir
Maned wolf
Nine-banded armadillo
Pacarana
Pallas's long-tongued bat
Puma
Pygmy marmoset
Silky anteater
Spix's disk-winged bat
Three-toed tree sloths
Vampire bat
White-faced saki
White-tailed deer

BOSNIA AND HERZEGOVINA
Common bentwing bat
Edible dormouse
Eurasian wild pig
European badger
Greater horseshoe bat
Red deer
Red fox

BOTSWANA
Aardvark
Aardwolf
African civet
Common genet
Common hippopotamus
Damaraland mole-rat
Egyptian slit-faced bat
Giraffe
Ground pangolin
Lion
Savanna elephant
Springhare

BRAZIL
Bald uakari
Blue whale

Boto
Brazilian free-tailed bat
Brown-throated three-toed sloth
Burmeister's porpoise
Capybara
Central American agouti
Collared peccary
Common bottlenosed dolphin
Common squirrel monkey
Coypu
Franciscana dolphin
Funnel-eared bat
Giant anteater
Goeldi's monkey
Greater bulldog bat
Greater dog-faced bat
Greater sac-winged bat
Hoffman's two-toed sloth
Humpback whale
Killer whale
Lowland tapir
Maned wolf
Masked titi
Nine-banded armadillo
Northern minke whale
Paca
Pacarana
Pallas's long-tongued bat
Parnell's moustached bat
Prehensile-tailed porcupine
Pygmy marmoset
Pygmy right whale
Pygmy sperm whale
Red deer
Rock cavy
Silky anteater
Smoky bat
Sperm whale
Spinner dolphin
Spix's disk-winged bat
Three-striped night monkey
Three-toed tree sloths
Vampire bat
Venezuelan red howler monkey
Water opossum

Weeper capuchin
White-faced saki
White-tailed deer

BULGARIA
Common bentwing bat
Edible dormouse
Eurasian wild pig
European badger
Gray wolf
Greater horseshoe bat
Harbor porpoise
Red deer
Red fox

BURKINA FASO
Aardvark
African civet
Common genet
Egyptian slit-faced bat
Rock hyrax
Senegal bushbaby

BURUNDI
Aardvark
African civet
Common bentwing bat
Common genet
Egyptian slit-faced bat
Gambian rat
Lord Derby's anomalure
Senegal bushbaby
South African porcupine

CAMBODIA
Asian elephant
Blue whale
Common bentwing bat
Common bottlenosed dolphin
Dugong
Eurasian wild pig
Greater horseshoe bat
Humpback whale
Indian muntjac
Lesser Malay mouse deer

Malayan tapir
Northern minke whale
Pileated gibbon
Pygmy sperm whale
Serow
Sperm whale
Spinner dolphin

CAMEROON
Aardvark
African civet
Blue whale
Chimpanzee
Common bottlenosed dolphin
Common genet
Dwarf epauletted fruit bat
Egyptian rousette
Forest elephant
Forest hog
Gambian rat
Greater cane rat
Humpback whale
Lord Derby's anomalure
Mandrill
Northern minke whale
Potto
Pygmy sperm whale
Rock hyrax
Senegal bushbaby
South African porcupine
Sperm whale
Spinner dolphin
Western gorilla
Western red colobus

CANADA
American bison
American black bear
American least shrew
American pika
American water shrew
Beluga
Bighorn sheep
Black-tailed prairie dog
Bobcat
California sea lion

Eastern chipmunk
Eastern mole
Ermine
Gray squirrel
Gray wolf
Harbor porpoise
Harp seal
Killer whale
Little brown bat
Moose
Mountain beaver
Muskrat
Narwhal
North American beaver
North American porcupine
North Atlantic right whale
Northern bottlenosed whale
Northern raccoon
Pallid bat
Polar bear
Pronghorn
Puma
Red deer
Red fox
Reindeer
Snowshoe hare
Southern flying squirrel
Star-nosed mole
Striped skunk
Virginia opossum
Walrus
White-tailed deer

CENTRAL AFRICAN REPUBLIC
Aardvark
African civet
Chimpanzee
Common genet
Dwarf epauletted fruit bat
Egyptian rousette
Forest elephant
Gambian rat
Giraffe
Greater cane rat
Lord Derby's anomalure

Rock hyrax
Senegal bushbaby
South African porcupine
Western gorilla
White rhinoceros

CHAD
Aardvark
African civet
Common genet
Dromedary camel
Egyptian slit-faced bat
Gambian rat
Ground pangolin
Mzab gundi
Rock hyrax
Senegal bushbaby
Spotted hyena
Trident leaf-nosed bat
White rhinoceros

CHILE
Alpaca
Ashy chinchilla rat
Blue whale
Brazilian free-tailed bat
Burmeister's porpoise
Common bottlenosed dolphin
Coypu
Degu
Humpback whale
Killer whale
Llama
Long-tailed chinchilla
Monito del monte
Northern minke whale
Pallas's long-tongued bat
Pearson's tuco-tuco
Pygmy right whale
Pygmy sperm whale
Red deer
Shepherd's beaked whale
Southern pudu
Sperm whale
Vampire bat

CHINA
Asian elephant
Baiji
Blue whale
Common bentwing bat
Common bottlenosed dolphin
Dugong
Edible dormouse
Ermine
European badger
Giant panda
Gray wolf
Greater horseshoe bat
Hairy-footed jerboa
Humpback whale
Indian muntjac
Kiang
Killer whale
Lar gibbon
Lesser Malay mouse deer
Moose
Mountain hare
Northern minke whale
Northern pika
Pygmy slow loris
Pygmy sperm whale
Red deer
Red fox
Red panda
Reindeer
Rhesus macaque
Serow
Siberian musk deer
Snow leopard
Sperm whale
Spinner dolphin
Tiger

COLOMBIA
Bald uakari
Blue whale
Boto
Brazilian free-tailed bat
Brown-throated three-toed
  sloth
Capybara

Central American agouti
Collared peccary
Colombian woolly monkey
Common bottlenosed dolphin
Common squirrel monkey
Cotton-top tamarin
Funnel-eared bat
Giant anteater
Goeldi's monkey
Greater bulldog bat
Greater sac-winged bat
Hispid cotton rat
Hoffman's two-toed sloth
Humpback whale
Killer whale
Llama
Lowland tapir
Nine-banded armadillo
Northern minke whale
Paca
Pacarana
Pallas's long-tongued bat
Parnell's moustached bat
Prehensile-tailed porcupine
Pygmy marmoset
Pygmy sperm whale
Silky anteater
Silky shrew opossum
Smoky bat
Sperm whale
Spinner dolphin
Spiny rat
Spix's disk-winged bat
Three-striped night monkey
Three-toed tree sloths
Vampire bat
Water opossum
White-faced saki
White-tailed deer
White-throated capuchin

CONGO
African civet
Blue whale
Common bottlenosed dolphin
Common genet

Dwarf epauletted fruit bat
Egyptian rousette
Egyptian slit-faced bat
Forest elephant
Forest hog
Humpback whale
Lord Derby's anomalure
Northern minke whale
Potto
Pygmy sperm whale
South African porcupine
Sperm whale
Spinner dolphin
Springhare
Western gorilla

COSTA RICA
American least shrew
Blue whale
Brazilian free-tailed bat
Brown-throated three-toed
  sloth
Central American agouti
Collared peccary
Common bottlenosed dolphin
Funnel-eared bat
Geoffroy's spider monkey
Giant anteater
Greater bulldog bat
Greater dog-faced bat
Greater sac-winged bat
Hispid cotton rat
Hoffman's two-toed sloth
Humpback whale
Killer whale
Nine-banded armadillo
Northern minke whale
Paca
Pallas's long-tongued bat
Parnell's moustached bat
Puma
Pygmy sperm whale
Silky anteater
Smoky bat
Sperm whale
Spinner dolphin

Spiny rat
Spix's disk-winged bat
Three-toed tree sloths
Vampire bat
Virginia opossum
Water opossum
White bat
White-tailed deer
White-throated capuchin

CROATIA
Blue whale
Common bentwing bat
Common bottlenosed dolphin
Edible dormouse
Eurasian wild pig
European badger
Greater horseshoe bat
Humpback whale
Northern minke whale
Pygmy sperm whale
Red deer
Red fox
Sperm whale

CUBA
Blue whale
Brazilian free-tailed bat
Central American agouti
Collared peccary
Common bottlenosed dolphin
Cuban hutia
Funnel-eared bat
Greater bulldog bat
Humpback whale
Killer whale
Northern minke whale
Pallid bat
Parnell's moustached bat
Pygmy sperm whale
Sperm whale
Spinner dolphin

CYPRUS
Blue whale

Common bottlenosed dolphin
Humpback whale
Northern minke whale
Pygmy sperm whale
Sperm whale

CZECH REPUBLIC
Black-bellied hamster
Common bentwing bat
Edible dormouse
Ermine
European badger
Greater horseshoe bat
Red deer
Red fox

DEMOCRATIC REPUBLIC OF THE CONGO
Aardvark
African civet
Blue whale
Checkered sengi
Chimpanzee
Common bentwing bat
Common bottlenosed dolphin
Common genet
Common hippopotamus
Dwarf epauletted fruit bat
Egyptian rousette
Egyptian slit-faced bat
Forest elephant
Forest hog
Gambian rat
Giraffe
Humpback whale
Lord Derby's anomalure
Mandrill
Northern minke whale
Okapi
Potto
Pygmy sperm whale
Rock hyrax
South African porcupine
Sperm whale

Spinner dolphin
Western gorilla
Western red colobus
White rhinoceros

DENMARK
Blue whale
Common bottlenosed dolphin
Ermine
Eurasian wild pig
European badger
Harbor porpoise
Humpback whale
Killer whale
North Atlantic right whale
Northern minke whale
Norway lemming
Pygmy sperm whale
Red deer
Red fox
Sperm whale
Western European hedgehog

DJIBOUTI
Aardvark
Blue whale
Common bottlenosed dolphin
Common genet
Dromedary camel
Dugong
Humpback whale
Northern minke whale
Rock hyrax
Senegal bushbaby
Sperm whale
Spinner dolphin

DOMINICAN REPUBLIC
Blue whale
Brazilian free-tailed bat
Common bottlenosed dolphin
Funnel-eared bat
Greater bulldog bat
Hispaniolan solenodon

Humpback whale
Killer whale
Northern minke whale
Parnell's moustached bat
Pygmy sperm whale
Sperm whale
Spinner dolphin

ECUADOR
Blue whale
Boto
Brazilian free-tailed bat
Brown-throated three-toed sloth
Capybara
Central American agouti
Collared peccary
Common bottlenosed dolphin
Galápagos sea lion
Giant anteater
Goeldi's monkey
Greater bulldog bat
Greater dog-faced bat
Greater sac-winged bat
Hoffman's two-toed sloth
Humpback whale
Killer whale
Llama
Lowland tapir
Nine-banded armadillo
Northern minke whale
Pacarana
Pallas's long-tongued bat
Pygmy marmoset
Pygmy sperm whale
Silky anteater
Silky shrew opossum
Sperm whale
Spinner dolphin
Spiny rat
Spix's disk-winged bat
Three-toed tree sloths
Vampire bat
Water opossum
White-faced saki
White-tailed deer

EGYPT
Blue whale
Common bottlenosed dolphin
Common genet
Dromedary camel
Egyptian rousette
Egyptian slit-faced bat
Egyptian spiny mouse
Eurasian wild pig
Greater horseshoe bat
Hardwicke's lesser mouse-
  tailed bat
Humpback whale
Northern minke whale
Pygmy sperm whale
Red fox
Rock hyrax
Sperm whale
Trident leaf-nosed bat

EL SALVADOR
Blue whale
Brazilian free-tailed bat
Brown-throated three-toed
  sloth
Collared peccary
Common bottlenosed dolphin
Funnel-eared bat
Geoffroy's spider monkey
Giant anteater
Greater bulldog bat
Greater sac-winged bat
Hispid cotton rat
Humpback whale
Killer whale
Nine-banded armadillo
Northern minke whale
Paca
Pallas's long-tongued bat
Parnell's moustached bat
Pygmy sperm whale
Silky anteater
Sperm whale
Spinner dolphin
Spix's disk-winged bat
Three-toed tree sloths

Vampire bat
Virginia opossum
Water opossum
White-tailed deer

EQUATORIAL GUINEA
African civet
Blue whale
Common bottlenosed dolphin
Common genet
Forest elephant
Humpback whale
Lord Derby's anomalure
Mandrill
Northern minke whale
Potto
Pygmy sperm whale
South African porcupine
Sperm whale
Spinner dolphin
Western gorilla

ERITREA
Aardvark
Blue whale
Common bottlenosed dolphin
Common genet
Dromedary camel
Dugong
Egyptian slit-faced bat
Humpback whale
Northern minke whale
Rock hyrax
Sperm whale
Spinner dolphin

ESTONIA
Blue whale
Common bottlenosed dolphin
Ermine
Eurasian wild pig
European badger
Gray wolf
Harbor porpoise
Humpback whale

Moose
Mountain hare
Northern minke whale
Red deer
Red fox
Sperm whale

ETHIOPIA
Aardvark
Common genet
Dromedary camel
Egyptian slit-faced bat
Forest hog
Grevy's zebra
Lion
Naked mole-rat
Rock hyrax
Senegal bushbaby
Thomson's gazelle

FINLAND
Blue whale
Common bottlenosed dolphin
Ermine
Eurasian wild pig
European badger
European otter
Gray wolf
Humpback whale
Moose
Mountain hare
Northern minke whale
Norway lemming
Red fox
Reindeer
Sperm whale
Western European hedgehog

FRANCE
Alpine marmot
Blue whale
Common bentwing bat
Common bottlenosed dolphin
Common genet
Edible dormouse

Ermine
Eurasian wild pig
European badger
European otter
Greater horseshoe bat
Harbor porpoise
Humpback whale
Killer whale
North Atlantic right whale
Northern bottlenosed whale
Northern minke whale
Pygmy sperm whale
Red deer
Red fox
Sperm whale
Western European hedgehog

FRENCH GUIANA
Blue whale
Capybara
Collared peccary
Common bottlenosed dolphin
Common squirrel monkey
Funnel-eared bat
Giant anteater
Greater bulldog bat
Greater dog-faced bat
Greater sac-winged bat
Humpback whale
Lowland tapir
Nine-banded armadillo
Northern minke whale
Paca
Pallas's long-tongued bat
Parnell's moustached bat
Prehensile-tailed porcupine
Pygmy sperm whale
Silky anteater
Smoky bat
Sperm whale
Spinner dolphin
Spix's disk-winged bat
Three-toed tree sloths
Vampire bat
Water opossum
Weeper capuchin

White-faced saki
White-tailed deer

GABON
African civet
Blue whale
Common bottlenosed dolphin
Common genet
Common hippopotamus
Dwarf epauletted fruit bat
Egyptian rousette
Forest elephant
Forest hog
Humpback whale
Lord Derby's anomalure
Mandrill
Northern minke whale
Potto
Pygmy sperm whale
South African porcupine
Sperm whale
Spinner dolphin
Western gorilla

GAMBIA
Aardvark
African civet
Blue whale
Common bottlenosed dolphin
Common genet
Gambian rat
Greater cane rat
Humpback whale
Killer whale
Northern minke whale
Pygmy sperm whale
Senegal bushbaby
South African porcupine
Sperm whale
Spinner dolphin
Western red colobus

GEORGIA
Common bentwing bat
Edible dormouse

Eurasian wild pig
European badger
Gray wolf
Harbor porpoise
Red deer
Red fox

GERMANY
Alpine marmot
Black-bellied hamster
Blue whale
Common bentwing bat
Common bottlenosed dolphin
Edible dormouse
Ermine
Eurasian wild pig
European badger
Greater horseshoe bat
Harbor porpoise
Humpback whale
Killer whale
North Atlantic right whale
Northern minke whale
Northern raccoon
Pygmy sperm whale
Red deer
Red fox
Sperm whale
Western European hedgehog

GHANA
Aardvark
African civet
Blue whale
Chimpanzee
Common bottlenosed dolphin
Common genet
Dwarf epauletted fruit bat
Egyptian rousette
Forest elephant
Forest hog
Gambian rat
Humpback whale
Lord Derby's anomalure
Northern minke whale
Potto

Pygmy sperm whale
Rock hyrax
Senegal bushbaby
South African porcupine
Sperm whale
Spinner dolphin
Western red colobus

GREECE
Blue whale
Common bentwing bat
Common bottlenosed dolphin
Edible dormouse
European badger
European otter
Gray wolf
Greater horseshoe bat
Harbor porpoise
Humpback whale
Northern minke whale
Pygmy sperm whale
Red deer
Red fox
Sperm whale

GREENLAND
Blue whale
Ermine
Harbor porpoise
Harp seal
Humpback whale
Killer whale
North Atlantic right whale
Northern bottlenosed whale
Northern minke whale
Polar bear
Reindeer
Walrus

GRENADA
Nine-banded armadillo
Pallas's long-tongued bat

GUAM
Marianas fruit bat

GUATEMALA
American least shrew
Blue whale
Brazilian free-tailed bat
Central American agouti
Collared peccary
Common bottlenosed dolphin
Funnel-eared bat
Geoffroy's spider monkey
Giant anteater
Greater bulldog bat
Greater dog-faced bat
Greater sac-winged bat
Hispid cotton rat
Humpback whale
Killer whale
Nine-banded armadillo
Northern minke whale
Paca
Pallas's long-tongued bat
Parnell's moustached bat
Puma
Pygmy sperm whale
Silky anteater
Sperm whale
Spinner dolphin
Spix's disk-winged bat
Vampire bat
Virginia opossum
Water opossum
White-tailed deer

GUINEA
Aardvark
African civet
Blue whale
Chimpanzee
Common bottlenosed dolphin
Common genet
Egyptian slit-faced bat
Forest hog
Gambian rat
Humpback whale
Killer whale
Northern minke whale
Pygmy hippopotamus

Pygmy sperm whale
Rock hyrax
Senegal bushbaby
South African porcupine
Sperm whale
Spinner dolphin

GUINEA-BISSAU
Aardvark
African civet
Blue whale
Common bottlenosed dolphin
Common genet
Forest hog
Gambian rat
Humpback whale
Killer whale
Northern minke whale
Pygmy sperm whale
Rock hyrax
Senegal bushbaby
South African porcupine
Sperm whale
Spinner dolphin
Western red colobus

GUYANA
Blue whale
Boto
Capybara
Collared peccary
Common bottlenosed dolphin
Common squirrel monkey
Funnel-eared bat
Giant anteater
Greater bulldog bat
Greater dog-faced bat
Greater sac-winged bat
Humpback whale
Lowland tapir
Nine-banded armadillo
Northern minke whale
Paca
Pallas's long-tongued bat
Parnell's moustached bat
Prehensile-tailed porcupine

Pygmy sperm whale
Silky anteater
Smoky bat
Sperm whale
Spinner dolphin
Spix's disk-winged bat
Three-toed tree sloths
Vampire bat
Water opossum
Weeper capuchin
White-faced saki
White-tailed deer

HAITI
Blue whale
Brazilian free-tailed bat
Common bottlenosed dolphin
Funnel-eared bat
Greater bulldog bat
Hispaniolan solenodon
Humpback whale
Killer whale
Northern minke whale
Parnell's moustached bat
Pygmy sperm whale
Sperm whale
Spinner dolphin

HONDURAS
American least shrew
Blue whale
Brazilian free-tailed bat
Brown-throated three-toed
  sloth
Central American agouti
Collared peccary
Common bottlenosed dolphin
Funnel-eared bat
Geoffroy's spider monkey
Giant anteater
Greater bulldog bat
Greater dog-faced bat
Greater sac-winged bat
Hispid cotton rat
Hoffman's two-toed sloth
Humpback whale

Killer whale
Nine-banded armadillo
Northern minke whale
Paca
Pallas's long-tongued bat
Parnell's moustached bat
Pygmy sperm whale
Silky anteater
Sperm whale
Spinner dolphin
Spiny rat
Spix's disk-winged bat
Three-toed tree sloths
Vampire bat
Virginia opossum
Water opossum
White bat
White-tailed deer
White-throated capuchin

HUNGARY
Black-bellied hamster
Common bentwing bat
Edible dormouse
Ermine
Eurasian wild pig
European badger
Greater horseshoe bat
Red deer
Red fox

ICELAND
Blue whale
Harbor porpoise
Humpback whale
Killer whale
North Atlantic right whale
Northern bottlenosed whale
Northern minke whale
Norway lemming

INDIA
Asian elephant
Blue whale
Common bentwing bat

Common bottlenosed dolphin
Dromedary camel
Dugong
Ermine
Eurasian wild pig
Ganges and Indus dolphin
Gray wolf
Greater horseshoe bat
Hardwicke's lesser mouse-
  tailed bat
Humpback whale
Indian crested porcupine
Indian flying fox
Indian muntjac
Indian rhinoceros
Kiang
Killer whale
Lion
Northern minke whale
Pygmy sperm whale
Red fox
Red panda
Rhesus macaque
Serow
Snow leopard
Sperm whale
Spinner dolphin
Tiger
Water buffalo

INDONESIA
Asian elephant
Babirusa
Blue whale
Bornean orangutan
Common bentwing bat
Common bottlenosed dolphin
Common tree shrew
Dugong
Eurasian wild pig
European otter
Humpback whale
Indian muntjac
Killer whale
Lar gibbon
Lesser Malay mouse deer

Malayan colugo
Malayan moonrat
Malayan tapir
Naked bat
Northern minke whale
Proboscis monkey
Pygmy sperm whale
Serow
Siamang
Sperm whale
Spinner dolphin
Sumatran rhinoceros
Tiger
Western tarsier

IRAN
Blue whale
Common bentwing bat
Common bottlenosed dolphin
Dromedary camel
Dugong
Edible dormouse
Egyptian rousette
Egyptian spiny mouse
Eurasian wild pig
European badger
Gray wolf
Greater horseshoe bat
Hairy-footed jerboa
Humpback whale
Indian crested porcupine
Killer whale
Northern minke whale
Pygmy sperm whale
Red deer
Red fox
Sperm whale
Spinner dolphin
Trident leaf-nosed bat

IRAQ
Dromedary camel
Egyptian spiny mouse
Eurasian wild pig
Gray wolf
Greater horseshoe bat

Red fox
Trident leaf-nosed bat

IRELAND
Blue whale
Common bottlenosed dolphin
Ermine
Eurasian wild pig
European badger
European otter
Harbor porpoise
Humpback whale
Killer whale
Mountain hare
North Atlantic right whale
Northern bottlenosed whale
Northern minke whale
Red deer
Red fox
Sperm whale
Western European hedgehog

ISRAEL
Blue whale
Common bottlenosed dolphin
Dromedary camel
Egyptian rousette
Egyptian slit-faced bat
Egyptian spiny mouse
Eurasian wild pig
Gray wolf
Hardwicke's lesser mouse-
  tailed bat
Humpback whale
Indian crested porcupine
Northern minke whale
Pygmy sperm whale
Red fox
Rock hyrax
Sperm whale
Trident leaf-nosed bat

ITALY
Alpine marmot
Blue whale

Common bentwing bat
Common bottlenosed dolphin
Edible dormouse
Ermine
Eurasian wild pig
European badger
Gray wolf
Greater horseshoe bat
Humpback whale
Killer whale
Mountain hare
Northern minke whale
Pygmy sperm whale
Red deer
Red fox
Sperm whale
Western European hedgehog

IVORY COAST
Aardvark
African civet
Blue whale
Chimpanzee
Common bottlenosed dolphin
Common genet
Dwarf epauletted fruit bat
Egyptian rousette
Forest elephant
Forest hog
Gambian rat
Humpback whale
Lord Derby's anomalure
Northern minke whale
Pygmy hippopotamus
Pygmy sperm whale
Rock hyrax
Senegal bushbaby
South African porcupine
Sperm whale
Spinner dolphin
Western red colobus

JAMAICA
Blue whale
Brazilian free-tailed bat
Common bottlenosed dolphin

Funnel-eared bat
Greater bulldog bat
Humpback whale
Killer whale
Northern minke whale
Pallas's long-tongued bat
Parnell's moustached bat
Pygmy sperm whale
Sperm whale
Spinner dolphin

JAPAN
Blue whale
Common bentwing bat
Common bottlenosed dolphin
Dugong
Ermine
Eurasian wild pig
European badger
European otter
Gray whale
Greater horseshoe bat
Harbor porpoise
Humpback whale
Killer whale
Marianas fruit bat
Mountain hare
Northern minke whale
Northern pika
Pygmy sperm whale
Reindeer
Siberian musk deer
Sperm whale
Spinner dolphin

JORDAN
Dromedary camel
Egyptian slit-faced bat
Egyptian spiny mouse
Eurasian wild pig
Gray wolf
Hardwicke's lesser mouse-
   tailed bat
Red fox
Rock hyrax
Trident leaf-nosed bat

KAZAKHSTAN
Black-bellied hamster
Common bentwing bat
Edible dormouse
Ermine
Eurasian wild pig
European badger
Gray wolf
Hairy-footed jerboa
Moose
Mountain hare
Red deer
Red fox
Snow leopard

KENYA
Aardvark
Aardwolf
African civet
Blue whale
Common bentwing bat
Common bottlenosed dolphin
Common genet
Dugong
Egyptian rousette
Egyptian slit-faced bat
Forest hog
Gambian rat
Giraffe
Greater cane rat
Grevy's zebra
Ground pangolin
Humpback whale
Kirk's dikdik
Lion
Lord Derby's anomalure
Naked mole-rat
Northern greater bushbaby
Northern minke whale
Potto
Pygmy sperm whale
Rock hyrax
Senegal bushbaby
South African porcupine
Sperm whale
Spinner dolphin

Springhare
Thomson's gazelle

KUWAIT
Egyptian spiny mouse
Gray wolf
Trident leaf-nosed bat

KYRGYZSTAN
Common bentwing bat
Edible dormouse
Ermine
Eurasian wild pig
European badger
Gray wolf
Red deer
Red fox
Snow leopard

LAOS
Asian elephant
Common bentwing bat
Eurasian wild pig
Greater horseshoe bat
Indian muntjac
Lesser Malay mouse deer
Malayan tapir
Pileated gibbon
Pygmy slow loris
Red fox
Red-shanked douc langur
Rhesus macaque
Serow

LATVIA
Blue whale
Common bottlenosed dolphin
Ermine
Eurasian wild pig
European badger
Gray wolf
Harbor porpoise
Humpback whale
Moose
Mountain hare

Northern minke whale
Red deer
Red fox
Sperm whale

LEBANON
Blue whale
Common bottlenosed dolphin
Dromedary camel
Egyptian spiny mouse
Hardwicke's lesser mouse-
  tailed bat
Humpback whale
Northern minke whale
Pygmy sperm whale
Sperm whale
Trident leaf-nosed bat

LESOTHO
Aardvark
African civet
Common bentwing bat
Common genet
Egyptian slit-faced bat
South African porcupine

LESSER ANTILLES
Blue whale
Brazilian free-tailed bat
Common bottlenosed dolphin
Funnel-eared bat
Greater bulldog bat
Humpback whale
Killer whale
Northern minke whale
Pygmy sperm whale
Sperm whale
Spinner dolphin

LIBERIA
Aardvark
African civet
Blue whale
Common bottlenosed dolphin

Common genet
Forest elephant
Forest hog
Humpback whale
Killer whale
Lord Derby's anomalure
Northern minke whale
Pygmy hippopotamus
Pygmy sperm whale
Rock hyrax
South African porcupine
Sperm whale
Spinner dolphin
Western red colobus

LIBYA
Blue whale
Common bottlenosed dolphin
Dromedary camel
Egyptian spiny mouse
Eurasian wild pig
Greater horseshoe bat
Humpback whale
Mzab gundi
Northern minke whale
Pygmy sperm whale
Red fox
Sperm whale
Trident leaf-nosed bat

LIECHTENSTEIN
Ermine
Eurasian wild pig
Greater horseshoe bat
Red deer
Red fox

LITHUANIA
Blue whale
Common bottlenosed dolphin
Edible dormouse
Ermine
Eurasian wild pig
European badger
Harbor porpoise

Humpback whale
Moose
Mountain hare
Northern minke whale
Red deer
Red fox
Sperm whale

LUXEMBOURG
Edible dormouse
Ermine
Eurasian wild pig
European badger
Greater horseshoe bat
Red deer
Red fox

MACEDONIA
Common bentwing bat
Edible dormouse
Eurasian wild pig
European badger
Gray wolf
Greater horseshoe bat
Red deer
Red fox

MADAGASCAR
Aye-aye
Blue whale
Common bentwing bat
Common bottlenosed dolphin
Common tenrec
Crowned lemur
Dugong
Fossa
Humpback whale
Indri
Killer whale
Milne-Edwards's sifaka
Northern minke whale
Old World sucker-footed bat
Pygmy sperm whale
Red mouse lemur

Red-tailed sportive lemur
Ringtailed lemur
Ring-tailed mongoose
Sperm whale
Spinner dolphin
White-footed sportive lemur
Yellow-streaked tenrec

MALAWI
Aardvark
African civet
Checkered sengi
Common bentwing bat
Common genet
Egyptian slit-faced bat
Gambian rat
Ground pangolin
South African porcupine

MALAYSIA
Asian elephant
Blue whale
Bornean orangutan
Common bentwing bat
Common bottlenosed dolphin
Common tree shrew
Dugong
Eurasian wild pig
Humpback whale
Indian muntjac
Killer whale
Lar gibbon
Lesser Malay mouse deer
Malayan colugo
Malayan moonrat
Malayan tapir
Naked bat
Northern minke whale
Proboscis monkey
Pygmy sperm whale
Serow
Siamang
Sperm whale
Spinner dolphin
Sumatran rhinoceros

MALI
Aardvark
African civet
Common genet
Dromedary camel
Egyptian rousette
Egyptian slit-faced bat
Gambian rat
Mzab gundi
Rock hyrax
Savanna elephant
Senegal bushbaby

MARIANA ISLANDS
Marianas fruit bat

MAURITANIA
Aardvark
Blue whale
Common bottlenosed dolphin
Dromedary camel
Humpback whale
Killer whale
Northern minke whale
Pygmy sperm whale
Sperm whale
Spinner dolphin

MEXICO
American black bear
American least shrew
Bighorn sheep
Black-tailed prairie dog
Blue whale
Bobcat
Brazilian free-tailed bat
Brown-throated three-toed
  sloth
California leaf-nosed bat
California sea lion
Central American agouti
Collared peccary
Common bottlenosed dolphin
Desert cottontail
Eastern mole

Funnel-eared bat
Geoffroy's spider monkey
Gray whale
Greater bulldog bat
Greater dog-faced bat
Greater sac-winged bat
Hispid cotton rat
Humpback whale
Killer whale
Little brown bat
Muskrat
Nine-banded armadillo
North American beaver
North American porcupine
Northern elephant seal
Northern minke whale
Northern raccoon
Paca
Pallas's long-tongued bat
Pallid bat
Parnell's moustached bat
Pronghorn
Puma
Pygmy sperm whale
Silky anteater
Sperm whale
Spinner dolphin
Spix's disk-winged bat
Striped skunk
Three-toed tree sloths
Valley pocket gopher
Vampire bat
Virginia opossum
Water opossum
White-tailed deer

MOLDOVA
Black-bellied hamster
Common bentwing bat
Edible dormouse
Eurasian wild pig
European badger
Gray wolf
Greater horseshoe bat
Red deer
Red fox

MONACO
European badger
Red fox

MONGOLIA
Ermine
Eurasian wild pig
Gray wolf
Hairy-footed jerboa
Moose
Mountain hare
Northern pika
Przewalski's horse
Red deer
Red fox
Reindeer
Siberian musk deer
Snow leopard

MOROCCO
Blue whale
Common bentwing bat
Common bottlenosed dolphin
Dromedary camel
Eurasian wild pig
European otter
Greater horseshoe bat
Harbor porpoise
Hardwicke's lesser mouse-tailed bat
Humpback whale
Killer whale
North Atlantic right whale
Northern bottlenosed whale
Northern minke whale
Pygmy sperm whale
Red deer
Red fox
Sperm whale
Spinner dolphin
Trident leaf-nosed bat

MOZAMBIQUE
Aardvark

African civet
Blue whale
Checkered sengi
Common bentwing bat
Common bottlenosed dolphin
Common genet
Common hippopotamus
Dugong
Egyptian rousette
Egyptian slit-faced bat
Gambian rat
Ground pangolin
Humpback whale
Killer whale
Lord Derby's anomalure
Northern minke whale
Pygmy sperm whale
Rock hyrax
South African porcupine
Sperm whale
Spinner dolphin
Springhare
White rhinoceros

MYANMAR
Asian elephant
Blue whale
Common bentwing bat
Common bottlenosed dolphin
Eurasian wild pig
Gray wolf
Greater horseshoe bat
Humpback whale
Indian flying fox
Indian muntjac
Kitti's hog-nosed bat
Lar gibbon
Lesser Malay mouse deer
Malayan moonrat
Malayan tapir
Northern minke whale
Pygmy sperm whale
Red fox
Red panda
Rhesus macaque
Serow

Sperm whale
Spinner dolphin
Tiger

NAMIBIA
Aardvark
African civet
Blue whale
Common bentwing bat
Common bottlenosed dolphin
Common genet
Common hippopotamus
Damaraland mole-rat
Dassie rat
Egyptian slit-faced bat
Giraffe
Grant's desert golden mole
Ground pangolin
Humpback whale
Killer whale
Kirk's dikdik
Northern minke whale
Pygmy sperm whale
Rock hyrax
Savanna elephant
Sperm whale
Springhare

NEPAL
Asian elephant
Common bentwing bat
Eurasian wild pig
Ganges and Indus dolphin
Gray wolf
Greater horseshoe bat
Indian crested porcupine
Indian muntjac
Indian rhinoceros
Kiang
Red fox
Red panda
Rhesus macaque
Serow
Snow leopard
Water buffalo

NETHERLANDS
Black-bellied hamster
Blue whale
Common bottlenosed dolphin
Ermine
Eurasian wild pig
European badger
Harbor porpoise
Humpback whale
Killer whale
Northern minke whale
Northern raccoon
Pygmy sperm whale
Red deer
Red fox
Sperm whale
Western European hedgehog

NEW ZEALAND
Blue whale
Brush-tailed rock wallaby
Common bottlenosed dolphin
Common brush-tailed possum
Dugong
Humpback whale
Killer whale
Lesser New Zealand short-
  tailed bat
Northern minke whale
Pygmy right whale
Pygmy sperm whale
Shepherd's beaked whale
Sperm whale

NICARAGUA
American least shrew
Blue whale
Brazilian free-tailed bat
Brown-throated three-toed
  sloth
Central American agouti
Collared peccary
Common bottlenosed dolphin
Funnel-eared bat
Geoffroy's spider monkey

Giant anteater
Greater bulldog bat
Greater dog-faced bat
Greater sac-winged bat
Hispid cotton rat
Hoffman's two-toed sloth
Humpback whale
Killer whale
Nine-banded armadillo
Northern minke whale
Paca
Pallas's long-tongued bat
Parnell's moustached bat
Pygmy sperm whale
Silky anteater
Sperm whale
Spinner dolphin
Spiny rat
Spix's disk-winged bat
Three-toed tree sloths
Vampire bat
Virginia opossum
Water opossum
White bat
White-tailed deer
White-throated capuchin

NIGER
Aardvark
Dromedary camel
Egyptian slit-faced bat
Gambian rat
Mzab gundi
Rock hyrax
Senegal bushbaby
Trident leaf-nosed bat

NIGERIA
Aardvark
African civet
Blue whale
Chimpanzee
Common bottlenosed dolphin
Common genet
Dwarf epauletted fruit bat

Egyptian rousette
Egyptian slit-faced bat
Gambian rat
Humpback whale
Lord Derby's anomalure
Northern minke whale
Potto
Pygmy sperm whale
Rock hyrax
Senegal bushbaby
South African porcupine
Sperm whale
Spinner dolphin
Western gorilla
Western red colobus

NORTH KOREA
Blue whale
Common bentwing bat
Common bottlenosed dolphin
Eurasian wild pig
Humpback whale
Killer whale
Northern minke whale
Northern pika
Pygmy sperm whale
Red deer
Siberian musk deer
Sperm whale
Spinner dolphin

NORWAY
Blue whale
Common bottlenosed dolphin
Ermine
Eurasian wild pig
European badger
European otter
Harbor porpoise
Humpback whale
Killer whale
Moose
Mountain hare
North Atlantic right whale
Northern bottlenosed whale

Northern minke whale
Norway lemming
Polar bear
Red deer
Red fox
Reindeer
Sperm whale
Western European hedgehog

OMAN
Blue whale
Common bottlenosed dolphin
Dromedary camel
Dugong
Egyptian rousette
Egyptian spiny mouse
Gray wolf
Humpback whale
Killer whale
Northern minke whale
Pygmy sperm whale
Rock hyrax
Sperm whale
Spinner dolphin
Trident leaf-nosed bat

PAKISTAN
Blue whale
Common bentwing bat
Common bottlenosed dolphin
Dromedary camel
Dugong
Eurasian wild pig
Ganges and Indus dolphin
Gray wolf
Greater horseshoe bat
Hardwicke's lesser mouse-
  tailed bat
Humpback whale
Indian flying fox
Indian muntjac
Indian rhinoceros
Kiang
Killer whale
Northern minke whale

Pygmy sperm whale
Red fox
Rhesus macaque
Snow leopard
Sperm whale
Spinner dolphin
Trident leaf-nosed bat

PANAMA
American least shrew
Blue whale
Brazilian free-tailed bat
Brown-throated three-toed
  sloth
Capybara
Central American agouti
Collared peccary
Common bottlenosed dolphin
Funnel-eared bat
Geoffroy's spider monkey
Giant anteater
Greater bulldog bat
Greater dog-faced bat
Greater sac-winged bat
Hispid cotton rat
Hoffman's two-toed sloth
Humpback whale
Killer whale
Nine-banded armadillo
Northern minke whale
Northern raccoon
Paca
Pallas's long-tongued bat
Parnell's moustached bat
Puma
Pygmy sperm whale
Silky anteater
Smoky bat
Sperm whale
Spinner dolphin
Spiny rat
Spix's disk-winged bat
Three-toed tree sloths
Vampire bat
Water opossum
White bat

White-tailed deer
White-throated capuchin

PAPUA NEW GUINEA
Blue whale
Common bentwing bat
Common bottlenosed dolphin
Dugong
Ground cuscus
Humpback whale
Killer whale
Northern minke whale
Pygmy sperm whale
Rufous spiny bandicoot
Short-beaked echidna
Sperm whale
Spinner dolphin
Sugar glider

PARAGUAY
Brazilian free-tailed bat
Brown-throated three-toed
  sloth
Capybara
Collared peccary
Coypu
Giant anteater
Greater bulldog bat
Maned wolf
Nine-banded armadillo
Paca
Pallas's long-tongued bat
Prehensile-tailed porcupine
Three-toed tree sloths
Vampire bat
Water opossum

PERU
Alpaca
Ashy chinchilla rat
Bald uakari
Blue whale
Boto
Brazilian free-tailed bat
Burmeister's porpoise

Capybara
Central American agouti
Collared peccary
Common bottlenosed
  dolphin
Giant anteater
Goeldi's monkey
Greater bulldog bat
Greater dog-faced bat
Greater sac-winged bat
Hoffman's two-toed sloth
Humpback whale
Killer whale
Llama
Lowland tapir
Maned wolf
Nine-banded armadillo
Northern minke whale
Pacarana
Pallas's long-tongued bat
Parnell's moustached bat
Pearson's tuco-tuco
Pygmy marmoset
Pygmy sperm whale
Silky anteater
Sperm whale
Spinner dolphin
Spix's disk-winged bat
Vampire bat
Water opossum
White-faced saki
White-tailed deer

PHILIPPINES
Blue whale
Common bentwing bat
Common bottlenosed
  dolphin
Dugong
Humpback whale
Naked bat
Northern minke whale
Philippine tarsier
Pygmy sperm whale
Sperm whale
Spinner dolphin

POLAND
Black-bellied hamster
Blue whale
Common bentwing bat
Common bottlenosed
  dolphin
Edible dormouse
Ermine
Eurasian wild pig
European badger
Greater horseshoe bat
Harbor porpoise
Humpback whale
Moose
Northern minke whale
Red deer
Red fox
Sperm whale

PORTUGAL
Blue whale
Common bentwing bat
Common bottlenosed
  dolphin
Common genet
Eurasian wild pig
European badger
European otter
Greater horseshoe bat
Harbor porpoise
Humpback whale
Killer whale
North Atlantic right whale
Northern bottlenosed whale
Northern minke whale
Pygmy sperm whale
Red deer
Red fox
Sperm whale
Western barbastelle
Western European hedgehog

PUERTO RICO
Blue whale
Brazilian free-tailed bat

Common bottlenosed
  dolphin
Funnel-eared bat
Greater bulldog bat
Humpback whale
Killer whale
Northern minke whale
Pygmy sperm whale
Sperm whale
Spinner dolphin

QATAR
Egyptian spiny mouse

ROMANIA
Black-bellied hamster
Common bentwing bat
Edible dormouse
Eurasian wild pig
European badger
Gray wolf
Greater horseshoe bat
Harbor porpoise
Red deer
Red fox

RUSSIA
Beluga
Black-bellied hamster
Blue whale
Common bentwing bat
Common bottlenosed
  dolphin
Edible dormouse
Ermine
Eurasian wild pig
European otter
Gray whale
Gray wolf
Harbor porpoise
Harp seal
Humpback whale
Killer whale
Moose
Mountain hare
Narwhal

Northern minke whale
Northern pika
Northern raccoon
Polar bear
Red deer
Red fox
Reindeer
Siberian musk deer
Snow leopard
Sperm whale
Tiger
Walrus
Western European hedgehog

RWANDA
Aardvark
African civet
Chimpanzee
Common bentwing bat
Common genet
Egyptian slit-faced bat
Gambian rat
Lord Derby's anomalure
Rock hyrax
Senegal bushbaby
South African porcupine

SAUDI ARABIA
Blue whale
Common bottlenosed dolphin
Dromedary camel
Dugong
Egyptian slit-faced bat
Egyptian spiny mouse
Gray wolf
Hardwicke's lesser mouse-
    tailed bat
Humpback whale
Indian crested porcupine
Northern minke whale
Pygmy sperm whale
Rock hyrax
Sperm whale
Spinner dolphin
Trident leaf-nosed bat

SENEGAL
Aardvark
African civet
Blue whale
Chimpanzee
Common bottlenosed dolphin
Common genet
Egyptian slit-faced bat
Gambian rat
Hardwicke's lesser mouse-
    tailed bat
Humpback whale
Killer whale
Northern minke whale
Pygmy sperm whale
Rock hyrax
Senegal bushbaby
South African porcupine
Sperm whale
Spinner dolphin
Western red colobus

SIERRA LEONE
Aardvark
African civet
Blue whale
Chimpanzee
Common bottlenosed dolphin
Common genet
Egyptian slit-faced bat
Forest hog
Gambian rat
Humpback whale
Killer whale
Lord Derby's anomalure
Northern minke whale
Potto
Pygmy hippopotamus
Pygmy sperm whale
Rock hyrax
Senegal bushbaby
South African porcupine
Sperm whale
Spinner dolphin
Western red colobus

SINGAPORE
Lesser Malay mouse deer

SLOVAKIA
Black-bellied hamster
Edible dormouse
Ermine
European badger
Greater horseshoe bat
Red deer
Red fox

SLOVENIA
Blue whale
Common bentwing bat
Common bottlenosed dolphin
Edible dormouse
Ermine
Eurasian wild pig
European badger
Greater horseshoe bat
Humpback whale
Northern minke whale
Pygmy sperm whale
Red deer
Red fox
Sperm whale

SOMALIA
Aardwolf
African civet
Blue whale
Common bentwing bat
Common bottlenosed dolphin
Common genet
Dromedary camel
Dugong
Egyptian slit-faced bat
Humpback whale
Kirk's dikdik
Naked mole-rat
Northern greater bushbaby
Northern minke whale
Pygmy sperm whale

Rock hyrax
Senegal bushbaby
South African porcupine
Sperm whale
Spinner dolphin

SOUTH AFRICA
Aardvark
Aardwolf
African civet
Black wildebeest
Blue whale
Cape horseshoe bat
Common bentwing bat
Common bottlenosed dolphin
Common genet
Damaraland mole-rat
Dassie rat
Egyptian rousette
Egyptian slit-faced bat
Gambian rat
Giraffe
Grant's desert golden mole
Ground pangolin
Humpback whale
Killer whale
Northern minke whale
Pygmy right whale
Pygmy sperm whale
Rock hyrax
Savanna elephant
Shepherd's beaked whale
South African porcupine
Southern tree hyrax
Sperm whale
Spinner dolphin
Springhare

SOUTH KOREA
Blue whale
Common bentwing bat
Common bottlenosed dolphin
Eurasian wild pig
Humpback whale
Killer whale

Northern minke whale
Pygmy sperm whale
Sperm whale
Spinner dolphin

SPAIN
Alpine marmot
Blue whale
Common bentwing bat
Common bottlenosed dolphin
Common genet
Edible dormouse
Eurasian wild pig
European badger
European otter
Gray wolf
Greater horseshoe bat
Harbor porpoise
Humpback whale
Killer whale
North Atlantic right whale
Northern bottlenosed whale
Northern minke whale
Pygmy sperm whale
Red deer
Red fox
Sperm whale
Western barbastelle
Western European hedgehog

SRI LANKA
Asian elephant
European otter
Indian crested porcupine
Indian flying fox
Indian muntjac

SUDAN
Aardvark
African civet
Blue whale
Chimpanzee
Common bottlenosed dolphin
Common genet

Common hippopotamus
Dromedary camel
Dugong
Dwarf epauletted fruit bat
Egyptian slit-faced bat
Gambian rat
Giraffe
Greater cane rat
Ground pangolin
Humpback whale
Northern minke whale
Pygmy sperm whale
Rock hyrax
Senegal bushbaby
South African porcupine
Sperm whale
Spinner dolphin
Spotted hyena
Thomson's gazelle
Trident leaf-nosed bat
White rhinoceros

SURINAME
Blue whale
Collared peccary
Common bottlenosed dolphin
Common squirrel monkey
Funnel-eared bat
Giant anteater
Greater bulldog bat
Greater dog-faced bat
Greater sac-winged bat
Humpback whale
Lowland tapir
Northern minke whale
Paca
Pallas's long-tongued bat
Parnell's moustached bat
Prehensile-tailed porcupine
Pygmy sperm whale
Silky anteater
Smoky bat
Sperm whale
Spinner dolphin
Spix's disk-winged bat
Three-toed tree sloths

Vampire bat
Water opossum
Weeper capuchin
White-faced saki
White-tailed deer

SWAZILAND
Aardvark
African civet
Common bentwing bat
Common genet
Egyptian slit-faced bat
Gambian rat
Giraffe
Ground pangolin
South African porcupine

SWEDEN
Blue whale
Common bottlenosed dolphin
Ermine
Eurasian wild pig
European badger
Gray wolf
Harbor porpoise
Humpback whale
Moose
Mountain hare
Northern minke whale
Norway lemming
Red deer
Red fox
Sperm whale
Western European hedgehog

SWITZERLAND
Alpine marmot
Common bentwing bat
Edible dormouse
Ermine
Eurasian wild pig
European badger
Greater horseshoe bat
Mountain hare
Red deer

Red fox
Western European hedgehog

SYRIA
Blue whale
Common bottlenosed dolphin
Dromedary camel
Egyptian spiny mouse
Eurasian wild pig
Gray wolf
Greater horseshoe bat
Hardwicke's lesser mouse-
  tailed bat
Humpback whale
Northern minke whale
Pygmy sperm whale
Red deer
Red fox
Sperm whale
Trident leaf-nosed bat

TAJIKISTAN
Common bentwing bat
Edible dormouse
Ermine
Eurasian wild pig
European badger
Gray wolf
Greater horseshoe bat
Red deer
Red fox
Snow leopard

TANZANIA
Aardvark
African civet
Blue whale
Checkered sengi
Chimpanzee
Common bentwing bat
Common bottlenosed dolphin
Common genet
Common hippopotamus
Dugong
Egyptian rousette

Egyptian slit-faced bat
Gambian rat
Giraffe
Greater cane rat
Ground pangolin
Humpback whale
Killer whale
Kirk's dikdik
Lion
Lord Derby's anomalure
Northern greater bushbaby
Northern minke whale
Pygmy sperm whale
Rock hyrax
Senegal bushbaby
South African porcupine
Sperm whale
Spinner dolphin
Springhare
Thomson's gazelle

THAILAND
Asian elephant
Blue whale
Common bentwing bat
Common bottlenosed dolphin
Common tree shrew
Dugong
Eurasian wild pig
Greater horseshoe bat
Humpback whale
Indian muntjac
Kitti's hog-nosed bat
Lar gibbon
Lesser Malay mouse deer
Malayan colugo
Malayan moonrat
Malayan tapir
Northern minke whale
Pileated gibbon
Pygmy sperm whale
Red fox
Rhesus macaque
Serow
Sperm whale

Spinner dolphin
Water buffalo

TOGO
Aardvark
African civet
Blue whale
Common bottlenosed dolphin
Common genet
Forest hog
Gambian rat
Humpback whale
Lord Derby's anomalure
Northern minke whale
Pygmy sperm whale
Rock hyrax
Senegal bushbaby
South African porcupine
Sperm whale
Spinner dolphin

TRINIDAD AND TOBAGO
Pallas's long-tongued bat
Prehensile-tailed porcupine
Silky anteater
Smoky bat
Vampire bat

TUNISIA
Blue whale
Common bentwing bat
Common bottlenosed dolphin
Common genet
Dromedary camel
Eurasian wild pig
European otter
Greater horseshoe bat
Humpback whale
Killer whale
Northern minke whale
Pygmy sperm whale
Red deer
Red fox
Sperm whale
Trident leaf-nosed bat

TURKEY
Blue whale
Common bentwing bat
Common bottlenosed dolphin
Edible dormouse
Egyptian rousette
Eurasian wild pig
European badger
Gray wolf
Greater horseshoe bat
Harbor porpoise
Humpback whale
Northern minke whale
Pygmy sperm whale
Red deer
Sperm whale

TURKMENISTAN
Common bentwing bat
Edible dormouse
Eurasian wild pig
European badger
Gray wolf
Greater horseshoe bat
Hairy-footed jerboa
Red deer
Red fox

UGANDA
Aardvark
African civet
Checkered sengi
Chimpanzee
Common bentwing bat
Common genet
Dwarf epauletted fruit bat
Egyptian rousette
Egyptian slit-faced bat
Forest hog
Gambian rat
Giraffe
Greater cane rat
Ground pangolin
Lord Derby's anomalure
Potto

Senegal bushbaby
South African porcupine
White rhinoceros

UKRAINE
Alpine marmot
Black-bellied hamster
Common bentwing bat
Edible dormouse
Ermine
Eurasian wild pig
European badger
Gray wolf
Greater horseshoe bat
Harbor porpoise
Moose
Red deer
Red fox

UNITED ARAB EMIRATES
Dromedary camel
Egyptian spiny mouse
Gray wolf
Trident leaf-nosed bat

UNITED KINGDOM
Blue whale
Common bottlenosed dolphin
Ermine
Eurasian wild pig
European badger
European otter
Greater horseshoe bat
Harbor porpoise
Humpback whale
Killer whale
Mountain hare
North Atlantic right whale
Northern bottlenosed whale
Northern minke whale
Pygmy sperm whale
Red deer
Red fox
Sperm whale

Western barbastelle
Western European hedgehog

UNITED STATES
American bison
American black bear
American least shrew
American pika
American water shrew
Beluga
Bighorn sheep
Black-tailed prairie dog
Blue whale
Bobcat
Brazilian free-tailed bat
California leaf-nosed bat
California sea lion
Collared peccary
Common bottlenosed dolphin
Desert cottontail
Eastern chipmunk
Eastern mole
Ermine
Giant kangaroo rat
Gray squirrel
Gray whale
Gray wolf
Harbor porpoise
Hawaiian monk seal
Hispid cotton rat
Humpback whale
Killer whale
Little brown bat
Moose
Mountain beaver
Muskrat
Narwhal
Nine-banded armadillo
North American beaver
North American porcupine
North Atlantic right whale
Northern bottlenosed whale
Northern elephant seal
Northern minke whale
Northern raccoon
Pallid bat

Polar bear
Pronghorn
Puma
Pygmy sperm whale
Red deer
Red fox
Reindeer
San Joaquin pocket mouse
Snowshoe hare
Southern flying squirrel
Sperm whale
Spinner dolphin
Star-nosed mole
Steller's sea cow
Striped skunk
Valley pocket gopher
Virginia opossum
Walrus
West Indian manatee
White-tailed deer

URUGUAY
Blue whale
Brazilian free-tailed bat
Burmeister's porpoise
Capybara
Collared peccary
Common bottlenosed dolphin
Coypu
Franciscana dolphin
Giant anteater
Humpback whale
Killer whale
Maned wolf
Northern minke whale
Pearson's tuco-tuco
Prehensile-tailed porcupine
Pygmy right whale
Red deer
Sperm whale
Vampire bat

UZBEKISTAN
Common bentwing bat
Edible dormouse

Eurasian wild pig
European badger
Gray wolf
Hairy-footed jerboa
Red deer
Red fox
Snow leopard

VENEZUELA
Blue whale
Boto
Brazilian free-tailed bat
Capybara
Collared peccary
Colombian woolly monkey
Common bottlenosed dolphin
Common squirrel monkey
Funnel-eared bat
Giant anteater
Greater bulldog bat
Greater dog-faced bat
Greater sac-winged bat
Hispid cotton rat
Hoffman's two-toed sloth
Humpback whale
Lowland tapir
Northern minke whale
Paca
Pacarana
Pallas's long-tongued bat
Parnell's moustached bat
Prehensile-tailed porcupine
Puma
Pygmy sperm whale
Silky anteater
Silky shrew opossum
Smoky bat
Sperm whale
Spinner dolphin
Spix's disk-winged bat
Three-striped night monkey
Three-toed tree sloths
Vampire bat
Venezuelan red howler
  monkey
Water opossum

Weeper capuchin
White-tailed deer

VIETNAM
Asian elephant
Blue whale
Common bentwing bat
Common bottlenosed dolphin
Dugong
Eurasian wild pig
Greater horseshoe bat
Humpback whale
Indian muntjac
Malayan tapir
Northern minke whale
Pygmy slow loris
Pygmy sperm whale
Red fox
Red-shanked douc langur
Rhesus macaque
Serow
Sperm whale
Spinner dolphin

YEMEN
Blue whale
Common bottlenosed dolphin
Dromedary camel
Dugong
Egyptian rousette

Egyptian slit-faced bat
Egyptian spiny mouse
Gray wolf
Hardwicke's lesser mouse-
    tailed bat
Humpback whale
Northern minke whale
Pygmy sperm whale
Rock hyrax
Sperm whale
Spinner dolphin
Trident leaf-nosed bat

YUGOSLAVIA
Alpine marmot
Blue whale
Common bentwing bat
Common bottlenosed dolphin
Edible dormouse
Ermine
Gray wolf
Greater horseshoe bat
Humpback whale
Northern minke whale
Pygmy sperm whale
Red deer
Sperm whale

ZAMBIA
Aardvark

Aardwolf
African civet
Checkered sengi
Common bentwing bat
Common genet
Common hippopotamus
Egyptian rousette
Egyptian slit-faced bat
Gambian rat
Giraffe
Ground pangolin
Lord Derby's anomalure
South African porcupine
Spotted hyena
Springhare

ZIMBABWE
Aardvark
African civet
Common bentwing bat
Common genet
Damaraland mole-rat
Egyptian rousette
Egyptian slit-faced bat
Gambian rat
Ground pangolin
Savanna elephant
South African porcupine
Spotted hyena
Springhare

Index

Italic type indicates volume number; **boldface** type indicates entries and their pages; (ill.) indicates illustrations.

Ant catchers. *See* Tamanduas

Antarctic fur seals, *3:* 675–76, 675 (ill.), 676 (ill.)

Antarctic minke whales, *4:* 786

Anteaters, *1:* 9, 178–82, **195–202**
    See also Echidnas; Numbats; Pangolins

Antechinus, *1:* 53

Antelopes, *4:* 969–87

Antilocapra americana. See Pronghorn

Antilocapridae. *See* Pronghorn

Antrozous pallidus. See Pallid bats

Ants
    eating, *1:* 9
    formacid, *5:* 991

Aotidae. *See* Night monkeys

Aotus trivirgatus. See Three-striped night monkeys

Apes, great, *3:* 423, **563–77**

Aplodontia rufa. See Mountain beavers

Aplodontidae. *See* Mountain beavers

Aquatic tenrecs, *2:* 232, 234

Arctic foxes, *3:* 583

Arctocephalus gazella. See Antarctic fur seals

Armadillos, *1:* 178–82, **203–11**

Armored rats, *5:* 1182

Arnoux's beaked whales, *4:* 751

Arra-jarra-ja. *See* Southern marsupial moles

Artiodactyla. *See* Even-toed ungulates

Asellia tridens. See Trident leaf-nosed bats

Ashy chinchilla rats, *5:* 1178, 1179–80, 1179 (ill.), 1180 (ill.)

Asian chevrotains, *4:* 927

Asian elephants, *4:* 813–14, 813 (ill.), 814 (ill.), 817

Asian false vampire bats, *2:* 324

Asian rhinoceroses, *4:* 849

Asiatic black bears, *3:* 593, 594, 595

Asiatic water shrews, *2:* 213–14

Asses, *4:* 848, 850, **854–64**

Astonishing Elephant (Alexander), *4:* 811

Ateles geoffroyi. See Geoffroy's spider monkeys

Atelidae. *See* Howler monkeys; Spider monkeys

Atherura species, *5:* 1111, 1112

Atlantic bottlenosed dolphins. *See* Common bottlenosed dolphins

Atlantic bottlenosed whales. *See* Northern bottlenosed whales

Australasian carnivorous marsupials, *1:* **51–55,** 75

Australian Bilby Appreciation Society, *1:* 77

Australian false vampire bats, *2:* 323, 324–25, 326–28, 326 (ill.), 327 (ill.)

Australian ghost bats. *See* Australian false vampire bats

Australian jumping mice, *5:* 1062–63, 1062 (ill.), 1063 (ill.)

Australian Koala Foundation, *1:* 109

Australian Platypus Conservancy, *1:* 22

Australian sea lions, *3:* 674

Australian water rats, *5:* 998

Avahis, *3:* **458–65**

Aye-ayes, *3:* 424, **475–79,** 477 (ill.), 478 (ill.)

Azara's agoutis, *5:* 1155

B

Babirusas, *4:* 894, 897–98, 897 (ill.), 899 (ill.)

Baboon lemurs, *3:* 459

Baboons, *3:* 424, 425, 426

Babyrousa babyrussa. See Babirusas

Bactrian camels, *4:* 917, 918

Badgers, *3:* 579, **614–27,** 629, 637

Bahaman funnel-eared bats, *2:* 379

Bahamian hutias, *5:* 1189

Baijis, *4:* 707, **714–18,** 716 (ill.), 717 (ill.)

Baird's beaked whales, *4:* 751

Balaena mysticetus. See Bowhead whales

Balaenidae. *See* Bowhead whales; Right whales

Balaenoptera acutorostrata. See Northern minke whales

Balaenoptera musculus. See Blue whales

Balaenopteridae. *See* Rorquals

Bald uakaris, *3:* 516, 520–22, 520 (ill.), 521 (ill.)

Baleen whales, *4:* 704–6, 777, 783–84, 787, 789, 795

Bamboo lemurs, *3:* 451

Banded anteaters. *See* Numbats

Bandicoots, *1:* 74–78, **79–87**
    See also Spiny bandicoots

Barbados raccoons, *3:* 581

Barbara's titis, *3:* 517

Barbastella barbastellus. See Western barbastelles

Barbastelles, western, *2:* 415–16, 415 (ill.), 416 (ill.)

Barred bandicoots. *See* Eastern barred bandicoots

Bathyergidae. *See* African mole-rats

Bats, *2:* **275–81**
    American leaf-nosed, *2:* **345–57**
    bulldog, *2:* **364–70**
    disk-winged, *2:* 384, **388–94,** 396
    false vampire, *2:* **323–29**
    free-tailed, *2:* 278, 279, **399–408**
    fruit, *2:* 277, 280, 282–97, 315, 345

Dog-faced bats, greater,
2: 309–10, 309 (ill.), 310 (ill.)
Dogs, 3: 578, 580, 581, **583–92**
prairie, 5: 998, 1015–16,
1015 (ill.), 1016 (ill.)
raccoon, 3: 583, 629
Dolichotis patagonum. See
Maras
Dolphins, 4: 703–8, 729,
737–48
baiji, 4: **714–18**, 716 (ill.),
717 (ill.)
boto, 4: **724–28**, 726 (ill.),
727 (ill.)
Franciscana, 4: **719–23**,
721 (ill.), 722 (ill.)
Ganges and Indus,
4: **709–13**, 711 (ill.), 712
(ill.)
Domestic cats, 3: 658
Domestic dogs, 3: 585
Domestic horses, 4: 848, 849,
852, 855–56
Domestic livestock, 4: 890
Domestic pigs, 4: 893, 894
Donkeys, 4: 856
Dormice, 5: **1087–92**
Douc langurs, red-shanked,
3: 537, 544–45, 544 (ill.),
545 (ill.)
Dourocouli. *See* Night
monkeys
Dracula (Stoker), 2: 279, 346
Dromedary camels, 4: 917,
919–20, 919 (ill.), 920 (ill.)
Dromiciops australis. See
Monitos del monte
Dromiciops gliroides. See
Monitos del monte
Dryland mouse opossums,
1: 25
Duck-billed platypus, 1: 1–6,
15–23, 20 (ill.), 21 (ill.)
Dugong dugon. See Dugongs
Dugongidae. *See* Dugongs; Sea
cows
Dugongs, 4: 828–32, **833–40**,
838 (ill.), 839 (ill.)

Dunnarts, 1: 54, 58
Dwarf epauletted fruit bats,
2: 293–94, 293 (ill.), 294 (ill.)
Dwarf gymnures, 2: 220
Dwarf lemurs, 3: **444–49**
Dwarf mongooses, 3: 638

E

Eagles, Philippine, 2: 270
Eared hutias, 5: 1189
Eared seals, 3: 579, 582,
673–83, 690
Earless seals. *See* True seals
Earth pigs. *See* Aardvarks
Eastern barred bandicoots,
1: 80, 83–84, 83 (ill.), 84 (ill.)
Eastern black gibbons, 3: 552
Eastern chipmunks,
5: 1013–14, 1013 (ill.), 1014
(ill.)
Eastern gray kangaroos,
1: 138–39, 138 (ill.), 139 (ill.)
Eastern moles, 2: 214, 216,
256, 258–59, 258 (ill.), 259
(ill.)
Eastern Pacific gray whales,
4: 781
Eastern pumas, 3: 658, 667
Eastern pygmy possums,
1: 150, 152–53, 152 (ill.),
153 (ill.)
Eastern red colobus monkeys,
3: 537
Eastern tarsiers, 3: 481
Eastern tube-nosed bats. *See*
Queensland tube-nosed bats
Eastern yellow-billed hornbills,
3: 638
Echidnas, 1: 1–6, **7–14**
Echimyidae. *See* Spiny rats
Echinosorex gymnura. See
Malayan moonrats
Echolocation, in bats, 2: 280
Echymipera rufescens. See
Rufous spiny bandicoots
Ectophylla alba. See White bats
Edentata, 1: 181

Edible dormice, 5: 1090–91,
1090 (ill.), 1091 (ill.)
Egg-laying mammals, 1: 5
See also specific species
Egyptian mongooses, 3: 639
Egyptian rousettes, 2: 290–92,
290 (ill.), 291 (ill.)
Egyptian slit-faced bats,
2: 319–21, 319 (ill.), 320 (ill.)
Egyptian spiny mice,
5: 1060–61, 1060 (ill.), 1061
(ill.)
Electroreceptors, 1: 4, 19
Elegant water shrews, 2: 248
Elephant seals, 3: 684, 691
northern, 3: 691, 695–97,
695 (ill.), 696 (ill.)
southern, 3: 578
Elephant shrews. *See* Sengis
Elephantidae. *See* Elephants
Elephants, 4: **808–19**, 821, 885
Elephas maximus. See Asian
elephants
Emballonuridae. *See* Ghost
bats; Sac-winged bats;
Sheath-tailed bats
Emotions, in elephants, 4: 811
Endangered Species Act (U.S.)
on gray wolves, 3: 587
on Sirenia, 4: 831
English Nature Greater
Horseshoe Bat Project, 2: 331
Epauletted fruit bats, dwarf,
2: 293–94, 293 (ill.), 294 (ill.)
Equidae. *See* Asses; Horses;
Zebras
Equus caballus przewalskii. See
Przewalski's horses
Equus grevyi. See Grevy's
zebras
Equus kiang. See Kiangs
Eremitalpa granti. See Grant's
desert golden moles
Erethizon dorsatum. See North
American porcupines
Erethizontidae. *See* New
World porcupines

Humans, 3: 423, **563–77,** 574 (ill.), 575 (ill.)

Humpback whales, 4: 797, 802–3, 802 (ill.), 803 (ill.)

Hutias, 5: **1188–93**

Hyaenidae. *See* Aardwolves; Hyenas

Hydrochaeridae. *See* Capybaras

Hydrochaeris hydrochaeris. See Capybaras

Hydrodamalis gigas. See Steller's sea cows

Hyenas, 3: 578, 580, **649–56**

Hylobates lar. See Lar gibbons

Hylobates pileatus. See Pileated gibbons

Hylobatidae. *See* Gibbons

Hylochoerus meinertzhageni. See Forest hogs

Hyperoodon ampullatus. See Northern bottlenosed whales

Hypsiprymnodon moschatus. See Musky rat-kangaroos

Hypsiprymnodontidae. *See* Musky rat-kangaroos

Hyracoidea. *See* Hyraxes

Hyraxes, 4: **820–27**

Hystricidae. *See* Old World porcupines

Hystricopsylla schefferi, 5: 1004

Hystrix africaeaustralis. See South African porcupines

Hystrix indica. See Indian crested porcupines

Hystrix species, 5: 1111–12

I

Iberian lynx, 3: 581, 658

Incan little mastiff bats, 2: 402

Incan shrew opossums, 1: 38–39

Indian crested porcupines, 5: 1115–16, 1115 (ill.), 1116 (ill.)

Indian flying foxes, 2: 288–89, 288 (ill.), 289 (ill.)

Indian muntjacs, 4: 937–39, 937 (ill.), 938 (ill.)

Indian rhinoceroses, 4: 874–75, 876, 880–82, 880 (ill.), 881 (ill.)

Indri indri. See Indris

Indriidae. *See* Avahis; Indris; Sifakas

Indris, 3: 424, 425, **458–65,** 462 (ill.), 463 (ill.)

Indus dolphins, 4: **709–13,** 711 (ill.), 712 (ill.)

Inia geoffrensis. See Botos

Iniidae. *See* Botos

Insectivora. *See* Insectivores

Insectivores, 2: **213–17,** 265

International Whaling Commission, 4: 780, 781, 789, 797, 799

Introduced species, 1: 65

Iranian jerboas, 5: 1047

Itjari-itjari. *See* Northern marsupial moles

IUCN Red List. *See* World Conservation Union (IUCN) Red List of Threatened Species

J

Ja slit-faced bats, 2: 318

Jackals, 3: **583–92**

Jamaican hutias. *See* Brown's hutias

Japanese macaques, 3: 423

Japanese sea lions, 3: 581

Javan pigs, 4: 894

Javan rhinoceroses, 4: 875, 876

Javan slit-faced bats, 2: 318

Javelinas. *See* Collared peccaries

Jerboas, 5: 997, 998, **1044–50**

Jerdon's palm civets, 3: 630

Juan Fernández fur seals, 3: 674

Jumping hares. *See* Springhares

Jumping mice, 5: **1044–50,** 1062–63, 1062 (ill.), 1063 (ill.)

K

Kakarratuls. *See* Southern marsupial moles

Kangaroo Island dunnarts, 1: 58

Kangaroo mice, 5: **1036–43**

Kangaroo rats, 5: 997, 998, **1036–43**

Kangaroos, 1: 26, 99–104, 130, **135–48**

    See also Rat-kangaroos

Karora, 1: 81

Kartana, I. Nyoman, 4: 928

Kerodon rupestris. See Rock cavies

Kiangs, 4: 860–61, 860 (ill.), 861 (ill.)

Killer whales, 4: 706, 737, 738, 741–43, 741 (ill.), 742 (ill.), 780

Kinkajous, 3: 580, 605, 606

Kipling, Rudyard, 3: 639

Kirk's dikdiks, 4: 981–82, 981 (ill.), 982 (ill.)

Kitti's hog-nosed bats, 2: 276, **312–15,** 313 (ill.), 314 (ill.)

Kloss gibbons, 3: 552

Koala bears. *See* Koalas

Koala lemurs, 3: 467

Koalas, 1: 26, 99–104, **105–10,** 107 (ill.), 108 (ill.)

Kogia breviceps. See Pygmy sperm whales

L

La Plata dolphins. *See* Franciscana dolphins

Lagomorpha, 5: **1200–1204,** 1224

Lagothrix lugens. See Colombian woolly monkeys

Lama glama. See Llamas

Myzopodidae. *See* Old World sucker-footed bats

Mzab gundis, 5: 1084–85, 1084 (ill.), 1085 (ill.)

N

Nail-tailed wallabies, bridled, 1: 144–45, 144 (ill.), 145 (ill.)

Naked-backed bats, 2: 358

Naked bats, 2: 403–5, 403 (ill.), 404 (ill.)

Naked bulldog bats. *See* Naked bats

Naked mole-rats, 5: 998, 1108–10, 1108 (ill.), 1109 (ill.)

Narwhals, 4: 767–76, 773 (ill.), 774 (ill.)

Nasalis larvatus. See Proboscis monkeys

Natalidae. *See* Funnel-eared bats

Natalus species, 2: 379

Natalus stramineus. See Mexican funnel-eared bats

Natterer's tuco-tucos, 5: 1168

Neobalaenidae. *See* Pygmy right whales

New South Wales Threatened Species Conservation Act, 2: 297

New World anteaters, 1: 9

New World leaf-nosed bats. *See* American leaf-nosed bats

New World marsupials, 1: 26

New World monkeys, 3: 423

New World opossums, 1: 24–36

New World porcupines, 5: 1121–28

New World sucker-footed bats. *See* Disk-winged bats

New Zealand long-eared bats. *See* Lesser New Zealand short-tailed bats

New Zealand Red Data Book, 2: 376

New Zealand short-tailed bats, 2: 371–77

Newman, Steve, 4: 811

Ngulia Rhino Sanctuary, 4: 876

Niangara free-tailed bats, 2: 402

Nicholson, Peter J., 1: 112

Nicobar tree shrews, 2: 265

Night monkeys, 3: 425, **509–15**

Nine-banded armadillos, 1: 179, 204, 205, 206–8, 206 (ill.), 207 (ill.)

Noctilio leporinus. See Greater bulldog bats

Noctilionidae. *See* Bulldog bats

Noctules, 2: 411

North African crested porcupines, 5: 1114

North American beavers, 5: 1026–27, 1026 (ill.), 1027 (ill.)

North American porcupines, 5: 1123–25, 1123 (ill.), 1124 (ill.)

North Atlantic humpback whales, 4: 803

North Atlantic right whales, 4: 789, 792–93, 792 (ill.), 793 (ill.)

North Pacific humpback whales, 4: 803

Northern bettongs, 1: 133–34, 133 (ill.), 134 (ill.)

Northern bottlenosed whales, 4: 751, 752–54, 752 (ill.), 753 (ill.)

Northern elephant seals, 3: 691, 695–97, 695 (ill.), 696 (ill.)

Northern fur seals, 3: 674

Northern greater bushbabies, 3: 441–42, 441 (ill.), 442 (ill.)

Northern hairy-nosed wombats, 1: 103, 111, 113

Northern marsupial moles, 1: 96

Northern minke whales, 4: 800–801, 800 (ill.), 801 (ill.)

Northern muriquis, 3: 527

Northern Pacific right whales, 4: 789

Northern pikas, 5: 1210–11, 1210 (ill.), 1211 (ill.)

Northern raccoons, 3: 605, 606, 607–9, 607 (ill.), 608 (ill.)

Northern sea lions, 3: 582

Northern short-tailed bats. *See* Lesser New Zealand short-tailed bats

Northern tamanduas, 1: 179, 195

Northern three-toed jerboas. *See* Hairy-footed jerboas

Norway lemmings, 5: 1056–57, 1056 (ill.), 1057 (ill.)

Nosy Mangabe Special Reserve, 3: 476

Notomys alexis. See Australian jumping mice

Notoryctemorphia. *See* Marsupial moles

Notoryctes typhlops. See Southern marsupial moles

Notoryctidae. *See* Marsupial moles

Numbats, 1: 9, 52, 53, **64–68,** 66 (ill.), 67 (ill.)

Nutrias. *See* Coypus

Nycteridae. *See* Slit-faced bats

Nycteris thebaica. See Egyptian slit-faced bats

Nycticebus pygmaeus. See Pygmy slow lorises

Nyctimene robinsoni. See Queensland tube-nosed bats

O

Oaxacan pocket gophers, 5: 1032

Ochotona hyperborea. See Northern pikas

Ochotona hyperborea yesoensis, 5: 1211

Ochotona princeps. See American pikas

Ochotonidae. *See* Pikas

Pteropodidae. *See* Old World fruit bats

Pteropus giganteus. See Indian flying foxes

Pteropus mariannus. See Marianas fruit bats

Pudu pudu. See Southern pudus

Pudus, southern, *4:* 946–47, 946 (ill.), 947 (ill.)

Puma concolor. See Pumas

Pumas, *3:* 658, 665–67, 665 (ill.), 666 (ill.)

Punarés, *5:* 1182

Pygathrix nemaeus. See Red-shanked douc langurs

Pygmy anteaters. *See* Silky anteaters

Pygmy fruit bats, *2:* 282

Pygmy gliders, *1:* 172–74, 175–77, 175 (ill.), 176 (ill.)

Pygmy hippopotamuses, *4:* 908, 909, 913–14, 913 (ill.), 914 (ill.)

Pygmy hogs, *4:* 892, 894

Pygmy marmosets, *3:* 423, 496, 505–7, 505 (ill.), 506 (ill.)

Pygmy mice, *5:* 996

Pygmy mouse lemurs, *3:* 423, 444

Pygmy possums, *1:* 101, 102, **149–53**

Pygmy rabbits, *5:* 1215

Pygmy right whales, *4:* 783–86, 785 (ill.), 786 (ill.)

Pygmy shrews, Savi's, *2:* 246

Pygmy sloths. *See* Monk sloths

Pygmy slow lorises, *3:* 428, 431–32, 431 (ill.), 432 (ill.)

Pygmy sperm whales, *4:* 765–66, 765 (ill.), 766 (ill.)

Pygmy squirrels, *5:* 1008

Q

Queensland tube-nosed bats, *2:* 295–97, 295 (ill.), 296 (ill.)

Querétaro pocket gophers, *5:* 1032

Quill pigs. *See* Old World porcupines

Quills, throwing, *5:* 1113

Quolls, spotted-tailed, *1:* 52

R

Rabbit-eared bandicoots. *See* Greater bilbies

Rabbits, *1:* 82, *5:* **1200–1204, 1213–22**

Raccoon dogs, *3:* 583, 629

Raccoons, *3:* 578, 579–80, 581, **605–13**

Rainforest bandicoots. *See* Spiny bandicoots

Rangifer tarandus. See Reindeer

Rat-kangaroos, *1:* **129–34**
    See also Musky rat-kangaroos

Rat opossums. *See* Shrew opossums

Rato de Taquara, *5:* 1183

Rats, *5:* 996–1000, **1051–68**
    cane, *5:* **1097–1102**
    chinchilla, *5:* **1177–81**
    dassie, *5:* **1093–96,** 1094 (ill.), 1095 (ill.)
    kangaroo, *5:* 997, 998, **1036–43**
    plains viscacha, *5:* 1173
    Polynesian, *2:* 373
    rock, *5:* 1173
    spiny, *5:* **1182–87,** 1185 (ill.), 1186 (ill.)
    water, *5:* 998
    See also Mole-rats; Moonrats

Red-backed squirrel monkeys, *3:* 488

Red-billed hornbills, *3:* 638

Red colobus
    eastern, *3:* 537
    western, *3:* 537, 538–40, 538 (ill.), 539 (ill.)

Red deer, *4:* 940–42, 940 (ill.), 941 (ill.)

Red foxes, *1:* 54, 65, 68, 134, *3:* 584, 588–89, 588 (ill.), 589 (ill.)

Red howler monkeys, Venezuelan, *3:* 528–30, 528 (ill.), 529 (ill.)

Red kangaroos, *1:* 101, 140–41, 140 (ill.), 141 (ill.)

Red List of Threatened Species. *See* World Conservation Union (IUCN) Red List of Threatened Species

Red mouse lemurs, *3:* 446, 447–48, 447 (ill.), 448 (ill.)

Red pandas, *3:* 579–80, 605, 606, 610–12, 610 (ill.), 611 (ill.)

Red ruffed lemurs, *3:* 450

Red-shanked douc langurs, *3:* 537, 544–45, 544 (ill.), 545 (ill.)

Red-tailed sportive lemurs, *3:* 469–71, 469 (ill.), 470 (ill.)

Red-toothed shrews, *2:* 248

Red wolves, *3:* 581, 584

Reindeer, *4:* 951–52, 951 (ill.), 952 (ill.)

Rhesus macaques, *3:* 426, 546–47, 546 (ill.), 547 (ill.)

Rhesus monkeys. *See* Rhesus macaques

Rhinoceros unicornis. See Indian rhinoceroses

Rhinoceroses, *4:* 821, 848–50, 852, 853, **874–86**

Rhinocerotidae. *See* Rhinoceroses

Rhinolophidae. *See* Horseshoe bats

Rhinolophus capensis. See Cape horseshoe bats

Rhinolophus ferrumequinum. See Greater horseshoe bats

Rhinopoma hardwickei. See Hardwicke's lesser mouse-tailed bats

Rhinopomatidae. *See* Mouse-tailed bats

Rhinos. *See* Rhinoceroses

Rhynchocyon cirnei. See Checkered sengis

Right whales, 4: 783, 787–94 *See also* Pygmy right whales

"Rikki-tikki-tavi" (Kipling), *3:* 639

Ring-tailed mongooses, *3:* 641–43, 641 (ill.), 642 (ill.)

Ringed seals, *3:* 594

Ringtail possums, 1: 154–60

Ringtailed lemurs, *3:* 451, 453–54, 453 (ill.), 454 (ill.)

Ringtails, *3:* 579, 605, 606
  common, *1:* 159–60, 159 (ill.), 160 (ill.)
  golden, *1:* 156
  green, *1:* 154
  See also Ringtail possums

River dolphins. *See* Baijis; Botos; Franciscana dolphins; Ganges dolphins; Indus dolphins

River horses. *See* Hippopotamuses

River otters, *3:* 614, 622

Rock cavies, *5:* 1139, 1142–43, 1142 (ill.), 1143 (ill.)

Rock hyraxes, *4:* 820, 821, 825–26, 825 (ill.), 826 (ill.)

Rock possums, *1:* 155

Rock rats, *5:* 1173

Rock wallabies
  brush-tailed, *1:* 142–43, 142 (ill.), 143 (ill.)
  yellow-footed, *1:* 101

Rodentia. *See* Rodents

Rodents, 4: 821, 5: 996–1002, 5: 1202

Rorquals, 4: 795–803

Rough-haired golden moles, *2:* 227

Rough-legged jerboas. *See* Hairy-footed jerboas

Roundleaf bats. *See* Old World leaf-nosed bats

Rousette bats, *2:* 283

Rousettes, Egyptian, *2:* 290–91, 290 (ill.), 291 (ill.)

Rousettus aegyptiacus. See Egyptian rousettes

Ruatan Island agoutis, *5:* 1155

Ruedas, Luis, *5:* 1215

Rufescent bandicoots. *See* Rufous spiny bandicoots

Ruffed lemurs, *3:* 450

Rufous sengis, *5:* 1223

Rufous spiny bandicoots, *1:* 91–93, 91 (ill.), 92 (ill.)

Russet mouse lemurs. *See* Red mouse lemurs

Russian desmans, *2:* 256, 257

Ruwenzori otter shrews, *2:* 233

S

Sac-winged bats, 2: 304–11

Saccopteryx bilineata. See Greater sac-winged bats

Saccopteryx species, *2:* 304, 306

Saguinus oedipus. See Cotton-top tamarins

Saimiri sciureus. See Common squirrel monkeys

Sakis, 3: 516–25

Salim Ali's fruit bats, *2:* 315

Salt-desert cavies, *5:* 1139, 1140

San Diego Zoo, *5:* 1136

San Joaquin pocket mice, *5:* 1039–40, 1039 (ill.), 1040 (ill.)

Sand puppies. *See* Naked mole-rats

Sand swimmers. *See* Yellow golden moles

Sandhill dunnarts, *1:* 54

Sandshoes, *5:* 1046

Sarcophilus laniarius. See Tasmanian devils

Sardinian pikas, *2:* 1203, *5:* 1207

Sauer, Martin, *4:* 835

Savanna baboons, *3:* 425

Savanna elephants, *4:* 815–16, 815 (ill.), 816 (ill.), 817, 818–19

Save the Bilby Fund, *1:* 82, 86

Savi's pygmy shrews, *2:* 246

Scalopus aquaticus. See Eastern moles

Scaly anteaters. *See* Pangolins

Scaly-tailed squirrels, 5: 1069–75

Scandentia. *See* Tree shrews

Scatterhoarding food, *1:* 125

Sciuridae, 5: 1008–21

Sciurus carolinensis. See Gray squirrels

Sclater's golden moles, *2:* 227

Sea cows, 4: 828–32, 833–40

Sea lions, 3: 581, 582, 673–83, 4: 707

Sea minks, *3:* 581

Sea otters, *3:* 579, 582, 614, *4:* 707

Seals, 4: 707
  crab-eater, *3:* 580
  eared, 3: 579, 582, 673–83, 690
  elephant, *3:* 578, 684, 691, 695–97, 695 (ill.), 696 (ill.)
  fur, 3: 673–83
  monk, *3:* 581, 582, 691, 698–700, 698 (ill.), 699 (ill.)
  ringed, *3:* 594
  true, 3: 579, 582, 690–701

Sei whales, *4:* 797

Self-anointing behavior, *2:* 220

Senegal bushbabies, *3:* 424, 437, 439–40, 439 (ill.), 440 (ill.)

Sengis, 5: 1223–28

Serows, *4:* 983–84, 983 (ill.), 984 (ill.)

Sewellels. *See* Mountain beavers

Shakespeare, William, *2:* 248

Shark Bay, Australia, *4:* 834

Sharks, tiger, *4:* 834

Sheath-tailed bats, *2: 304–11*
Sheep, *4: 888, 890, 969–87*
Shepherd's beaked whales, *4: 749, 755–56, 755 (ill.), 756 (ill.)*
Short-beaked echidnas, *1: 2–3, 5, 7–8, 9, 11–13, 11 (ill.), 12 (ill.)*
Short-nosed echidnas. *See* Short-beaked echidnas
Short-tailed bats, New Zealand, *2: 371–77*
Short-tailed chinchillas, *5: 1131*
Short-tailed opossums, gray, *1: 28*
Short-tailed shrews, *2: 247, 248*
Shrew moles, *2: 255–62*
Shrew opossums, *1: 37–43*
Shrews, *2: 213–14, 215, 216, 246–54*
    otter, *2: 232, 233, 234*
    tree, *2: 263–68, 1202, 5: 1224*
    true, *1: 37, 5: 1224*
    See also Sengis
Siamangs, *3: 552, 559–61, 559 (ill.), 560 (ill.)*
Siberian musk deer, *4: 935–36, 935 (ill.), 936 (ill.)*
Siberian pikas. *See* Northern pikas
Sifakas, *3: 425, 458–65*
Sigmodon hispidus. See Hispid cotton rats
Silky anteaters, *1: 179, 180, 195, 196, 198–99, 198 (ill.), 199 (ill.)*
Silky shrew opossums, *1: 38–39, 40, 41–42, 41 (ill.), 42 (ill.)*
Silky tuco-tucos, *5: 1167*
Silverbacks, *3: 564, 568*
Sirenia, *4: 828–32*
Skunks, *3: 578, 579, 614–27, 637*
Sleep, dolphins, *4: 720*

Slender gray lorises, *3: 428*
Slender lorises, *3: 428–29*
Slit-faced bats, *2: 316–22*
Sloth bears, *3: 593, 594, 595*
Sloth lemurs, *3: 459*
Sloths, *1: 178–82*
    three-toed tree, *1: 178, 181, 189–94*
    two-toed tree, *1: 178, 180, 183–88*
    West Indian, *1: 183–88*
Slow lorises, *3: 428*
Small-eared galagos. *See* Northern greater bushbabies
Small-eared shrews, *2: 247*
Small mouse-tailed bats, *2: 299*
Small Sulawesi cuscuses, *1: 116*
Smoky bats, *2: 383–87, 385 (ill.), 386 (ill.)*
Smooth-tailed tree shrews, Bornean, *2: 265*
Smooth-toothed pocket gophers. *See* Valley pocket gophers
Snow leopards, *3: 668–69, 668 (ill.), 669 (ill.)*
Snowshoe hares, *5: 1214, 1216–17, 1216 (ill.), 1217 (ill.)*
Snub-nosed monkeys, *3: 426, 537*
Social tuco-tucos, *5: 1167, 1168*
Solenodon paradoxus. See Hispaniolan solenodons
Solenodons, *2: 215, 240–45*
Solenodontidae. *See* Solenodons
Somali sengis, *5: 1225*
Sorex palustris. See American water shrews
Soricidae. *See* Shrews
South African porcupines, *5: 1117–19, 1117 (ill.), 1118 (ill.)*
South American beavers. *See* Coypus

South American mice, *5: 1051, 1052*
South American rats, *5: 1051, 1052*
Southern brown bandicoots, *1: 76, 80*
Southern dibblers, *1: 54*
Southern elephant seals, *3: 578*
Southern flying squirrels, *5: 1011–12, 1011 (ill.), 1012 (ill.)*
Southern hairy-nosed wombats, *1: 103, 111, 112*
Southern marsupial moles, *1: 96, 97–98, 97 (ill.), 98 (ill.)*
Southern muriquis, *3: 527*
Southern opossums, *1: 28*
Southern pudus, *4: 946–47, 946 (ill.), 947 (ill.)*
Southern tamanduas, *1: 179, 195*
Southern tree hyraxes, *4: 823–24, 823 (ill.), 824 (ill.)*
Southern two-toed sloths. *See* Linné's two-toed sloths
Species, introduced, *1: 65*
    See also specific species
Spectacled bears, *3: 593, 594, 595*
Spectacled porpoises, *4: 729–30, 731*
Spectral vampire bats, *2: 345, 347*
Sperm whales, *4: 758–66, 761 (ill.), 762 (ill.)*
Spermaceti, *4: 759*
Spider monkeys, *3: 425, 526–35*
Spinner dolphins, *4: 706, 746–47, 746 (ill.), 747 (ill.)*
Spiny anteaters. *See* Echidnas
Spiny bandicoots, *1: 74, 75, 88–93*
Spiny mice, Egyptian, *5: 1060–61, 1060 (ill.), 1061 (ill.)*
Spiny rats, *5: 1182–87, 1185 (ill.), 1186 (ill.)*

on western barbastelles,
  2: 416
on western gorillas, *3:* 570
on white bats, *2:* 356
on woolly monkeys,
  3: 534
on Xenarthra, *1:* 181
World Wildlife Fund, *4:* 797
Wroughton free-tailed bats,
  2: 402

X

Xenarthra, *1:* **178–82**

Y

Yapoks. *See* Water opossums
Yellow-bellied gliders, *1:* 163
Yellow-breasted capuchins,
  3: 488
Yellow-footed rock wallabies,
  1: 101
Yellow golden moles, *2:* 226
Yellow-streaked tenrecs,
  2: 237–38, 237 (ill.), 238 (ill.)
Yellow-tailed woolly monkeys,
  3: 527
Yellow-winged bats, *2:* 324,
  325

Yellowstone National Park,
  3: 587
Yerbua capensis. See Springhares

Z

Zalophus californianus. See
  California sea lions
Zalophus wollebaeki. See
  Galápagos sea lions
Zebras, *4:* 848–50, 852,
  854–64
Zenkerella species, *5:* 1069
Ziphiidae. See Beaked whales